Emotion Focused Therapy for Youth

This edited collection is the first book of its kind to apply the theory, research, and teaching of emotion focused therapy to youth and their families, equipping clinicians and students with the practical skills to facilitate individual, dyadic, and parent sessions confidently.

Mirisse Foroughe is joined by an impressive group of internationally acclaimed contributors, including clinician-scientists and scholars, as well as the developer of Emotion Focused Therapy, Dr. Leslie Greenberg. This clinical manual offers a trauma-informed perspective on how to apply EFT for youth in primary care as well as more complex mental health difficulties. The manual begins with an incredibly user-friendly overview of core EFT principles before moving on to clinical applications with individual youth, parents, and dyads. The contributors then address how EFT can be implemented with specific client populations, such as youth with anxiety, depression, and borderline personality disorder, before examining important considerations that clinicians should bear in mind when working with parent and youth trauma and complex clinical presentations.

Interweaving a trauma-informed perspective throughout, the manual is filled with practical summary tables, helpful tips, and eye-catching illustrations to ensure it is useful for students and experienced therapists. *Emotion Focused Therapy for Youth* is essential reading for marriage and family therapists, clinical social workers, and other mental health professionals working with youth and their families.

Dr. Mirisse Foroughe completed her doctoral studies at York University and now directs the Family Psychology Centre and the Emotion Transformation Institute in Toronto. She has received numerous awards and accolades for her work, including the CPA 2017 PFC Innovative Service Award and the OPA 2019 Harvey T. Brooker Award for Excellence in Clinical Teaching.

Emotion Focused Therapy for Youth

The Clinical Manual

Edited by Mirisse Foroughe

Routledge
Taylor & Francis Group
NEW YORK AND LONDON

Designed cover image: Getty Images

First published 2023
by Routledge
605 Third Avenue, New York, NY 10158

and by Routledge
4 Park Square, Milton Park, Abingdon, Oxon, OX14 4RN

Routledge is an imprint of the Taylor & Francis Group, an informa business

ISBN: 9781032112312 (hbk)
ISBN: 9781032112299 (pbk)
ISBN: 9781003218968 (ebk)

DOI: 10.4324/9781003218968

Typeset in Adobe Caslon Pro
by Newgen Publishing UK

CONTENTS

BRIEF BIOGRAPHY OF DR. FOROUGHE, EDITOR

Dr. Mirisse Foroughe is a clinical psychologist and Director of Clinical Training and Research at the Family Psychology Centre. She has over 15 years of experience providing assessment and treatment to children and families utilizing emotion focused therapeutic approaches. After completing a Master's degree in Health Psychology, Dr. Foroughe completed her doctorate degree in Clinical-Developmental Psychology at York University with a focus on family-based therapy. She was Ontario's first full-time child and family psychologist in a family health team. Dr. Foroughe currently oversees clinical services at the Family Psychology Centre and directs the Emotion Transformation Lab. She has received numerous awards and accolades for her work, including the OPA Ruth Berman Early Career Psychologist Award, the CPA 2017 PFC Innovative Service Award, and the 2019 OPA Harvey Brooker Award for Excellence in Clinical Teaching. She holds adjunct faculty positions with York University and the University of Waterloo and is an Adjunct Clinical Supervisor for OISE at the University of Toronto.

LIST OF CONTRIBUTORS

Dr. Leslie S. Greenberg, Ph.D., C. Psych. Distinguished Research Professor, York University, and developer of EFT

Dr. Robert T. Muller, Ph.D., C. Psych. Professor of Clinical Psychology, York University, and Director of the Trauma & Attachment Lab

Sarah Thompson, Ph.D., C. Psych. Adjunct Faculty, Dept. of Psychology, Toronto Metropolitan University, and Director of Transforming Emotions Transforming Emotions

Lucas Liu, B.A.H., Emotion Transformation Lab and REACh Lab

Angela Ashley, B.Sc.H., Emotion Transformation Lab, The Addiction and Mental Health Lab, Toronto Metropolitan University

Imayan Neela, B.Sc.H., Emotion Transformation Lab, McMaster University/ Hamilton Health Sciences

George A. Langdon, B.A.H., TULiP Lab, Emotion Transformation Lab, Trauma & Attachment Lab

Serena Darking, B.Sc.H., Emotion Transformation Lab, Trauma & Attachment Lab, The Till Lab

PREFACE

I attended my first emotion focused therapy (EFT) training in 2010. At that single day training on EFT for Depression, I took 31 pages of notes while Dr. Leslie Greenberg spoke in the packed lecture hall at York University in Toronto.

> "You can't change what happened, but you can change how you feel about what happened."
> "You have to get to place before you can leave it."
> "Pain is a compass."
> "You have to feel it to heal it."

I didn't quite understand the meaning of these assertions, but they sounded intriguing, and I wanted to learn more. Many years later, I find that I continue to learn so much from the EFT community—a generous and brilliant group of people who can analyze 20 seconds of video at a level of detail only matched by acting coaches and police detectives. Of course, the attention that EFT pays to minute detail in human behaviour is not concerned with performance or objective truth, but with the journey of self-healing.

In my work as a child and adolescent psychologist, I have found EFT to be the single most impactful model for working productively and directly with emotion. As in the adult-focused model, EFT for youth (EFT-Y) focuses on relationship and alliance building and technical skills for working with emotion in the moment. It provides specific roadmaps for helping youth work with their emotions by helping clinicians know what to do, why to do it, when to do it, and how much to do it.

In these chapters, you will not find a manual or checklist of what should happen in each session. Rather, you will strengthen the ability to notice, identify, and deepen understandable emotion-based processes that occur in the therapy session. EFT's marker-driven approach helps to develop an "if–then" blueprint of clinical decisions—if you find yourself here, then this is where you could go, and this is how to go about it. It's like a therapist GPS: the more you use it, the wider and more detailed your roadmap becomes. This marker-driven approach provides us with the flexibility to make clinical decisions in the moment and based on the client in front of us. Each of our clients is unique, and EFT-Y does not follow a one-size-fits-all recipe. We constantly evaluate our next step based on where we are but also on who we are with, how our relationship is doing, and how much this client can tolerate right now.

Many youth come to therapy when there have been painful or overwhelming experiences in their lives. It's true that they cannot change the fact that these experiences took place, but how do they feel when they remember these experiences? How much do they suffer as a result? And what other feelings can they access? EFT's emotion transformation process simply and brilliantly demonstrates how emotions can undo other emotions and reduce suffering. It also provides us with keys to unlock productive emotion processing along the way.

In the search for their own path to healing, EFT-Y directs youth to their emotions as a fundamental meaning system. Each emotion provides clues to how a person is experiencing their world while also organizing them to think and act in certain ways. In our practice of EFT-Y, we have found that the client-centred emphasis is much appreciated by youth. In addition to praising the fact that there's no workbook and no homework, young people often recognize that EFT-Y is individualized for them and places them at the centre of the process:

> "I like that you don't really know what we are going to do in therapy that day until I start feeling something important. It's really about me and what I feel, not like someone is telling me what to think or what to do."

EFT engages youth and requires their active involvement. This necessarily challenges emotion avoidance:

> "It's definitely not boring and it's impossible to zone out for the whole session like I have in therapy before."

In fact, young people tell us that EFT feels undeniably authentic"

> "I literally can't lie to myself when I'm in the chairs. There's nowhere to hide. Sometimes I feel things that I didn't even know were there, so I actually know myself better now and I'm more honest with myself because of this."

As child and adolescent therapists, the potential for greater engagement, self-awareness, and authenticity for our clients is a compelling reason to learn EFT. We have adapted EFT for youth based on ten years of clinical research. We observed recordings of therapy sessions, identified key moments in therapy, and mapped ideal therapist responses that helped youth make real changes in their inner experience and their lives.

In this book, we share with you our emotion focused therapy model for youth as well as special considerations for the populations we see most often in child and adolescent practice. Chapter 1 provides a dynamic introduction to the broader model and theory of change in EFT. Chapter 2 outlines core EFT applications for youth including the use of empathic responses and evocative tasks to identify and begin to treat a youth's core wound or to pave the way for parent–child therapy. Chapters 3 and 4 are focused on working with primary caregivers and the clinical decision points related to involving caregivers in a youth's therapy. Chapters 4 through 8 share our application of EFT-Y for specific presenting concerns (anxiety, depression, borderline personality traits, and trauma), offering theoretical considerations, technical adaptations, and practical tips to help engage youth in an emotion focused intervention.

When we work directly with emotions, youth build their capacity for processing emotion and their openness to the therapeutic process. Productive engagement with emotion and emotional memories, without emphasizing coping- or avoidance-based methods such as distraction, behavioural shaping, or changing thoughts, can provide youth with evidence of their own emotional resilience and self-directed healing. It is an exercise in concentration, focusing inwards, and attending fully to their own feelings and sensations. Whereas self-conscious thoughts or feeling pushed to change can impede therapeutic engagement, being immersed in their own experience can allow therapy to move forward.

Perhaps the most satisfying aspect of using EFT-Y in our practice has been the increased confidence and hope for improvement that our therapists see in their young clients. All too often, children or teens who do not progress quickly in treatment are perceived as being unmotivated or not ready for therapy. EFT-Y encourages us to instead consider and address the emotional blocks that get in the way of positive treatment response. Does the youth feel worried that they cannot tolerate the emotions that will come up in therapy? Are they feeling guilty or ashamed about something that has happened? Are they concerned that they will make themselves vulnerable and end up feeling alone? Have they learned that their feelings and needs are too much for others to handle? There are many emotion blocks that can prevent youth from engaging in and benefiting from therapy. Without attending to these blocks, youth may leave therapy believing that they "tried therapy but it doesn't work." We use EFT-Y to change that.

The EFT community is inspiring. Collectively, they have spent half a century studying precisely how and why therapy works and have produced volumes of literature and training videos. When you are first learning, I encourage you not to concern yourself with the outstanding scholarship on therapy process or the seamless transition from task to resolution in an EFT demonstration video. Instead, just start with the moment you are in, the client in front of you, and a focus on your client's emotion. The process is in the name of the therapy itself. Be *emotion focused* in the content you bring attention to, the words you use, the nonverbal behaviours you watch for, and the way you connect with physical sensations in your own body. Keep doing these things and you will be on your way to practising EFT-Y with your own clients and in your own way. From there, allow the road maps in this book to help guide you on your journey to discovering the power of centring emotion in the therapy room and in your practice. Your clients, of all ages, will thank you for it.

Mirisse Foroughe

1
EMOTION FOCUSED THERAPY

Sarah Thompson and Les Greenberg

The brain is an almost mystical entity in its complexity. Its processing power, its capacity for retention of memory, the depth of human experience that it generates, and, of course, the tremendous growth occurring throughout childhood and adolescence are all quite simply amazing. I think about these things often when reflecting on change in psychotherapy—wondering what is happening as someone shifts from feeling shut down, self-loathing, painfully anxious, or irritable to the warmth of self-compassion, the calm of self-soothing, and the healthy emotional flexibility that can follow deep transformational work.

In this chapter, we lay out the theory and practice of emotion focused therapy (EFT) in accessible terms. We briefly introduce you to EFT, its origins, and the research base that supports it. Then, we move on to a bit about the brain (trust us, it will be worth it!) and what fundamental processes we are working with as we facilitate change in psychotherapy. We will highlight how EFT uses six change processes to transform emotion with emotion through early, middle, and late phases of therapy, and how we help clients to rewire old, stuck emotional patterns to create feelings and responses that are anchored in the "here and now." We end by translating theory into practice

DOI: 10.4324/9781003218968-1

through the case of "Clara," a fictional client based on composites of real clients we have worked with in our practices over the years. Fundamentally, we believe that, once you understand the basic change processes in psychotherapy, it's easier to be a flexible and effective clinician—and that's what this chapter is all about.

EFT: Origins and Research

If EFT were the child of prior therapeutic models, it would belong to Rogers's client-centred therapy (Rogers, 1957; Gendlin, 1996) and Perls's Gestalt therapy (Gendlin, 1996; Perls et al., 1951), achieving a strong blend of some of the best qualities of each parent model. Developed by Dr. Leslie Greenberg, Dr. Laura Rice, and Dr. Robert Elliott, beginning in the late 1970s (Greenberg et al., 1996; Elliott & Greenberg, 2021), this therapy arose from the basic research question of what differentiated strong versus poor outcome therapies—fundamentally asking the question, "When therapy works, why?" Researchers carefully analyzed client-centred therapy sessions using both video and session transcripts and using line-by-line analysis of therapist and client speech to determine what patterns occurred between therapist and client that predicted positive and negative outcomes over the course of therapy. The results of several decades of painstaking research can be boiled down to one, rather complicated, sentence:

> Moderate to high **aroused emotions** that
> are **deeply experienced** and **reflected** on
> in order to make **narrative sense**
> in the context of
> an **empathically-attuned** relationship
> with a **good working alliance**
> with a therapist who is **present**
> predicts therapeutic outcome.
>
> (Greenberg & Warwar, 2019)

While we will spend the rest of this chapter unpacking this sentence, decades later, EFT is a tested therapy model that excels in working directly with a client's emergent emotional experience. EFT has been demonstrated to be effective in creating lasting therapeutic change in the treatment of social anxiety (Elliott, 2013; Shahar et al., 2017), generalized anxiety (Timulak & McElvaney, 2018; Watson & Greenberg, 2017), depression (Elliott et al., 2013; Goldman et al., 2006; Watson et al., 2003), childhood trauma (Paivio & Pascual-Leone, 2010), and eating disorders (Dolhanty & Lafrance, 2019).

Why Work with Emotion?

> ***Fun Facts about the Brain***
>
> Our brains are incredibly complex. Neuroscientists estimate that our brains contain roughly 120 billion neurons (Dance, 2020). That's equivalent to about one-third of all the stars in the whole Milky Way galaxy (Voytek, 2013)! Each neuron is estimated to have 7–10,000 connections with other neurons (Dance, 2020), with each neuron firing 1–200 times per second (Bryant, 2013). Just take a moment to try to wrap your own brain around that.

While not all therapies acknowledge the centrality of emotion, the majority of clients in our practices come in with reports of *feeling* bad in some way or another. Throughout this chapter, we'll refer to the case of Clara. She is a 16-year-old whose mother called our clinic after they had been struggling for months to manage Clara's anxiety related to school and friendships. Although Clara has a number of close friends, when she is invited out to parties or social gatherings, she worries that no one really wants her to come, and she will somehow make a fool out of herself. Her mom reports that she often finds it hard to comfort Clara, who spends hours getting ready to go out, which often includes bouts of tearful self-doubt. For Clara, coming to therapy is all about wanting to *feel* better.

In this chapter, we define emotion as an automatic unfolding process that occurs in our nervous system in response to changes in our environment. Mediated by neurotransmitter and hormone levels (LeDoux, 1998), these processes impact our breathing, muscle tension, blood flow, memory, attention, and thought patterns (Levenson, 1994). For example, when we feel fear, we experience:

- Physiological changes in our body: our heart rate and breathing increase; we may sweat or shake.
- Changes in our thought patterns: we may be more likely to believe that our environment is unsafe or that we are unable to cope.
- Changes in our perception and accessible memories: we monitor our environment for signs of danger; we most easily remember times when we have been scared in the past.
- Changes in motivation and action: this leads us to seek safety.

As therapists, we can often observe the impact of these changes in a person's posture, movement, tone of voice, and more. These changes are important to pay attention to because they can guide us to the heart of a client's experience. For example, in early sessions with Clara, we noticed that she often spoke quietly while looking down at the floor when talking about herself, sometimes with a tear in her eye.

Emotion Schemes

We use the term "emotion scheme" to refer to the (not so simple) whole experience of a certain emotion state and what is then activated in one's body and mind (Elliott & Greenberg, 2021). Figure 1.1 reflects five key component processes of the emotion scheme of shame as we observe them with Clara. We can help clients deepen their emotions by exploring different aspects of the emotion scheme.

Follow Emotion to the Heart of the Matter

Leaning into the heart of clients' painful feelings helps to heal and transform stuck emotional processes. How do we know this? By understanding what is happening in the brain during therapy.

Fundamentally, therapy is about helping our nervous systems learn, and learning is about creating and modifying memory. When we help clients become aware of their emotions, tolerate their emotions, and follow where their emotions lead, we more quickly arrive at the core of what brings clients

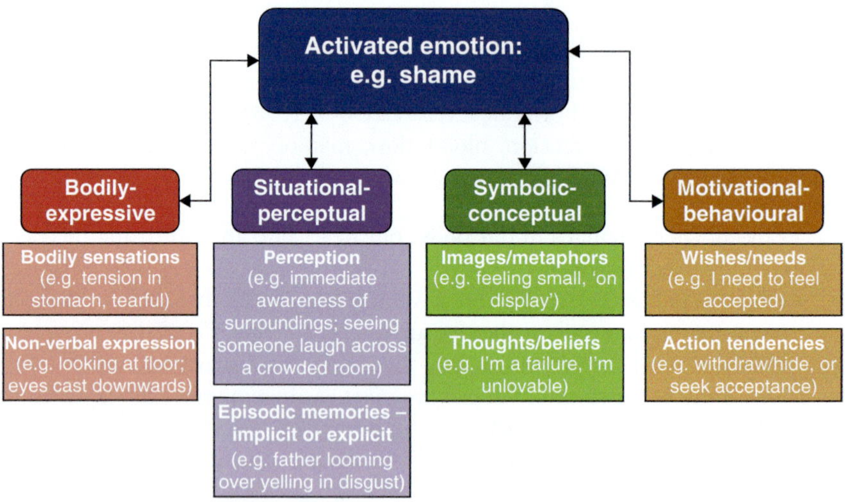

Figure 1.1 Shame as an Emotion Scheme.

Adapted from Elliott and Greenberg, 2021.

into therapy. One of the processes associated with this is state-dependent memory.

State-dependent memory is a well-researched phenomenon. When we feel a strong emotion, we are most likely to recall memories from the last time we felt that way (Eich et al., 1994). As EFT therapists, we speak of following "the pain compass" (Goldman & Greenberg, 2015), a process in which we empathically reflect, follow, and deepen those aspects of the client's experience that are accompanied by signs of painful or difficult expressed emotion. If a client spends a few minutes telling us about their weekend and expresses anger and hurt in the second last sentence, we can focus on and empathically reflect the hurt that they shared, probing gently to focus the client in this area. In EFT, we make use of the phenomenon of state-dependent memory, trusting that, as we follow the pain and evoke problematic aspects of a client's emotional experience, the most relevant thoughts, memories, and meaning will emerge.

You've Got to Feel It to Heal It

Once we've arrived at the heart of a client's experience, what do we do? We help clients feel it to heal it—literally. This is based on two principles:

1. Neuroplasticity: neurons that fire together, wire together.
2. Memory reconsolidation: how we change memories.

Neurons That Fire Together, Wire Together

Our brain is composed of billions of neurons organized into networks of interconnected cells, something psychologist Francis Stevens (2022) likens to a three-dimensional spider-web of interconnecting threads and nodes. The threads represent individual neurons (cells), and the nodes are where the cells connect. Each time we activate a pathway through the web, the neurons along that path fire with tiny electrical signals. Only when a pathway is "firing" can it create links to new pathways, creating new connections or nodes. Essentially, when firing, the pathway becomes plastic and ready for change (Lane et al., 2015). This process underpins the saying "neurons that fire together, wire together."

This is important to understand as EFT clinicians. If we simply help our clients *talk about* emotion, we are most able to help clients make changes in how and what they *think* about emotions—change happens in the part of the brain where we understand and make sense of emotion. If we help our clients *feel* their emotions, we are most able to help them make changes in the parts of their brain that create automatic emotion-based responses to their environments—literally changing emotion with emotion. In EFT, we aim to help clients "fire up" parts of the brain associated with feeling old, painful, stuck feelings while also "firing up" parts of the brain that feel adaptive healthy emotions. Neurons that fire together, wire together, resulting in brand new feelings.

How We Change Memories

Stevens (2022) talks about *affect reconsolidation*, a process based on a growing body of literature related to memory (Nadel et al., 2012, 2000). What this research tells us is that each time we recall a memory—each time we pull up a memory out of our brain's filing system—if the memory meets new contradictory experience, the memory becomes labile (changeable) and is changed a little bit before it goes back into the filing system. Each time we remember something and what we expect to encounter differs from what happens in our environment, the memory itself is altered in the process and is reconsolidated as an updated memory (Fernández et al., 2016). This is captured in Figure 1.2.

If, while a strong emotion is activated, we can help a client to have a new emotional experience, the memory that gets re-encoded will be sent back to the filing system with the new emotion attached to it and with new meaning associated with it. While we can't change the past, we can change the feelings that come when we remember the past.

Now, here is where it gets tricky. If we help a client to pull a big emotional memory out of storage and we do not help the client to feel something new, we may just reinforce the old memory, repeating the same connections and strengthening them. The strength of these "wired" connections in our brains is impacted by repetition (Nadel et al., 2007). Memories of new experiences become more easily reactivated with repetition—this is why regular review of

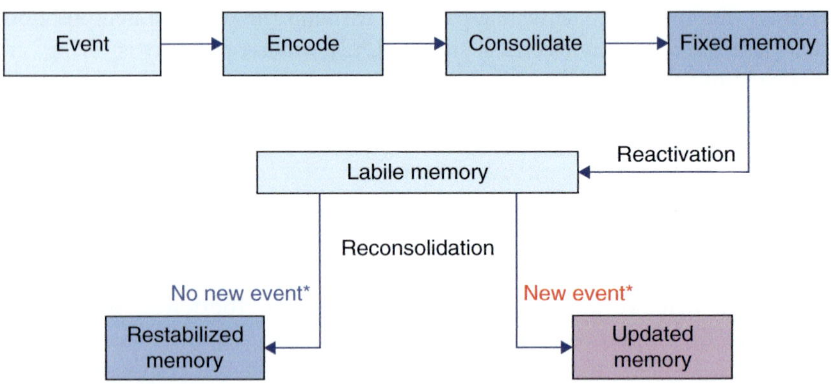

Figure 1.2 Making and Updating Memories.

Adapted from Nadel et al., 2012, p. 1641.

new material (as opposed to last-minute cramming) is so helpful before tests and exams (Nadel et al., 2007).

If we switch our metaphor up a bit, we can think of Clara as having a fear-shame superhighway running through her brain—thick pathways that have been well maintained and repeatedly repaved. In contrast, pathways associated with pride, confidence, and feelings of safety have not been fired up very often and, thus, are not well maintained or well connected to her fear-shame superhighway. These more positive feelings are hard to trigger and tend to be weaker. In order to strengthen connections to positive feelings and associated memories, we have to repeatedly help Clara activate new feelings and connections and tie them into her existing superhighways. Think of building new ramps on to and off of the fear-shame superhighway until the highway itself is so altered that it is no longer recognizable, with as many routes characterized by confidence, safety, and pride as by fear or shame. What a different road trip that would be!

There is just one more important point to consider: timing. Research suggests that a memory can be sent back to long-term storage in an altered state when we recall a memory and then have a new experience within the next several minutes to a few hours (Nader et al., 2013). On a practical level, this means that we want to fully activate old, stuck, painful emotions in session and then co-activate fresh, new adaptive emotions *in the same session* (Lane et al., 2015). If we go back to our superhighway metaphor, we want to help Clara feel her stuck anxiety, fear, and shame in session and then feel safe, soothed, confident, or proud in the same session. This allows us to help her to build on-ramps and off-ramps connecting one highway to another and changing her overall emotional experience. If we help Clara to experience stuck old feelings in one session and then fresh new feelings in the next session, it's like we're helping Clara to travel (and repave) the old superhighway in one session and then travel (and repave) the new highway in the next session, without changing either route and connecting them together. This process is outlined in Figure 1.3.

The Type of Emotion You Work with Matters

As therapists, we know that emotions are key to the change process, and that there is healing power in following a client's emotional process closely and empathically. However, many therapists find it a challenge to articulate why helping clients attend to, work with, and express their emotions is more effective sometimes and less impactful at other times. Through EFT, we learn that the *type* of emotion we are working with is the key to understanding this puzzle.

In EFT, we refer to three broad types of emotion: **primary**, **secondary**, and **instrumental** (Greenberg, 2015, Chapter 2). Only one of these types of emotion gives us immediately useful information about what we need to feel better, along with a push in a specific direction to get that need met. The other categories of feelings need a bit more decoding before they can be helpful to us or our clients.

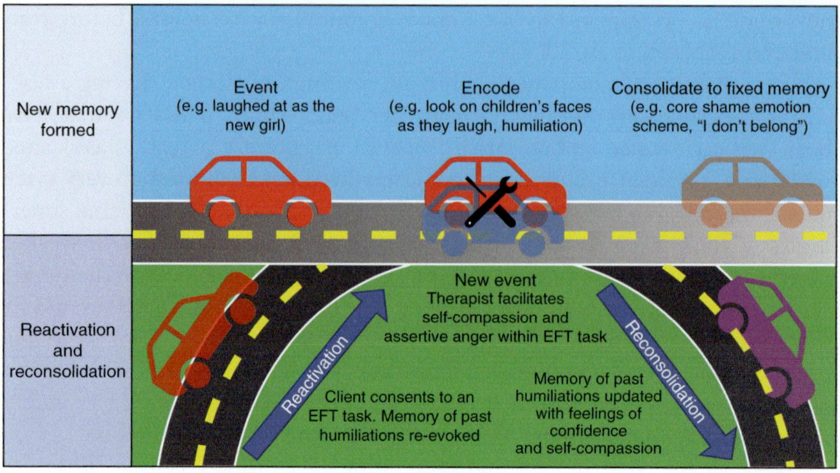

Figure 1.3 Memory Consolidation and Reconsolidation.

Adapted from Nader et al., 2013.

Primary emotions are the first thing we feel in response to a change in our environment. They are a reaction to an event or situation and they can be maladaptive or adaptive. It's important to note that words such as "adaptive" and "maladaptive" are not meant to pass judgement on the individual feelings; rather, these words refer to whether or not the information provided by the emotion will lead us towards what we need (adaptive) or away from what we need (maladaptive).

Primary Adaptive Emotions

Primary adaptive emotions are the ones that give us immediately useful information. Our emotion systems have evolved to be rapid signal detection systems, alerting us to the details in our environments that most need our attention (Hoscheidt et al., 2013; LaBar & Cabeza, 2006; McGaugh, 2003; Roozendaal et al., 2009). For example, when organized in calm satisfaction, our attention may be flexibly deployed, turning inwards towards pleasant daydreams, solving problems, being creative, or simply attending to things we enjoy around us. When organized in fear, our attention is oriented towards signs of potential danger in the environment, and, once we have perceived and addressed any threat, a healthy fear signal is turned off. These "here and now" responses to our environments help us to know what we need and are fundamentally adaptive emotional responses.

As a therapist, these tips can help you identify primary adaptive emotions:

- These feelings seem fresh and new (not old, repetitive, and stuck).
- They are experienced at an intensity that matches the current situation.

When a client is feeling a primary adaptive emotion, we want to help them attend to this feeling, understand what it is telling them about their environment and what they need, and then act on the information appropriately within their current environment. If Clara is feeling scared that she will fail a test because she has skipped classes and has not opened a book, we want to help her to attend to this feeling. It is telling her that she's in danger of violating her own standards and action is needed.

Table 1.1 provides examples of primary adaptive feelings and the needs and healthy action tendencies associated with each one. As EFT clinicians, these concepts help us to understand and make meaning of our clients' emotions.

Primary Maladaptive Emotions

Primary maladaptive emotions can be very intense, both for our clients and for us as therapists as we bear witness. They tend to have the quality of feeling repetitive, stuck, old, and familiar for clients (Elliott & Greenberg, 2021; Greenberg, 2002). The problem with primary maladaptive feelings is that they tell us more about what has happened to a client in the past (and about what they needed "then and there") than about what is happening or is needed in the "here and now."

For example, clients with pervasive anxiety can be viewed as struggling with underlying disavowed and undifferentiated pain, experiencing surface symptoms of worry and anxiety as a way both to maintain a sense of control and to avoid feared internal states or feared external outcomes. These underlying dreaded internal states—typically loneliness, shame, or fear—are the primary maladaptive emotions that are perpetually triggered and that underlie surface symptoms (Timulak & McElvaney, 2018; Watson & Greenberg, 2017).

In general, the unmet need and the action tendency will be the same whether I am feeling primary adaptive or primary maladaptive emotion. The difference is that primary maladaptive feelings are like the emotion part of an old memory—they are not truly a reaction to current circumstances and can lead to reactions that are not helpful. For example, a child may naturally feel frustration when they can't do something new. With support, they may overcome their frustration to persevere, succeed, and enjoy a (primary adaptive) sense of accomplishment. If, instead, the child is humiliated by a parent each time they make a mistake, the child may learn to respond to mistakes with shame, withdrawing and giving up in the face of challenge in all situations. This

Table 1.1 Primary Adaptive Emotions.

Situation	*Emotion*	*Need*	*Adaptive Action*
Loss of someone or something important	**Sadness**	Comfort	Express pain to elicit comfort and connection. If that's not possible, withdraw and disengage
Violation (attack on self, family, possessions, goals, values)	**Anger**	Protect boundaries, dignity	Raise my voice, stand up for myself, seek distance
Danger	**Fear/anxiety**	Safety	Flee, freeze, seek protection
Having acted inappropriately or revealed a social defect	**Shame**	Protect or repair social standing or connection with others	Hide, correct, or express awareness of impropriety
Harming a valued other	**Guilt**	Repair the damage	Apologize, make amends
Offensive, dirty, indigestible object or person	**Disgust**	Reject noxious object or person	Expel, avoid
Psychological injury	**Emotional pain**	Disengage to prevent further injury	Withdraw into self to heal if possible
Novel, unknown, unexpected stimuli	**Interest/curiosity**	Explore, understand	Attend, approach, engage, immerse
Achievement of goal, task, need, or connection	**Joy/happiness**	Savour and share	Stop and appreciate, let others know, strengthen connections
Suffering of a vulnerable other	**Compassion**	Provide caregiving	Offer comfort, soothing, support, validation

Adapted from Greenberg and Paivio, 1997, and Elliott and Greenberg, 2021.

would be an example of the development of a primary maladaptive emotion scheme of shame.

As a therapist, we can pay attention to these patterns to help identify primary maladaptive emotions:

- These feelings seem familiar, stuck, repetitive, and uncomfortable.
- They are experienced at an intensity that often does not match the current situation.

When a client is feeling primary maladaptive emotions, we want to help them fully explore, express, and transform these primary emotions. As therapists, we can do this by helping clients:

- Acknowledge and name their old, stuck feelings.
- Express what they are truly feeling and what they need.
- Feel and express new feelings that emerge in session.

As emotion focused therapists, we can remember that, after old, stuck, familiar feelings have been fully activated, we want to help clients experience and deepen emerging primary adaptive emotions in the same session so that we can alter the emotion superhighways in their brains—changing emotion with emotion! We will explore an example of this later in this chapter through the case of Clara as we explore the middle phase of therapy through the lens of EFT.

Table 1.2 lists the three types of primary maladaptive feeling we typically see in our clients. Being familiar with each of these emotion schemes will help you to spot them in your clients' stories.

Secondary Emotions

As an earlier career clinician, I (ST) often followed feelings in session based on their intensity rather than on their quality. I assumed that the strongest feelings must be the most important ones to follow to facilitate positive change. Often, I was just plain wrong.

While primary feelings are our first reactions to an event, **secondary feelings** are *reactions to our own reaction.* Secondary feelings are commonly learned through emotion-socialization processes and will vary across cultures and across time (Kitzmann, 2012). We are taught by our parents, friends, teachers, and even pop culture how to feel about our own emotional reactions. For example, young boys in some cultures may be told to stop crying or "toughen up" when they express sadness or fear (Pollack, 1999). Little girls may be told to "stop being so bossy" when they assert themselves (Lamb & Brown, 2007). In this type of socialization process, boys may learn to feel ashamed of fear and vulnerability, while girls may learn to feel ashamed of their assertiveness and desires.

Table 1.2 Primary Maladaptive Feelings.

Primary Maladaptive Emotion	*I Feel …*	*In the Past, I Experienced …*	*When I Feel This, My Body Has Learned to …*	*What I Needed and Continue to Need Is …*
Shame	Flawed, worthless, defective, small, deserving of mistreatment	Humiliation, rejection, judgement	Shrink away, hide	To be valued, accepted, and appreciated
Fear	Scared, terrified, like I'm "falling apart," "losing myself," may include dissociation	Uncontrollable danger or being abandoned by caregivers	Flee/freeze/ appease, or monitor myself (appearance, behaviour) to remain appealing to others	Safety, control, mastery, protection, stability
Sadness/ aloneness	Empty, profoundly alone, lonely, missing others	Exclusion, loss, neglect	Remain separate, avoid rejection, or try desperately or overwhelmingly to connect	(To reach out for) closeness, support, love, connection, inclusion

Adapted from Timulak and Pascual-Leone, 2015.

Like primary maladaptive emotions, secondary emotions do not provide good information about what we need to feel better in the moment. They tell us more about how we have been raised and the social rules we have internalized. Social rules about emotion expression are important—they may help us to understand how best to express ourselves in our local environment (once we know our primary adaptive feelings) in order to access what we truly need (Foroughe, 2018; Greenberg et al., 1996). However, at other times, secondary feelings may cover up or get in the way of knowing how we really feel (our primary feelings) and what we really need.

As therapists, we can pay attention to these patterns to help identify secondary emotions:

- They are reactions to reactions.
- They may not readily shift or change with empathic reflection and validation. For example, validating anxiety or hopelessness does not tend to be

helpful or emotionally transformative. In contrast, validating deep sadness tends to leave a client feeling more understood and seen … which feels *good.*

When a client is feeling secondary emotion, we can follow these steps:

- Listen carefully to uncover the client's primary reaction to a situation or event.
- Reflect and validate the secondary emotion ("I understand it just leaves you feeling so worried and anxious").
- Then empathically reflect and explore the primary feeling to get to the heart of the matter ("and I imagine somehow that underneath all that anxiety, you just never quite feel good enough?").

Instrumental Emotions

Instrumental feelings are the final category we will consider here. **Instrumental feelings** are expressed purposefully to influence others around us. They do not match what we are *actually* experiencing. For example, a client may present a light and happy exterior to others even when they are really feeling anxious, fearful, or ashamed, so that no one will see the parts of themself that they find to be shameful.

As a therapist, we can use these tips to help identify instrumental emotions:

- Verbal expression doesn't seem to match nonverbal expression.
- When a client is expressing instrumental emotion, we can do the following:
  - Understand the *function* of instrumental emotions (what is the client trying to achieve?).
  - Help your client assess whether this form of expression is helping or hindering them in accessing what they really need.

When we think of Clara's story and as we observe how Clara expresses herself in therapy, we begin to surmise that Clara is living with core shame (feeling "not good enough" or "not smart enough") along with fear of lonely abandonment (afraid people will leave her if they see her flaws, leaving her alone in the world). Clara's predominant secondary emotion is anxiety—feelings of shakiness and self-doubt when she feels vulnerable to criticism or rejection. At times, she instrumentally expresses confidence or happiness, even when she doesn't feel it, in order to feel safe and fit in without appearing vulnerable.

How Much Is Too Much?

As clinicians learning EFT for the first time, we often ask ourselves how much emotion is "too much" emotion? This is a very good question, as our goal is to help clients process emotions productively, not to retraumatize clients or to rehearse and strengthen unhelpful emotional response patterns. Psychotherapy research beginning with EFT and moving on to additional modalities has demonstrated that depth of emotional experience in session is a predictor of positive outcome in therapy and is likely a common factor across all therapy modalities (Pascual-Leone & Yeryomenko, 2016). Why might this be the case?

As it turns out, the brain encodes memories differently in high versus low emotion situations (Nadel & Jacobs, 1998; Cahill, 2000; McGaugh, 2003; Murty et al., 2010; Phelps, 2004). Memories encoded in moments of high-intensity emotion (as in dysregulation or trauma) are more likely to be remembered implicitly as fragments of information taken in by our senses—a sudden intrusive image, a sound, a sensation in our body, a smell (Van der Kolk, 2002). Memories that are encoded when emotions are regulated tend to be well organized, with a beginning, middle, and end, and with meaning that is clearer to us (Pannu Hayes et al., 2010). When individuals remember something, they tend to re-experience the emotion they felt at the time of encoding or reconsolidation (Lane et al., 2015). For example, I may remember instances of overwhelming childhood abuse, as I recalled them the last time with my therapist, with self-compassion and a sense of both safety and agency (not as a flashback as though it's happening to me again in the here and now, with all of the feelings of shame and fear washing over me).

To optimize working directly with emotion in EFT, we want clients' feelings to be activated at a moderate level, so they are neither numbing nor overwhelming, allowing memories to be activated and then reconsolidated in regulated and meaningful ways. In fact, one reason that building rapport may be so important across therapies is that a sense of safety is associated with low physiological arousal (Abelson et al., 2010, cited in Lane et al., 2015, p. 16), which in turn allows for both self-reflection and reflecting to understand others' intentions and experience (Amodio & Frith, 2006; Lane et al., 2009; Thayer et al., 2012).

To determine if a client is feeling the "right amount" of emotion, ask yourself if:

- Verbal and nonverbal cues (vocal tone, posture, facial expressions) tell us that emotion is activated; *and*
- Clients are also able to speak and make meaning of their experiencing.

This now brings us to understanding EFT as a model. EFT includes a series of research-based techniques that systematically help clients to deepen their emotions in session, shifting from *talking about* emotion to *experiencing and expressing* emotion efficiently and effectively in a regulated manner, before

Table 1.3 Six Emotion Change Processes in EFT.

Function	*Process*
Access and express emotion effectively	1. Help clients **know what they feel** by increasing emotional awareness and helping clients put words or images to different feelings
	2. Help clients **say how they really feel** by learning to express primary emotions directly rather than expressing secondary emotions or stopping themselves from expressing emotion altogether
Regulate and understand emotion	3. Help clients **regulate emotion**—developing confidence that they can safely manage strong emotion
	4. Help clients **reflect on emotion**, understanding the meaning behind their feelings and the unmet needs they reveal
Transform emotion	5. Work in session to **change emotion with emotion**. Help your client activate primary maladaptive emotions. Then, using EFT techniques, help your client to feel and express something fresh, adaptive, and new
	6. **Change emotion with corrective emotional experience with an attuned other**. Help your client activate primary maladaptive emotions. Respond with empathy, congruence, and unconditional positive regard to help your client feel safe, accepted, relieved, and soothed

having a new emotional experience in the same session (Elliott et al., 2004; Lane et al., 2015).

How EFT Changes Emotion with Emotion

EFT is organized around six emotion change processes (Greenberg, 2010; Vrana & Greenberg, 2018). These are highlighted in Table 1.3. The first four processes ensure that clients have the building blocks necessary for the final two processes.

What Does EFT Look Like in Practice?

EFT can be organized broadly into early, middle, and late phases of treatment. Below, we outline the clinical focus in each phase of treatment. Then, we'll see how each phase looks through excerpts of sessions with Clara.

What Do I Do in the Early Phase of Treatment?

- Build trust and safety.
- Assess emotional processing style.

- Notice and follow the pain compass to the heart of the matter.
- Begin to build your case formulation and treatment plan.

Build Bond, Trust, and Safety

In the early stages of treatment, clients are typically nervous. They may be concerned about judgement from the therapist, may feel ashamed of themselves, or even scared of feeling their emotions in the presence of another. In the first few sessions, we focus on building rapport and trust in the bond between therapist and client based on Rogers's (1957) three fundamental principles of person-centred therapy: **empathy**, **congruence**, and **unconditional positive regard**. We convey to the client our understanding, acceptance, and validation of their emotions within the context of their lived experience, helping the client to feel seen, respected, accepted, and safe in their pain and vulnerability. Our primary therapeutic tool is empathic responding.

Assess Client Emotional Processing Style

In this early phase, we listen to client content (presenting issues, history, treatment goals) while also attending to *how* the client shares their experience. We assess for and focus on the first four emotion change processes. To assess emotional processing style, ask yourself if your client can:

1. Know how they feel by:
    - Identifying sensations in their body—noticing and naming physical sensations that signal that a feeling is alive.
    - Naming different emotions with words, images, or metaphors.

2. Say how they really feel by:
    - Expressing what they are actually feeling rather than masking their underlying emotion or expressing something else instead.
3. Feel their emotions in a regulated way.
4. Reflect on their emotions to understand the information contained within.

To help assess your client's emotional processing style, periodically ask your client "What happens inside as you say this?"

- Use empathic conjecture and reflection to help your client find the right words to convey what they feel underneath the surface.
- Notice whether your client can regulate emotion in session and ask how clients handle their biggest feelings when alone.

- Help clients identify what they need to feel better when a strong feeling is present.

If a client struggles with any of these basic processes, help your client to build these skills first so that they are able to experience, work with, and express emotions safely in therapy.

Notice and Follow the Pain Compass to the Heart of the Matter
Notice emotion when it arises. It will lead you to the heart of the client's story. This can be as simple as noting when a client briefly tears up, when their voice cracks or becomes choked up, or when a client's facial expression changes to show a new emotional experience. Remember, secondary feelings such as anxiety, hopelessness, and anger can be signs that something more vulnerable lurks underneath. When emotions are present, how you respond can lead to further deepening or to moving away from emotion (Prenn, 2011). Follow the pain compass by:

- Slowing down and speaking softly.
- Keeping your reflections short and simple. Don't distract your client from their emotion with questions or fancy interpretations!
- Empathically reflecting on the emotion you are seeing (rather than the content you are hearing). Name the feeling and bring attention to it.
- Validating emotion. Let your client know that what they are feeling makes sense to you given their lived experience.

Begin to Build Your Case Conceptualization
Agreement between client and therapist on a shared treatment focus by the fifth session of therapy predicts outcome following treatment (Watson & Greenberg, 1996). As we identify presenting issues, relevant history, emotion processing style, and any barriers to working productively with emotion, we begin to develop a case formulation which we share with the client in an open and transparent manner before we enter the middle phases of treatment, usually around session three or four. We use the acronym MENSIT (Goldman & Greenberg, 2015) to help us to track six variables that are central to case formulation and treatment planning in EFT:

- **M**arkers: a verbal or nonverbal signal that a client's core painful emotion has been activated in the moment.

- **E**motion: primary maladaptive emotions that are unhelpful, repetitive, and stuck in the client's presentation.
- **N**eeds that remain unmet.
- **S**econdary emotions: a client's common reactions to their own underlying primary feelings.
- **I**nterruption of emotion: a client's idiosyncratic patterns of stopping themself from feeling.
- **T**hemes: a client's central narratives about self and/or others in the world.

What Do I Do in the Middle Phase of Treatment?

The middle phase represents the bulk of our active treatment in EFT. As therapists, we aim to:

- Build productive processing skills (when necessary).
- Transform primary maladaptive emotion schemes.

Build Productive Processing Skills (If Needed)

To help your clients notice physical sensations and better identify different feelings that arise, techniques such as focusing (Elliott et al., 2004; Gendlin, 1996), targeted use of empathy statements (Greenberg et al., 2008), and validation form the core approach. Many resources exist to support clients who need to develop their capacity to accept, tolerate, and regulate their feelings, and a full recounting goes beyond the scope of this chapter. Examples include DBT (Linehan, 1993; Marra, 2005) and mindfulness training (Neff & Germer, 2013).

Transform Primary Maladaptive Emotion Schemes

Many of the unique contributions of EFT to psychotherapeutic intervention lie in this area. In EFT, we have identified many markers that tell us that an emotion process is active for the client (Elliott & Greenberg, 2021; Elliott et al., 2004). Each marker directs us to an associated task or set of steps that allow us to help the client work directly at an emotion focused level. These include relationship tasks, empathy-based tasks, experiencing tasks, and enactment tasks. Table 1.4 provides a sample of EFT tasks.

We will briefly consider the example of a worry dialogue task (Figure 1.4) to explore how a marker and a task work together to assist in changing emotion with emotion. The task is initiated when a marker for worry dialogue is presented. This may consist of a client worrying or catastrophizing in session. After introducing the task, two chairs are set up facing one another. The therapist will prompt the client to move back and forth between the chairs focusing on a different aspect of the client's experience in each chair.

We will start by asking the client to switch to the new chair, asking the client to enact their anxious critic - the part of themselves that induces the secondary anxiety or worry. We will use the term the "Frightener" to refer to this part. We ask the client to imagine that they, as the Frightener, are speaking to the part of themselves that just wants to be okay. The client enacts the Frightener, expressing a typical sequence of worries and fears aloud, making explicit the process through which they scare themselves. The therapist helps the client to move from more global fears to specific negative beliefs about the self or the world.

As primary maladaptive vulnerable emotion is evoked, the client moves back to their original chair, which we will call the "Experiencer" chair. In this chair, the client is directed to become aware of what happens in their body as they receive these messages from the Frightener. We help clients to notice and name the impact of this self-treatment upon their nervous system, differentiating embodied sensations into distinct feelings, each with an embedded need. As clients access these deeper underlying feelings, the therapist assists them to become aware of and then express associated unmet needs. This may include a need for greater accuracy or fairness in expectations, support to take risks, acknowledgement of strengths and competencies, or simply silence. Often the expression of need is accompanied by evocation of primary adaptive emotion such as a shift to assertive anger, self-compassion, or simply a sense of deserving something different.

Returning to the Frightener chair, the client is asked to respond to the need articulated by the Experiencer. This typically results in one of two outcomes. In the first, the Frightener softens in response to witnessing evoked fear and pain, expressing a desire to help rather than hurt and experientially shifting from anxiety to primary sadness, fear, or pain. At the same time, the client often becomes aware of underlying values that have been associated with this negative self-treatment such as wanting to protect the self from feared outcomes. Alternatively, the Frightener may heighten, reverting to catastrophizing, often with indications of a desire to protect the Experiencer from some feared and intolerable outcome but without any reduction in this negative self-treatment.

The movement between chairs is continued until the Experiencer is able to assert boundaries, acknowledge current capacities, and identify a need to take risks and grow. This may include soothing of the Frightener from the position of a strengthened Experiencer.

The resulting contact and negotiation between distinct affect states (e.g., secondary anxiety, primary fear, primary sadness) result in new emotional experience and a new integration of meaning and experience, changing emotion with emotion. The co-activation of primary maladaptive and primary adaptive emotions in a single session, followed by noticing and making meaning of changes in the client's experience, is central to creating enduring change. We'll take a closer look at how this works below when we follow Clara's progress through the middle phase of therapy.

Table 1.4 Sample Emotion Focused Therapy Markers and Tasks.

Marker	*Task Name*	*Goal*	*Outcome*
Client feels confused or overwhelmed by too many problems	Clearing a space	Help client identify and name each problem and develop a working distance from problems and associated emotions	Client identifies priority for therapeutic focus
Client reports a confusing, vague, or unclear felt sense in their body	Focusing	Differentiate and symbolize the felt sense to shift internal experience and understand the meaning	Client becomes clearer on what they are feeling and what they need
Client is criticizing themself (name calling, focused on "shoulds," putting themself down)	Self-critical dialogue	Help client differentiate the part of self that is critical from the part that is impacted by self-criticism. Help client identify what they really need in order to evoke primary adaptive feelings	Critic softens into self-compassion; new treatment of self emerges
Client is worrying or catastrophizing	Worry dialogue	Help client differentiate the part of self that catastrophizes from the part that is impacted by worry. Help client identify what they really need and how they are protecting themself	Frightener softens into sadness, fear, and pain Experiencing self strengthens into self-acceptance, self-compassion, and empowering anger

Table 1.4 Cont.

Marker	*Task Name*	*Goal*	*Outcome*
Client stops themself from feeling	Self-interruption	Help client to identify: (1) verbal messages that stop emotion from being experienced and/or expressed *and* (2) physical changes that stop emotion (e.g., holding breath, tensing muscles)	Allowing emotion to be experienced and expressed
Client experiences lingering, stuck, repetitive negative feeling about a significant other	Unfinished business	Help client to enact the negative part of the other, become aware of the impact of this treatment on themself, and identify their unmet need to evoke primary adaptive feelings	Change in the client's automatic internal or external emotional response to the other

Adapted from Elliott and Greenberg, 2021.

What Do I Do in the Late Phase of Treatment?

This phase of treatment generally unfolds over two to six sessions, depending on the length of treatment.

- Help clients grieve and let go of the impact of their previous pain.
- Consolidate gains, meaning, and personal narrative.

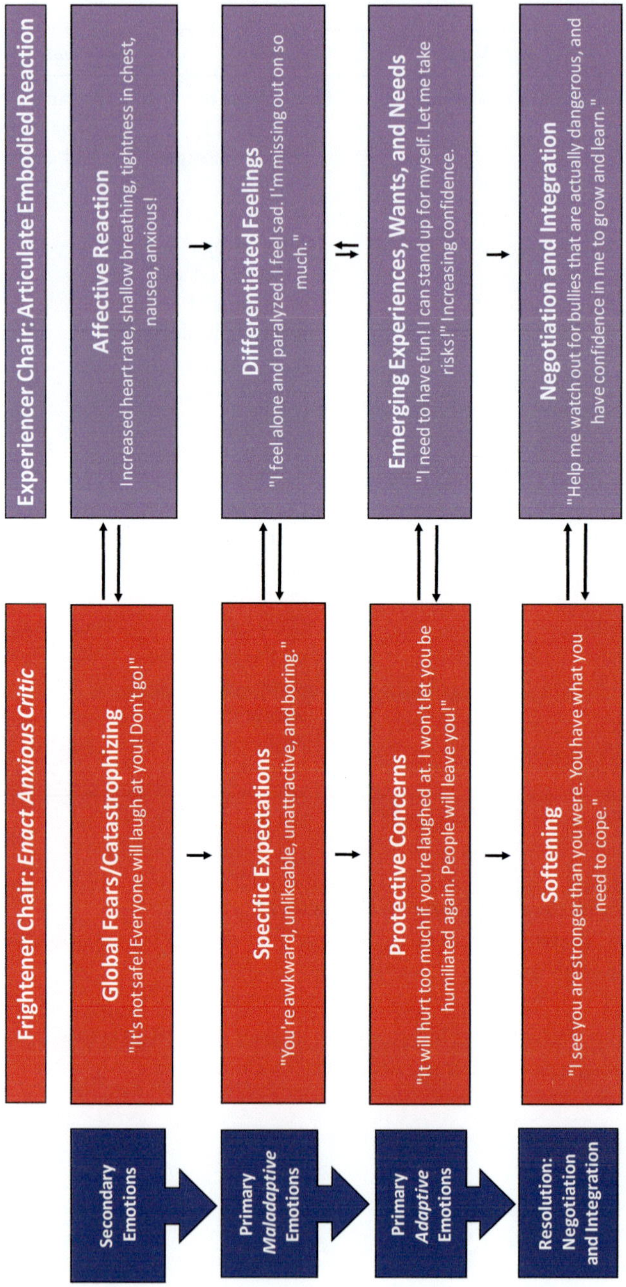

Figure 1.4 Model for Worry Dialogue Task.

Help Clients Grieve and Let Go of the Impact of Their Previous Pain
Late phases of therapy often focus on grieving the losses associated with living with painful feelings and symptoms for so long. Through this process, we help clients consolidate changes, let go of past hurts and their previously enduring influence, and move into a sense of agency and hope. This phase of therapy often commences when a planned time-limited course of treatment is coming to an end or when clients begin to consistently report and demonstrate understandable responses to present circumstances rather than responding in familiar, old, stuck, painful ways—in other words, when significant EFT markers no longer present in session.

Consolidate Gains, Meaning, and Personal Narrative
This phase of therapy often involves a return to *talking about* emotion as clients come to narrate and make meaning of changes that have occurred in therapy, including updating their view of themselves. For example, after a client experiences a stable decrease in anxiety alongside increasing self-confidence, the client may shift from understanding themself as a pervasively anxious person to understanding that they suffered from anxiety for many years as a result of prior lived experience, and that they are now able to walk through life with greater calm, confidence, and self-acceptance.

EFT from Beginning to End

In Figure 1.5, we see the evidence-based model of change in EFT summarizing changes in client emotional experience through treatment phases (Pascual-Leone, 2018; Pascual-Leone & Greenberg, 2007). EFT is a sophisticated model with a strong evidence base. If this chapter has intrigued you, additional training and supervision will help guide your learning journey (see iseft.org for further information).

Clinical Vignette: Case of Clara

Let's take a closer look at the early, middle, and late phases of emotion focused therapy through the case of Clara. Again, the case of Clara is based on a composite of clients we have worked with throughout our careers.

Early Phase

Therapist: Hi, Clara. It's nice to meet you today. How are you feeling as you come in? [Welcome and orient to inner world from the first session.]

Clara: [Smiling nervously] I'm ok. A bit nervous I guess. [Noting the client is able to name and express internal experience; appears willing to engage.]

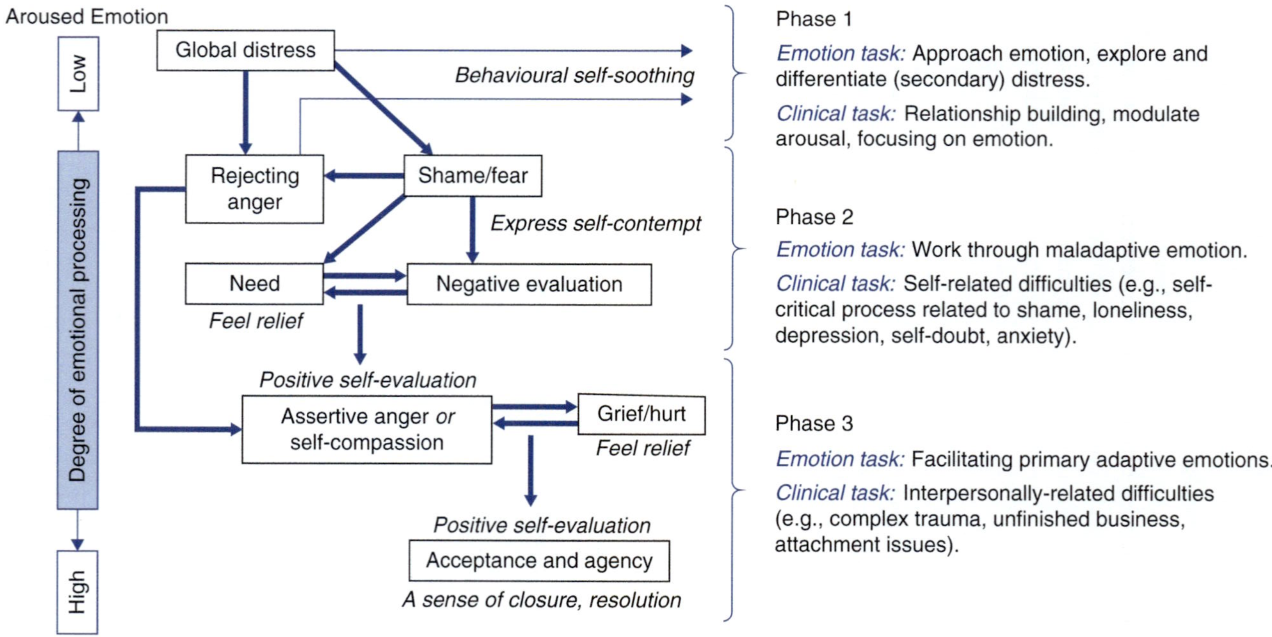

Figure 1.5 The Sequential Model of Emotional Processing.

Modified from Pascual-Leone, 2018, p. 167; Pascual-Leone & Greenberg, 2007.

Therapist: Of course, it's a bit of a nerve-wracking thing starting therapy, isn't it? [Provide normalization, validation, and orientation to therapy to help soothe anxiety and orient Clara to what is expected.] My hope for the first couple of sessions is to just take some time to get to know each other. I'd love to listen and understand what brings you in, and I may have some questions from time to time. I also welcome any questions you may have. By the third or fourth session, I'd like to share my thoughts with you about how I understand what is going on to see if we're on the same page, and I'll share my thoughts on how I may be able to help. Does that work on your end?

Clara: [Clara nods]

Therapist: Great. So, Clara, I understand from your mom that you may live with a lot of anxiety in your life? Can you tell me a bit about that to help me understand? [Inviting the client to share her experience in her own words, I will listen respectfully with empathy, congruence, and unconditional positive regard to build rapport while I listen for content and *how* Clara expresses herself.]

Clara: Um. Well, yeah, I get pretty anxious, I guess.

Therapist: Yeah, I imagine that may be hard at times. Can you tell me more about that?

Clara: Well … I get pretty good grades I guess but, like, I'm always … I'm always, well, I just never feel like it's enough and I get so stressed. It's like people think I'm really smart, but they don't see that it's just because I'm studying all the time. I don't think I'm actually very smart. [Said in a quiet voice. We simply note this marker for self-criticism, which we'll attend to as we enter the middle stages of therapy if this marker persists.]

Therapist: Oh, so it feels like your good grades don't really have anything to do with *you*, it's just that you work really hard at it.

Clara: Yeah.

Therapist: And I guess it kind of feels like, if you let off at all, somehow it will all come crumbling down, or people will somehow see that you're not really that smart after all?

Clara: Yeah. [Beginning to tear up a bit.]

Therapist: I imagine that's kind of scary? [Empathic conjecture based on a sign of pain that may lead us to the heart of the matter.]

Clara: [Clara nods; appears choked up, unable to speak.]

Therapist: Clara, can we just pause here for a moment. This is so painful. Can you take a moment, and just tell me what happens inside as I say this?

Clara: Inside?

Therapist: Yes, what happens in your body as you hear me say this? It's like there is a tear that comes to your eye, and it's almost like it's hard to speak? [This question both begins to socialize and orient Clara to turning her attention inwards and allows for further assessment of Clara's emotion processing style.]

Clara: [Clara nods] Well, I guess I just feel really crappy …

Therapist: Mm-hmm … Just really crappy. This is just really painful. And what else do you notice in your body right now?

Clara: … Just kind of shaky and … small, I guess. It's a bit hard for me to talk about myself …

In the first session, we go on to explore anxiety triggers and responses at home and at school and then talk a little about life at home. I can see it's hard for Clara to talk about her dad, and I know from an intake meeting with her mom that Dad had "a temper" and was often "hard on Clara." She also reveals heightened anxiety before social gatherings, with fears of not fitting in or appearing foolish. Our pace is slow, my voice is gentle, and my primary interventions are empathy statements and exploratory questions.

In terms of the six emotional change processes, we see that Clara is able to know and say how she feels. She can express her secondary feelings (anxiety) and she may have a sense of her own underlying primary maladaptive shame (feeling "small" or "not really good to hang around with") and fear (fear that others will reject her), but we will need to learn more about this over time. She is able to regulate emotion in session, and we will explore in early sessions what happens when she feels strong feelings alone. Although we are not yet focused on changing emotion with emotion (change process 5), Clara is not shamed or rejected as she begins to share her internal world with her therapist. Rather, the therapist responds with empathy, congruence, and acceptance, which may begin to load on changing emotion through corrective emotional experience (change process 6).

In the first three sessions, we see signs of the pain compass in her vocal tone and her shift towards tearfulness. From this early exchange, we begin to see the basic elements of our case conceptualization emerging, captured through the acronym MENSIT:

- Markers: self-criticism, worry.
- Emotion: shame, fear.
- Need: acceptance and belonging.
- Secondary emotions: anxiety.
- Interruption of emotion: we know this likely happens, but don't yet know how.
- Themes: fear of rejection by others, feeling not good enough.

Middle Phase

In the middle phase of therapy, we are seeking to assist clients in building emotion-regulation skills when necessary and are then moving into active work using marker-driven therapeutic tasks. Clara is already able to regulate her affect, so we begin working to evoke her maladaptive emotion schemes for the purpose of changing emotion with emotion.

In the first five to ten minutes of the fifth session, we explore how Clara is feeling coming into session today (stressed) and how she was feeling after our last session. She advises that she felt "ok," which suggests that pacing has been fine, and Clara has been working within her window of tolerance. In this excerpt, we focus on what is at the forefront for Clara this week.

Clara: I'm so scared to go to this party … but I can't not go. But if I go, I just know I'm going to do something stupid. I hate it when people laugh at me! [Therapist notes a marker for a worry split—fears that she will look "stupid" in front of others.]

Therapist: Yeah, there are so many layers here—I'm scared of being judged whether I go or not, but I guess underneath it all, I'm just so scared of looking foolish. [Therapist seeks to confirm the marker and uses "I" language to stay close to the client's experience.]

Clara: Yes!

Therapist: Right. And this is such a familiar feeling, isn't it?

Clara: I mean, it's not there all the time, but every time someone wants to go out and do something, or I get invited to something, it's just … there.

Therapist: Okay, could we maybe work with this a little bit today, because I think there are some pretty tough feelings under all of this anxiety? [Therapist seeks client's willingness to engage in a task, conjecturing underlying primary emotion.]

Clara: [Client nods]

Therapist: Okay, I'm just going to pull up this chair. [Therapist brings up a new chair and has Clara turn her chair so that she is directly facing the new chair.] I just want you to come and sit over here for a moment. [Therapist points to the new chair.] In this chair, I want you to be that voice in your head that says that you'll do something stupid; that others will laugh at you. In that chair, [therapist points to her original chair] I want you to just imagine the part of you that just wants to feel okay—that wants to be able to enjoy her life. Can you do that? [Therapist sees client nod.] Okay, so I want you to *be* the voice in your head that scares you about going to the party. I want you to do it.

Clara: What, so, like I'm talking to myself?

Therapist: Yes. I know it's a bit strange [therapist normalizes], but it can really help us to sort out all these different feelings and thoughts underneath all of this anxiety. So, see if you can just tell her … what … it's like "you shouldn't go to the party. You'll just make a fool of yourself." [Therapist inviting client to enact the Frightener using "you" language.]

Clara: Yeah, you can't go to this party. You don't know what to wear. You'll have no one to hang out with. You'll just feel awkward and uncomfortable all night. You'll just say something stupid and everyone will laugh. Actually, they'll just laugh at you behind your back! [Therapist notes from Clara's history that Clara does have good friends, and that there are no interpersonal skills deficits. Rather, Clara's presentation is consistent with social anxiety—she believes that others don't like her when her own core shame is evoked. Statements such as "They all …" and "No one …" are often signs of what we call projected self-criticism—a process that happens when we assume that others view us the way that we view ourselves in our worst moments.]

Therapist: Yes, can you tell her what it is about her that makes people laugh at her? Like, what is it about her? [Therapist helps Clara be *specific* about what it is about *her* that her anxious critic targets in order to activate core emotion schemes and associated self-referential beliefs.]

Clara: Well, you're just … you never know what to say. You're a total airhead. You don't really understand half the jokes, and then you laugh when you shouldn't, and you just look like an idiot! [Clara begins to tear up, suggesting that her stuck, painful feelings are getting activated.]

Therapist: Okay, switch. Come over here. [Therapist directs her to move back to her original chair to **enact the Experiencer**.] Clara, what happens inside as you hear this? What actually happens in your body? [Therapist helps client tune into her embodied emotional reaction.]

Clara: Inside?

Therapist: Yes, what happens in your body?

Clara: [Client pauses and is attending inwards.] I just feel so stupid.

Therapist: Yes, and what sensations do you notice in your body? [Therapist is refocusing on bodily felt experience rather than cognitions.]

Clara: Well … [looking tearful] my stomach hurts, and it's hard to breathe, and I just keep imagining people laughing at me. I feel about two inches tall … and … I just sort of want to curl up and hide!

After taking some time to explore aspects of Clara's evoked emotion scheme of shame (her felt sense, how the voice makes her feel, memories of past humiliations that begin to come to her, how this experience impacts her behaviour), we help her to express this experience to the anxious critic in her own words. Then, we help Clara to access what it is that she needs from the critic. Asking clients to identify and express this need typically begins to activate new primary adaptive feelings such as self-compassion or assertive anger (Greenberg, 2004, 2015).

Clara: When you talk to me this way, I'm too scared to show my face! I feel sick to my stomach and I can't even breathe! I just want to curl up in the dark and hide!

After processing her shame-based feelings of not being acceptable, of not fitting in and feeling unwanted, the therapist guides Clara towards her adaptive need embedded within her shame scheme.

Therapist: Yes, and when it just hurts so much, what is it that you actually need from your critic? [Therapist says in a gentle tone, aligned with Clara's pain.]
Clara: What I need from that part over there?
Therapist: Yes—what do you need from it, when it just hurts so much?
Clara: [Client crying] I just want it to stop.
Therapist: Yes, so tell her: Stop it! You're hurting me.
Clara: Yeah, stop it! You're hurting me! I can't do anything when you're talking all the time and saying these horrible things about me. It really hurts and … and … and I just want to run away and hide. But … but then … then I just feel like such a loser when I'm alone.
Therapist: Yes, so tell her again what you need. It's like, I need you to stop it! And maybe …
Clara: Stop it! And maybe … I don't know. Like, I just need you to stop it. And, it's not fair! You're not being fair! [Clara begins to shift from primary maladaptive shame to assertive anger in response to her expression of need.]
Therapist: Yes, tell her what's not fair about it.
Clara: It's not fair! I … I do have friends and they like me—I know they do! I know Michelle doesn't see me as fake or awkward. And, she knows how bad my anxiety gets—she gets anxious too. And Marcus and his friends are just stupid—they laugh at everyone—it's not just me. I just need you to back off! And … and let me hang out with the people I actually feel comfortable with!

We spend some time here assisting Clara in fully articulating her need, in deepening into and arriving at primary adaptive emotion in the moment, expressing assertive anger and a sense of deserving something different. In alignment with the fifth intervention process, changing emotion with emotion, we have helped Clara move from activated secondary anxiety to primary maladaptive shame to co-activation of healthy assertive anger. She has shifted from wanting to pull away and hide towards a desire to affirm her healthy connections and live life. When the need has been fully articulated, we ask the client to shift back to the critic chair to respond as the critic.

Therapist: Good. Good. Clara, come back to this side. [Therapist points to the other chair.] As the critic, how do you respond?
Clara: Well … I don't know. [Pauses, reflecting] It's like, I don't want to hurt her. And, I don't want her to feel so alone.
Therapist: Tell her.
Clara: I … I don't want to hurt you, and I can see how scared and alone you feel, but … I also really don't want you to get laughed at again. [Here, we see the emergence of a **self-protective function** of the Frightener.]
Therapist: Yes, so it's just too scary to back off. Something really bad might happen? And then what might happen?
Clara: You'd … you'd just be all alone, I guess. You'd have no friends … and that would be so terrible.
Therapist: It almost sounds like you just want so badly to protect her? You don't want her to be alone?
Clara: Yes!

When worry is present in worry dialogues, it is very common that the Frightener plays a self-protective function (Watson & Greenberg, 2017). Once uncovered, this often feels like a revelation to the client (another new primary adaptive emotional experience!) and leads to a softening and negotiation of needs between the Frightener and the Experiencer. Typically, in moving towards resolution, we see a strengthening of the experiencing self organized around a desire for freedom to take greater risks to allow for growth and connection. In Clara's case, memories of being bullied and ostracized after moving to a new school in Grade 4 emerge, with a strong desire to never feel those painful feelings again. Moving through the task, Clara recognizes that her life is now very different. She's no longer the new girl. She has solid friendships and she is strong enough to handle some teasing from Marcus and his friends—including standing up to them if she needs to. This task ends with improved integration between these two parts of self, accompanied by a shift in dominant emotion patterns over time from anxiety and underlying shame to greater self-compassion and confidence.

A given marker will typically re-emerge throughout the course of therapy as repetition and emotional intensity will be required for learning and reconsolidation to reliably produce a new emotional response to old stimuli.

Late Phase

We know that therapy is moving towards ending when markers related to the client's initial goals no longer emerge with any frequency, and new goals and markers have not emerged. For Clara, this might look like a gradual reduction in anxiety, with more of her time spent thinking about her daily affairs, enjoying downtime with her friends, and being focused on completing tasks that are important to her. In the final stages of therapy with Clara, we focus on helping her notice and narrate changes she has experienced in herself over the course of therapy, coming to see herself as a person who used to be very anxious but who now has more confidence in herself based on her actual daily experiences.

Conclusion

Often, youth enter therapy reluctantly; this may be owing to fear of judgement, or not looking for another adult in their lives to try and "fix" them, label them, or tell them what to do. For many decades, there have been two opposing therapeutic approaches available for youth: highly structured, didactic, cognitive and behavioural therapies versus unstructured supportive counselling. During this same time period, emotion focused therapy developed from a process-experiential examination of how people and relationships transform into an efficacious therapeutic approach with applications to individuals with depression, generalized anxiety, trauma, and more. Recently, clinician-scientists in the field have theorized that EFT may have transdiagnostic therapeutic value. In adapting EFT to a new population, we stand on the shoulders of eminent researchers, clinical teachers and supervisors, and particularly psychologists who embody the clinician-scientist-scholar model (Raimy, 1950). Indeed, there is more process research conducted for EFT than for any other therapeutic intervention—we not only know that it works, but we know a lot about *how* it works, the timing of specific aspects of the process, and more. This is quite an impressive accomplishment for a therapy that is so practical, concrete, and technically proficient that it could have easily overshadowed the strong theoretical base on which it rests. EFT-Y provides us with the opportunity to provide youth with a new experience in therapy: one in which they are seen as whole people with permission to feel seemingly opposing things at the same time, and one in which their health-seeking self is honoured and supported so that they can lead themselves to healing.

References

Abelson, J. L., Khan, S., Young, E. A., & Liberzon, I. (2010). Cognitive modulation of endocrine responses to CRH stimulation in healthy subjects. *Psychoneuroendocrinology*, *35*(3), 451–459. https://doi.org/10.1016/j.psyneuen.2009.08.007

Amodio, D. M., & Frith, C. D. (2006). Meeting of minds: The medial frontal cortex and social cognition. *Nature Reviews Neuroscience*, 7, 268–277. https://doi.org/10.1038/nrn1884

Bryant, A. (2013, August 27). Ask a neuroscientist! What is the synaptic firing rate of the human brain? *NeuWrite West*. www.neuwritewest.org/blog/4541

Cahill, L. (2000). Neurobiological mechanisms of emotionally influenced, long-term memory. *Progress in Brain Research*, *126*, 29–37. https://doi.org/10.1016/S0079-6123(00)26004-4

Dance, A. (2020, August 18). Making and breaking connections in the brain. *Knowable Magazine.* https://knowablemagazine.org/article/health-disease/2020/what-does-a-synapse-do
Dolhanty, J., & LaFrance, A. (2019). Emotion-focused family therapy for eating disorders. In L. S. Greenberg and R. N. Goldman (Eds.), *Clinical handbook of emotion-focused therapy* (pp. 403–424). American Psychological Association.
Eich, E., Macaulay, D., & Ryan, L. (1994). Mood dependent memory for events of the personal past. *Journal of Experimental Psychology: General*, *123*(2), 201–215. https://doi.org/10.1037/0096-3445.123.2.201
Elliott, R. (2013). Person-centered/experiential psychotherapy for anxiety difficulties: Theory, research and practice. *Person-Centered & Experiential Psychotherapies*, *12*(1), 16–32. https://doi.org/10.1080/14779757.2013.767750
Elliott, R., & Greenberg, L. S. (2021). *Emotion-focused counselling in action.* Sage.
Elliott, R., Greenberg, L. S., Watson, J., Timulak, L., & Freire, E. (2013). Research on humanistic-experiential psychotherapies. In M. J. Lambert (Ed.), *Bergin & Garfield's handbook of psychotherapy and behavior change* (pp. 495–538). John Wiley.
Elliott, R., Watson, J. E., Goldman, R. N., & Greenberg, L. S. (2004). *Learning emotion-focused therapy: The process–experiential approach to change.* American Psychological Association. https://doi.org/10.1037/10725-000
Fernández, R. S., Boccia, M. M., & Pedreira, M. E. (2016). The fate of memory: Reconsolidation and the case of prediction error. *Neuroscience & Biobehavioral Reviews*, *68*, 423–441. https://doi.org/10.1016/j.neubiorev.2016.06.004
Foroughe, M. (Ed.). (2018). *Emotion focused family therapy with children and caregivers: A trauma-informed approach* (1st ed.). Routledge. https://doi.org/10.4324/9781315161105
Gendlin, E. T. (1996). *Focusing-oriented psychotherapy: A manual of the experiential method.* New York: Guilford Press.
Goldman, R. N., & Greenberg, L. S. (2015). *Case formulation in emotion-focused therapy: Co-creating clinical maps for change.* American Psychological Association. https://doi.org/10.1037/14523-000
Goldman, R. N., Greenberg, L. S., & Angus, L. (2006). The effects of adding emotion-focused interventions to the client-centered relationship conditions in the treatment of depression. *Psychotherapy Research*, *16*, 536–546. https://doi.org/10.1080/10503300600589456
Greenberg, L. S. (2002). Integrating an emotion-focused approach to treatment into psychotherapy integration. *Journal of Psychotherapy Integration*, *12*(2), 154. https://doi.org/10.1037/1053-0479.12.2.154
Greenberg, L. S. (2004). Emotion–focused therapy. *Clinical Psychology & Psychotherapy*, *11*(1), 3–16. https://doi.org/10.1002/cpp.388
Greenberg, L. S. (2010). Emotion-focused therapy: A clinical synthesis. *Focus*, *8*(1), 32–42. https://doi.org/10.1176/foc.8.1.foc32
Greenberg, L. S. (2015). *Emotion-focused therapy: Coaching clients to work through their feelings* (2nd ed.). American Psychological Association. https://doi.org/10.1037/14692-000
Greenberg, L. S., & Paivio, S. C. (1997). *Working with emotions in psychotherapy.* Guilford Press.
Greenberg, L. S., Rice, L. N., & Elliott, R. K. (1996). *Facilitating emotional change: The moment-by-moment process.* Guilford Press.
Greenberg, L. S., & Warwar, S. H. (2019). *Skills training in a comprehensive set of tools for working directly with emotion* [PowerPoint slides]. Workshop lecture.

Greenberg, L. S., Warwar, S. H., & Malcolm, W. M. (2008). Differential effects of emotion-focused therapy and psychoeducation in facilitating forgiveness and letting go of emotional injuries. *Journal of Counseling Psychology*, *55*(2), 185–196. https://doi.org/10.1037/0022-0167.55.2.185

Hoscheidt, S., Dongaonkar, B., Payne, J., & Nadel, L. (2013). Emotion, stress, and memory. In D. Reisberg (Ed.), *Oxford handbook of cognitive psychology* (pp. 557–70). Oxford University Press.

Kitzmann, K. M. (2012). Learning about emotion: Cultural and family contexts of emotion socialization. *Global Studies of Childhood*, *2*(2), 82–84. https://doi.org/10.2304/gsch.2012.2.2.82

LaBar, K. S., & Cabeza, R. (2006). Cognitive neuroscience of emotional memory. *Nature Reviews Neuroscience*, *7*(1), 54–64. https://doi.org/10.1038/nrn1825

Lamb, S., & Brown, L. M. (2007). *Packaging girlhood: Rescuing our daughters from marketers' schemes*. St. Martin's Press.

Lane, R. D., McRae, K., Reiman, E. M., Chen, K., Ahern, G. L., & Thayer, J. F. (2009). Neural correlates of heart rate variability during emotion. *Neuroimage*, *44*(1), 213–222. https://doi.org/10.1016/j.neuroimage.2008.07.056

Lane, R. D., Nadel, L., Greenberg, L, and Lee, R. (2015). The integrated memory model: A new framework for understanding the mechanisms of change in psychotherapy. *Behavioral and Brain Sciences*, *38*. https://doi.org/10.1017/S0140525X15000011

Lane, R. D., Ryan, L., Nadel, L., & Greenberg, L. (2015). Memory reconsolidation, emotional arousal, and the process of change in psychotherapy: New insights from brain science. *Behavioral and Brain Sciences*, *38*. https://doi.org/10.1017/S0140525X14000041

LeDoux, J. (1998). *The emotional brain: The mysterious underpinnings of emotional life*. Simon & Schuster.

Levenson, R. W. (1994). Human emotions: A functional view. In P. Ekman & R. J. Davidson (Eds.), *The nature of emotion: Fundamental questions* (pp. 123–126). New York: Oxford University Press.

Linehan, M. M. (1993). *Cognitive-behavioral treatment of borderline personality disorder*. Guilford Press.

Marra, T. (2005). *Dialectical behavior therapy in private practice: A practical and comprehensive guide*. New Harbinger.

McGaugh, J. L. (2003). *Memory and emotion: The making of lasting memories*. Columbia University Press.

Murty, V. P., Ritchey, M., Adcock, R. A., & Labar, K. S. (2010). fMRI studies of successful emotional memory encoding: A quantitative meta-analysis. *Neuropsychologia*, *48*(12), 3459–3469. https://doi.org/10.1016/j.neuropsychologia.2011.02.031

Nadel, L., Campbell, J., & Ryan, L. (2007). Autobiographical memory retrieval and hippocampal activation as a function of repetition and the passage of time. *Neural Plasticity*, *2007*, 1–14. https://doi.org/10.1155/2007/90472

Nadel, L., Hupbach. A., Gomez, R., & Newman-Smith. K. (2012). Memory formation, consolidation and transformation. *Neuroscience and Biobehavioral Reviews*, *36*(7), 1640–1645. https://doi.org/10.1016/j.neubiorev.2012.03.001

Nadel, L., & Jacobs, W. J. (1998). Traumatic memory is special. *Current Directions in Psychological Science*, *7*(5), 154–157. https://doi.org/10.1111/1467-8721.ep10836842

Nadel, L., Samsonovich, A., Ryan. L., & Moscovitch, M. (2000). Multiple trace theory of human memory: Computational, neuroimaging, and

neuropsychological results. *Hippocampus*, *10*(4), 352–368. https://doi.org/10.1002/1098-1063(2000)10:4%3C352::AID-HIPO2%3E3.0.CO;2-D
Nader, K., Hardt, O., & Lanius R. (2013). Memory as a new therapeutic target. *Dialogues in Clinical Neuroscience*, *15*(4), 475–486. https://doi.org/10.31887/DCNS.2013.15.4/knader
Neff, K. D., & Germer, C. K. (2013). A pilot study and randomized controlled trial of the mindful self-compassion program. *Journal of Clinical Psychology*, *69*(1), 28–44. https://doi.org/10.1002/jclp.21923
Paivio, S. C., & Pascual-Leone, A. (2010). *Emotion-focused therapy for complex trauma.* American Psychological Association.
Pannu Hayes, J., Morey, R. A., Petty, C. M., Seth, S., Smoski, M. J., McCarthy, G., & LaBar, K. S. (2010). Staying cool when things get hot: Emotion regulation modulates neural mechanisms of memory encoding. *Frontiers in Human Neuroscience*, *4*(230), 1–10. https://doi.org/10.3389/fnhum.2010.00230
Pascual-Leone, A. (2018). How clients "change emotion with emotion": A programme of research on emotional processing. *Psychotherapy Research*, *28*(2), 165–182. https://doi.org/10.1080/10503307.2017.1349350
Pascual-Leone, A., & Greenberg, L. S. (2007). Emotional processing in experiential therapy: Why "the only way out is through." *Journal of Consulting and Clinical Psychology*, *75*(6), 875–887. https://doi.org/10.1037/0022-006X.75.6.875
Pascual-Leone, A., & Yeryomenko, N. (2016). The client "experiencing" scale as a predictor of treatment outcomes: A meta-analysis on psychotherapy process. *Psychotherapy Research*, *27*(6), 653–665. http://doi.org/10.1080/10503307.2016.1152409
Perls, F. S., Hefferline, R. F., & Goodman, P. (1951). *Gestalt therapy.* New York: Julian Press.
Phelps, E. A. (2004). Human emotion and memory: Interactions of the amygdala and hippocampal complex. *Current Opinion in Neurobiology*, *14*(2), 198–202. http://doi.org/10.1016/j.conb.2004.03.015
Pollack, W. (1999). *Real boys: Rescuing our sons from the myths of boyhood.* Holt Paperbacks.
Prenn, N. (2011). Mind the gap: AEDP interventions translating attachment theory into clinical practice. *Journal of Psychotherapy Integration*, *21*(3), 308–329. https://doi.org/10.1037/a0025491
Raimy, V. C. (Ed.) (1950). *Training in clinical psychology.* New York: Prentice-Hall.
Rogers, C. R. (1957). The necessary and sufficient conditions of therapeutic personality change. *Journal of Consulting Psychology*, *21*(2), 95–103. https://doi.org/10.1037/h0045357
Roozendaal, B., McEwen, B. S., & Chattarji, S. (2009). Stress, memory and the amygdala. *Nature Reviews Neuroscience*, *10*(6), 423–433. https://doi.org/10.1038/nrn2651
Shahar, B., Bar-Kalifa, E., & Alon, E. (2017). Emotion-focused therapy for social anxiety disorder: Results from a multiple-baseline study. *Journal of Consulting and Clinical Psychology*, *85*(3), 238–249. doi:http://dx.doi.org/10.1037/ccp0000166
Stevens, F. L. (2022). *Affective neuroscience in psychotherapy: A clinician's guide for working with emotions.* Routledge.
Thayer, J. F., Åhs, F., Fredriskon, M., Sollers, J., & Wager, T. D. (2012). A metaanalysis of heart rate variability and neuroimaging studies: Implications for heart rate variability as a marker of stress and health. *Neuroscience and Behavioral Reviews*, *36*(2), 747–756. https://doi.org/10.1016/j.neubiorev.2011.11.009
Timulak, L., & McElvaney, J. (2018). *Transforming generalized anxiety: An emotion-focused approach.* Routledge.

Timulak, L., & Pascual-Leone, A. (2015). New developments for case management in emotion-focused therapy. *Clinical Psychology and Psychotherapy*, *22*(6), 619–636. https://doi.org/10.1002/cpp.1922

Van der Kolk, B. A. (2002). Trauma and memory. *Psychiatry and Clinical Neurosciences*, *52*(S1), S52-S64. https://doi.org/10.1046/j.1440-1819.1998.0520s5S97.x

Voytek, B. (2013, May 20). *Are there really as many neurons in the human brain as stars in the Milky Way?* Scitable by Nature Education. www.nature.com/scitable/blog/brain-metrics/are_there_really_as_many/

Vrana, G., & Greenberg, L. (2018). Overview of emotion-focused therapy. In *Emotion focused family therapy with children and caregivers* (1st ed., pp. 1–22). Routledge. https://doi.org/10.4324/9781315161105-1

Watson, J. C., Gordon, L. B., Stermac, L., Kalogerakos, F., & Steckley, P. (2003). Comparing the effectiveness of process-experiential with cognitive-behavioral psychotherapy in the treatment of depression. *Journal of Consulting and Clinical Psychology*, *71*, 773–781.

Watson, J. C., & Greenberg, L. S. (1996). Pathways to change in the psychotherapy of depression: Relating process to session change and outcome. *Psychotherapy: Theory, Research, Practice, Training*, *33*(2), 262–274. https://doi.org/10.1037/0033-3204.33.2.262

Watson, J. C., & Greenberg, L. S. (2017). *Emotion-focused therapy for generalized anxiety disorder.* American Psychological Association. https://doi.org/10.1037/0000018-000

2

Emotion Focused Therapy for Youth

Mirisse Foroughe

Many youth do not want to be in therapy and want even less to work on feeling painful emotions while in therapy. And yet, to feel better, the emotional need is to heal the core maladaptive emotion that they have, which is often linked to the oldest, longest, and most impactful relationship in their life to this point. We cannot change what we desire and are compelled to seek it. One of the most compelling desires is that of seeking the proximity or approval of our parents. For some, it is proximity, closeness, and to be loved that is needed above all else. For others, it is approval, respect, and to be seen for who they are. While the object of their desire may be the caregiver, the desire itself is **emotion**. *The entire goal of therapy is to feel more one way and less another* (Greenberg, 2021). And, in most people, the way they are feeling can be observed empirically—unlike thought, emotion can be seen and felt and heard—observed by you, the therapist. Is your patient saying they are angry but crying? Dismissing that someone matters to them while clenching their fists? What is their nonverbal communication telling you, and is it congruent with their narrative?

Human connection is far from simple, and our understanding of it has only begun to take shape. Emotion focused therapy for youth offers an approach that

DOI: 10.4324/9781003218968-2

is honest about both the complexity and uncertainty involved in supporting children and youth to find their way to emotional health. To support our adaptation of emotion focused therapy (EFT) for this population, we have found it valuable to follow the path that EFT clinicians and researchers have paved in drawing from emotion science, the study of nonverbal behaviour, and our understanding of each youth's functioning within their complex system. This understanding can be based on the youth's own perspective, parent perspectives, collateral sources, as well as our own emotional reactions, empirical observations, and empathic inferences that we make as a therapist. Taken together, these sources of information help to create as complete a view as we can have so that we can support our young clients. Of course, as EFT teaches us in the tradition of humanistic psychotherapy, we can never be an expert on another person; we can, however, use empathy to allow us imaginative entry into the youth's experience.

EFT-Y: Assessment Tasks

Assessing Motivation

When working with youth, in contrast to therapy with adults, there is a greater chance of encountering scepticism—either in the youth themselves or from others in their life—and what may appear to be "low motivation." What does this actually mean? What exactly is "motivation"? In our view, motivation is a term that describes the net effect of two or more emotions in conflict: if a soldier feels a little annoyed at doing 50 push-ups but is quite fearful of disobeying a direct order from his commanding officer, he may do the push-ups and appear "motivated." If a child is excited to earn an "A" on their oral presentation but terrified about being laughed at by kids in the class, they may not go through with the presentation—does this mean they are not motivated? The term motivation does not give us any information about what the actual "motive" is in either of these cases—*it is emotion that underlies our motives and drives our behaviour*. When we stop concerning ourselves with assessing motivation, assuming instead that every youth has a part of themselves that very much wants to feel better, we can focus on the therapeutic bond and ally with the health-seeking part of the client in front of us. This humanistic stance has practical implications for the way we talk to clients; we can focus on the emotion driving their behaviour rather than passing judgement on them for not seeming ready or not appearing motivated.

Assessing Emotion

Most youth seek therapy for emotional difficulties of one type or another: feeling sad, anxious, angry, scared, being unable to deal with their emotions, feeling too little, feeling too much, or otherwise not being able to access or express their emotions in a way that is adaptive to their current needs. Support with activating emotion—or "up-regulating"—may be needed if youth are numbing their feelings, emotionally shut off, or pushing feelings down. Support with deactivating emotion—"down-regulating"—is more appropriate for youth in a heightened state of emotional arousal, overwhelmed by their emotions, or not yet able to tolerate the emotion arousal that they experience. The EFT-Y model views affect regulation as a core motive of therapy. However, the focus on emotion is not about feeling "good" or feeling pleasure—for example, a high-achieving student does not feel "pleasure" in studying for hours to prepare for exams or even in sitting the exams themselves, but the experiences bring other emotions to them, such as feelings of competence and mastery. Of course, all therapy addresses emotion, whether directly or indirectly, but EFT emphasizes the processing and transformation of emotion in a systematic way, beginning with the emotion assessment.

Emotion Assessment: What to Assess

When we conduct an emotion assessment for youth, we are asking ourselves to observe and attend to *what*, *how*, and *how much they feel*. This includes the basic emotions that they are presenting with, as well as the emotion schemes that have developed over time as they tried to feel certain ways and not others. **Emotion** is defined as a complex state that results in physical and psychological change, influences what we think and what we do, and alerts us to threat and to actions that will help us survive. Initially, the work with youth involves helping them approach their feelings. Even this first task can be highly threatening for youth in therapy:

> I was completely terrified coming into the first few sessions. I thought I would lose control, it would hurt so much, and that it would be totally overwhelming, like I wouldn't be able to handle it and would die or something.
>
> (Eva, aged 12)

Another part of the emotion assessment is *assessing the youth's current comfort level with emotion* so that we can provide appropriate support as we offer opportunities for them to notice their own emotional experiences. As our assessment progresses, we can differentiate between different categories of emotion. **Primary adaptive emotions** are biologically adaptive because they give us helpful information. They are "gut feelings"—fear of an oncoming car when we cross the street or sadness about a loss that we experienced—and will call the body to act in ways that aid survival. **Primary maladaptive** emotions are a function of memory. At one point, they were adaptive (fear in the midst of an angry parent expressing harsh criticism) but are no longer serving us (fear in the midst of a child bullying us or a teacher expressing constructive criticism). **Secondary emotions** come second and mask the primary emotion—such as feeling ashamed of our sadness, scared of our anger, or angry at our feelings of shame. **Instrumental** emotions are employed to achieve an aim, such as expressing sadness to manipulate or anger to keep someone at bay. The client isn't necessarily doing this with awareness and may be offended or hurt if the instrumental emotion is called out. It can be helpful to simply tend to what is driving the instrumental emotion, which is typically a need for validation or support.

How to Assess

From the first moments of the initial session, the emotion assessment of the client begins. We follow what our client says and does and note how they follow what we pay attention to: research into the EFT process shows us that clients are eight times more likely to follow our focus on emotion if we include this focus in the last part of our statement (Greenberg, 2021). So, if a youth says: "I was scared when I went to the party and there were so many people there, it was crowded, and we stayed really late," and we respond with a question about how many people were there or what they were doing, the youth will likely respond with more "content" or non-experiential information. But, if we respond to the same youth with: "Wow, so it was a lot to take in and you stayed a long time—and you remember being scared," they will be much more likely to follow our focus on their experiential, emotional process rather than offer more content about the party. What this tells us is that our responses are important, influential, and capable of drawing the youth's attention to their own internal processes. Most youth will begin by narrating an event or experience, focusing primarily on who was involved and what each person said or did. With targeted responses, we can help youth move to a deeper level of experience:

Table 2.1 Deeping the Level of Experience.

Level of Experience	*Client Statement*	*Therapist Response*
Behaviour	My mom wasn't even listening to me	What does that mean to you?
Meaning	I don't matter to her	Picture your mom here and tell her
Expression	It's like I don't matter to you	Tell her how that makes you feel
Internal	It feels awful, like you don't see me	I feel invisible and worthless …

In our emotion assessment, we use all of our empirical senses as well as our own gut reactions to notice and draw out the youth's emotional experience. While most therapists are accustomed to taking notes tracking the content of what the client is saying, it can be especially helpful to track the process of how the client is presenting and what you notice about them—and, internally, within yourself—as they talk, draw, or play. Videotaping sessions is invaluable for EFT training and practice, as only so much of the nonverbal behaviour and live emotion process can be captured by even the most prolific note-taker. As well, it is very difficult to be fully present and in contact with our client when we are writing notes. As EFT depends on in-session processes, effective timing, and empathic attunement, it is optimal to videorecord sessions and not take any notes during the session at all. If videorecording is not possible, another option would be to audiotape sessions so that the content and vocal changes can be tracked.

For younger clients, accessing the pathway to primary maladaptive emotions seems to be much quicker than it is for older adolescents. However, clients young and old will often do their best not to feel, not to express, and not to talk about primary maladaptive emotions. As therapists, we may feel very uncomfortable at first when we notice how uncomfortable the client is as we approach their primary maladaptive emotions. Building on the strategies relayed in Chapter 1, there are some helpful ways to recognize the primary maladaptive emotion that begins to emerge as youth begin to focus on their core pain:

- The feeling that the client doesn't like feeling.
- What they are "defending" against.
- What is at the root of their avoidance.
- Fear, anger, sadness, shame, disgust, and helplessness are the usual suspects.
- Self-critics "evoke" and "incite" these emotions.
- Secondary emotions "cover" and "mask" these emotions.
- Blocks/self-interruptions try to stop the client from feeling these emotions.
- They were once adaptive but are now happening in different situations, where they are not adaptive anymore.
- Your client may be "triggered" to feel the primary maladaptive emotion over and over.
- Sometimes they don't know why they keep feeling this way (problematic reaction).
- Sometimes they are aware of it, but don't realize that they are evoking it themselves (self-critic or anxiety split).
- Usually, the root is within a primary attachment relationship (unfinished business).

Productive Emotional Processing

When we work with emotion that is "live" in a therapy session, there are specific elements that will aid us in productive emotional processing with youth: (1) We have to be working with the youth's primary emotion—if it's not the primary emotion, it's not productive processing. (2) The youth needs to be able to extract useful information from the emotion—this information is typically relevant to the goals of therapy. (3) The youth must be "contactfully aware," meaning that they are both experiencing and able to talk about their experience of the emotion. (4) The youth needs to be accepting of the emotion and feeling a sense of agency over it. (5) Emotion arousal should be moderate to high, so that the youth is not overwhelmed by the emotion or stuck in it—they can be struggling, but should not be out of control or shut down—not above 80% arousal is an approximate gauge. (6) The youth can be supported to differentiate between distinct parts of themselves and be able to differentiate the emotion being processed from other emotions. The more of these elements present, the better—this is not a linear sequence (Greenberg & Pascual-Leone, 2022), and so these elements can be present and facilitated in any order. Through the Youth Emotion Transformation Study, the EFT tasks listed in Table 2.2 have been employed successfully with children and adolescents aged 9–17 to support productive emotional processing.

EFT-Y Experiential Tasks

Youth can be engaged in emotion focused chair work for a range of concerns, with some modifications and clinical considerations unique to their age and developmental needs. These unique intervention strategies, as well as strategic, ethical, systemic, and organizational (SESO) considerations, can develop and support an effective therapeutic process.

SESO

Prior to employing EFT-Y, the SESO framework can guide our biopsychosocial, developmental formulation of the youth's current needs and supports. Strategic considerations include deciding if, when, and how to involve a caregiver in the therapeutic process (see Chapters 3 and 4); whether to introduce EFT symbolically, within a play or art therapy context, or to employ primarily verbal dialogue with youth; and determining the youth's developmental stage in relation to social communication, language, and learning abilities—as many youth are sent to therapy by their caregivers, we need to determine if the youth's "symptoms" may actually be age- and stage-appropriate. Ethical considerations involve weighing the risks and benefits of intervention, such as the decision to evoke emotion in a youth if their caregivers are not yet prepared to provide emotional support. Systemic

Table 2.2 List of Potential Markers and Corresponding EFT Tasks.

Marker	*Task Name*	*Goal*	*Outcome*
Youth feels stressed or overwhelmed by too many concerns	Clearing a space	Internal focus to identify and name each concern; note physical sensations; develop a working distance from concerns and associated emotions	Youth can "put things away" when they need to; can determine a priority for current therapeutic focus
Client feels confused, unsure how they feel, or has an unclear, vague felt sense in their body	Empathic responding, focusing	Reflect, differentiate, explore, symbolize, etc. the felt sense to shift internal experience to level of expressed emotion; explore client's understanding and meaning-making	How the youth feels and what they need becomes clearer; better able to express self; feeling of safety and acceptance in the therapeutic relationship
Client is criticizing themself (name calling, focused on "shoulds," putting themselves down)	Self-critical dialogue	Help client differentiate the part of self that is critical from the part that is impacted by self-criticism; help client identify what they really need in order to evoke primary adaptive feelings	Critic softens into self-compassion; new treatment of self emerges
Client is worrying or catastrophizing	Worry dialogue	Help client differentiate the part of self that catastrophizes from the part that is impacted by worry; help client identify what they really need and how they are protecting themselves	Frightener softens into sadness, fear, and pain; experiencing self strengthens into self-acceptance, self-compassion, and empowering anger
Client stops themself from feeling	Self-interruption	Help client to identify: (1) verbal messages that stop emotion from being experienced and/or expressed *and* (2)	Allowing emotion to be experienced and expressed

Table 2.2 Cont.

Marker	*Task Name*	*Goal*	*Outcome*
		physical changes that stop emotion (e.g., holding breath, tensing muscles)	
Client struggling to access emotion or experiencing repetitive negative feeling about a caregiver	Witness Your Parent (WYP)	Help client to enact the negative part of the other, become aware of the impact of this treatment on themselves, and identify their unmet need to evoke primary adaptive feelings	Accessing and expressing feelings held inside, whether or not they relate to the parent; sharing cut-off parts of the Self
Client has unresolved or hurt feelings; has not expressed feelings to the parent; client worried about burdening parent or afraid of parent's reaction to their feelings	Parent as Witness (PAW)	Client visualizes their parent and shares hurt or unresolved feelings, processing their own feelings throughout; can also imagine parent's response—most likely response, ideal response, and feared response	A step towards resolving intrafamilial tension *or* accessing support in sharing feelings, experiences, and needs; what is shared may or may not be about the parent–child relationship, and parent response may or may not be attuned
Client has unresolved feelings or hurt in relation to a caregiver; has felt abandoned, unfairly treated, or harshly criticized by parent; has completed PAW and is able to tolerate activation/ process further	Open for Business (OFB)	Client may begin by visualizing parent and expressing feelings or by enacting parent's maladaptive response (historical or current); empty-chair dialogue continues with several switches between parent chair and self chair in the search for attunement and relief	Transforming emotion scheme; accessing attuned support from the parent or from the Self

Notes. Adapted Elliot and Greenberg (2021).

considerations allow us to reflect on the family, school, culture, and societal systems in which the youth is situated, as well as the strengths and resources within these systems. Finally, organizational considerations involve taking into account the services, supports, and structures within the therapy centre or organization—how can we utilize or adapt the organization to optimize positive outcomes for this youth?

Intervention Strategies

Self-interruption is a task that can be appropriate right from the outset of EFT-Y, when youth may struggle even with acknowledging that there may be a reason to consider emotion focused work as part of their journey of healing. For others, once a core emotion begins to be noticed—for example, the slightest felt sense of sadness in the throat or concern in the chest—there is a quick re-regulation and denial that the feeling was important or even noticed at all. For Tanya, this is where the self-interruption task was helpful.

Clinical Case Dialogue

Client Details: Tanya, age 15
Clinical Diagnoses: Generalized Anxiety Disorder, Obsessive-Compulsive Disorder
Previous Diagnoses: Anorexia Nervosa, Restricting Subtype (Resolved)
Marker: Client responded "I'd rather not" when asked about engaging in emotion work
Task: Self-Interruption

Tanya was in agreement with therapy for generalized anxiety as well as OCD symptoms and had specific goals that were age-appropriate (e.g., "I want to be able to do things with my friends without second-guessing myself," "I don't want to be making my bed for thirty minutes until it looks just right and then turning to look at it again ten times before I leave the room"), but she was unsure about the utility of engaging in emotion focused tasks, responding with "I'd rather not" when emotion focused tasks were first raised. In the second session, she and her therapist discussed this issue, and Tanya was engaged in the task of processing self-interruption:

Tanya: I don't really see the point of, like, going back to the past and stuff … I don't really need to deal with that and there's enough going on like right now so …

Therapist: So going back seems like it would be …

Tanya: A waste of time! [chuckles]

Therapist: Right, so it makes sense of course not to want to waste time especially after last session when you shared with me all the goals that you have right now.

Tanya: Exactly. So there's no point in wasting time on other things.

Therapist: There's part of you that says it's pointless, it's a waste of time to go back. And if you do try and go back and remember these things that happened and how they felt, maybe you'll be taking time away from going forward, and maybe you'll get stuck there in the remembering, or … something negative …

Tanya: Well, I dunno about that. Just that there's no point.

Therapist: Okay, right. And before we decide to move on and not look back, can we try something? Can you separate out the part of you that is telling you very clearly not to look back, that's telling you just to forget it, and not do that. Can you picture that part of you over here [points to space across the client] on that chair or bench there?

Tanya: Okay …? [reluctantly agrees and looks to the space across]

Therapist: And if the part over there is saying absolutely don't look back, do not do it, what's left over here inside of yourself? If we separate that other part out.

Tanya: I don't know.

Therapist: Let's see. Can you switch over here and be the part of you that is telling you not to look back to the past and all the stuff that happened there? Come over here and be that part.

Tanya: [Client switches to Self-Interrupter chair.]

Therapist: Picture yourself where you were just sitting. As the part that stops you, interrupts you when you try and look back at the past, tell her not to do it. Stop yourself.

Tanya: Put it out of your mind

Therapist: Right, put it out of your mind. Do it some more. Really convince yourself.

Tanya: Everything's fine. Don't deal with it.

Therapist: Everything's fine. And don't deal with it … tell her exactly what not to deal with

Tanya: [Silent: tension in chest, face, frozen, still, throat clenched.]

Therapist: Remind her what she can't deal with.

Tanya: Don't [voice cracks]

Therapist: Aha, don't let yourself feel sad, or …?

Tanya: Don't let yourself feel anything [draws breath, slight shake of head]

Therapist: Don't let her feel—tell her not to feel and stop her from feeling right now. How do you stop her?

Tanya: I remind her of what can happen.

Therapist: Right, do it now, remind her.

Tanya: Remember what happened when you thought of Dad? And cried for three days? Do you really want to go back to that? That's what I thought. So don't do it again. Let's just get skinny and everything will be fine.

Therapist: Switch [client switches back to Self chair]. What happens here for you when she reminds you of those painful times? How do you feel right now?

Tanya: I don't … I feel nothing.

Therapist: Right, so it's effective, it worked—tell her that. When you remind me of those times, I can't feel. You stop me from feeling.

Tanya: But I want her to stop me.

Therapist: Right, so it's "You stop me from feeling and you stop me from even wanting to feel."

Tanya: [Silent]

Therapist: She's very effective, right? How much power does she have compared to you? If it's a 100% total, what percentage split do you each have? Is 90:10? 50:50?

Tanya: It's 99:1.

Therapist: Tell her what it's like to be up against that. Tell her "When you do this to me, I have almost no power left … I feel powerless."

Tanya: [Silent: strong inhale, no exhale, tension in chest, face, throat clenched]

Therapist: What's happening right now in your body? What do you notice in your throat and chest?

Tanya: It feels tight.

Therapist: Okay, you feel this tightness … where do you notice it right now?

Tanya: It's in my face and all the way down to my stomach—like I swallowed a brick.

Therapist: Right, and speak from that tense place and tell her: when you do this, it's like you put this brick here and I feel all tightened up …

Tanya: I feel completely blocked. Frozen. Like I can't be a person. Like I have to stay shut in or else.

Therapist: I have to stay shut in … or else … [two-second pause] … or else what?

Tanya: Or else … she knows.

Therapist: Okay, switch back to the other chair. Now be the interrupter and stop yourself from being a full person. You have to stay shut in or else …

Tanya: Or else you'll have nobody. Nobody wants to be there for you. You'll be alone.

Therapist: Switch [client switches]. How do you feel now, hearing her say that?

Tanya: Scared?

Therapist: Where do you feel it? Can you get a sense of it in your body?

Tanya: Here [touches chest]. I feel scared.

At this stage, the task can change to **anxiety split** or **self-critic split**, detailed in Chapters 5 and 6, respectively, depending on the emotional quality and impact of the split self. If the split is creating emotional overwhelm and anxiety, the anxiety split is more appropriate. If the split is harshly critical and inciting shame or deep sadness, the self-critic split may be more appropriate. Sometimes it's difficult to know before you start, but you can always follow the client's process and re-route to the other task. However, as a result of the self-interruption task in the case example above, there is now a "live" emotion in the therapy room and it can be furthered along the emotion transformation process. The self-interruption task may be needed several times for the same client, either in the same session or a future session, to allow core emotions to become accessible and knowable. The self-interruption process allows for emotions to be identified and symbolized, as well as incorporated into the co-created case formulation between therapist and client.

Transdiagnostic Approach: Core Empathic Responses

While several of the chapters in this manual are dedicated to specific diagnostic presentations among youth, there has been a recent shift in the literature towards a transdiagnostic model of understanding and treating mental health disorders (Barlow et al., 2017; Pearl & Norton, 2017; Sloan et al., 2017; Timulak & Keogh, 2021). EFT is an approach that fits well within this model, with "emotion dysregulation" as the core deficit and driver of symptoms across all manifestations of mental health disorders, and productive emotion processing as a core mechanism of healthy emotion integration, or recovery. Empathic responding, one of the primary components of EFT-Y practice, is designed to facilitate productive emotion processing if used at the right time in the client's process and in the context of a strong therapeutic bond. The timing of use is determined by the goal and function of the task within a particular session.

Empathic Affirmation

Empathic affirmation can be used when youth are struggling with self-related emotional pain such as shame, worthlessness, and vulnerability (Pos & Greenberg, 2007). This therapist response task takes priority over any other task within the EFT therapeutic process. When a client shares a deeply personal experience with the therapist for the first time, the therapist's task is to accept and affirm the youth's emotions. During this process, the therapist should not push the youth for deeper inner exploration so as not to heighten the existing vulnerabilities. It is important for the therapist to clearly convey that they are on their client's side (Greenberg, 2017) by validating their experiences with responses such as: "That must have really hurt you," "I imagine you feel so betrayed." Through empathic affirmation, the youth can begin to work towards self-acceptance and self-affirmation with the support of their therapist as other primary emotions are addressed: "The goal is acceptance of emotion. Self-acceptance and self-awareness are interconnected. To truly know something about oneself, one must accept it" (Greenberg, 2017).

Validation

Feelings are always valid. Validation is the unconditional acceptance of feelings and is a crucial component of EFT's empathic affirmation process. It involves letting the youth know you understand where they are coming from, and that their emotions, thoughts, needs, and reactions make sense. It is the process of being non-judgemental and conveying phrases of acceptance. The therapist reinforces that the youth is entitled to their emotional response and experience. A clear message is given that there is nothing wrong or deficient about their response; for example, "Yes, when you are in this kind of pain, of course you have a hard time concentrating; that is completely normal." Validation is important at any time when the youth shares vulnerable feelings and extremely important for newly expressed primary emotion. Using validation will allow the child to explore their emotional responses more willingly, as they do not feel ashamed or judged or the need to justify (Greenberg, 2010). Ultimately, the main function of validation is to legitimize responses and support youth to continue to explore how they construct their experience and their interactions. Validation also builds alliance, as it allows the youth to see the therapist as a safe and understanding figure (Greenberg, 2010). Finally, validation encourages an alliance with the therapist. Rebellion follows rejection (Ginott et al., 2009), and validation is the opposite of rejection.

Empathic Attunement

Empathic attunement is best described through metaphors such as taking a walk in the person's shoes or joining them on the same wavelength (Bohart & Greenberg, 1997). This refers to the process of emotional and kinaesthetic (using your body) responding to the youth's current experiences. Attunement refers to an accepting stance that tries to "lean into" the client's experience—in other words, what it must feel like to be the youth in that moment. The goal is to communicate, in every way possible, that you are clearly tracking and following the client's experience. To this end, close attention is paid to both the content of the youth's responses and the manner in which they are expressed—how are they feeling as they speak? What do their voice, breath, face, and body convey as they share their experiences (Bohart & Greenberg, 1997)? As an EFT therapist, a primary goal is to actively immerse yourself in the client's world, using your verbal and nonverbal communication to convey understanding (Elliot et al., 2004). Attunement responses are often short utterances and body language that join with what the youth is experiencing in the moment. Your facial expressions, tone, and bodily sensations can match or mirror the intensity of the client's experience (Bohart & Greenberg, 1997). For instance, if youth demonstrate a quicker rate of speech accompanied by a nervous look on their face when relating a distressing situation, you can approach, but not fully mirror, this intensity in your response by nodding quickly in agreement, opening your eyes wider, sitting up straight, and moving closer to them. Importantly, empathic attunement is the basis for all empathic responding (Elliot et al., 2004) because it requires us to feel what they feel, or at least imagine ourselves in their place.

Reflection

Empathic attunement also includes the process of reflection. Reflection, as described by Carl Rogers, gives the therapist the opportunity to repeat the youth's sentiments back to them, in a paraphrased or expanded version, while validating the experience and ensuring that they feel heard and understood (Elliott, 2012).

Evocative Responding

Evocative responding originates from the Latin word *evocare*, meaning "to call" (Lebow, 2012). This involves the therapist asking when, what, where, and how questions to bring up the youth's primary emotions and gain a deeper understanding of their experience (Elliot et al., 2004). The therapist elicits and captures the implicit aspects of a youth's experience in a tentative, open-to-being-corrected manner. EFT-Y therapists often ask questions about the youth's present experience, including internal responses and reactions to in-session dynamics. For example, (a) "What's happening right now, as you say, 'I can't take this anymore?' What's that like for you?" or (b) "Your face just seemed to change now; can you tell me what is happening for you?" The main functions of evocative responding are to increase awareness and expand elements of experience to help reorganize the experience. Additional functions are to access unclear or marginalized elements of experience and encourage exploration and engagement with the youth's experience.

Empathic evocation involves the therapist's use of dramatic and expressive language, often extrapolating from what the client has already shared and speaking in the client's voice (Elliot et al., 2004). The purpose of this technique is to assist the youth in accessing experiences, meanings, and emotional schemes (Elliot et al., 2004). Using metaphors and vivid imagery is helpful and allows for the possibility of retrieving new information (Bohart & Greenberg, 1997). Although some youth struggle with symbolic language, many grasp it quite easily. It can be helpful to try just using metaphor and imagery and seeing how the youth respond. We can also employ non-verbal symbolism if needed, especially for younger children. In interactions with youth with intense emotional responses, we might use empathic evocation less often if the youth are readily emotionally activated. Conversely, if youth tend to employ deactivating strategies, are dismissive of emotional pain, or have difficulty expressing vulnerability, empathic evocation can serve as a highly challenging but highly effective intervention.

Heightening

Heightening is the process of repeating the youth's sentiments or using imagery to make their experience more vivid (Elliot et al., 2004). The therapist highlights specific responses or interactions to intensify the youth's emotional experience. For example,

- "So it feels like you're drowning … so when you think of your friends laughing at you and not caring about what you have to say, you feel like you're drowning in an ocean of pain and nobody sees, nobody seems to care."
- "It seems like this is incredibly difficult for you, like standing there and trying to speak to someone, anyone, just to know you're not alone, but no one can understand you. You feel so alone when this comes up, and it's unbearable and makes you think that you don't want to be on this earth anymore."
- "So when you're at this birthday party, you feel like you don't really belong there, you get thoughts like 'I'm so awkward. No one here even likes me. Everyone must think I'm such a loser.' This makes you feel worthless, unimportant, so you resort to drinking or hurting yourself, numbing yourself to make these thoughts stop."

This enables the client to better engage with their experience, as it is made more evident. Heightening highlights and intensifies key emotions, vivifies experiences, and encourages new formulations of experience.

Reflecting Underlying Emotions

Reflecting underlying emotions involves recognizing emerging emotions and integrating them into the youth's self-understanding (Pos & Greenberg, 2007). The therapist offers reflections that draw upon emotions that are not immediately apparent to the youth. For instance,

> "Of course you panic and feel fear when you argue with your best friend. If this person abandons you, you might feel like you will be alone again,

> and like you might not even be worth being loved or cared for because you're 'overly dramatic,' or 'too needy,' or just simply not good enough."

The benefits of reflecting emotions are that we focus the therapy process on feelings, clarify the emotional responses underlying interactional positions, and bring the youth's inner experiences into their awareness.

Empathic Conjecture

Empathic conjectures are guesses or hypotheses made by the therapist regarding the youth's unexpressed thoughts and feelings (Elliot et al., 2004). The therapist can offer insight and share their perspective using a nonauthoritarian approach, clearly open to being corrected (Bohart & Greenberg, 1997). Empathic conjectures are useful in guiding young clients to explore their experiences more thoroughly and to put these experiences into words. The therapist works on the edge of a youth's experience to move them forward in their experience such that a new meaning can emerge. Often, these conjectures address the attachment fears related to self and others. The therapist should ask fit questions, conveying "does that fit?", to determine if their interpretations match the youth's inner experience (Elliot et al., 2004). For example, (a) "You don't believe that you will ever gain control over your emotions, and they will continue to ruin your life and your relationships, is that right?" or (b) "I am getting the idea that underneath your anger you may feel some fear and sadness. Am I getting that right, that really you are feeling fear and sadness, and you are acting angry because feeling vulnerable is too hard?" The main function of this process is to promote more contact and awareness of emotional experience, meanings, or action tendencies.

Nonverbal Communication Training

Over 60% of communication is nonverbal. With a client population including children as young as nine years of age, attunement to nonverbal communication is even more important. In the practice of EFT, we want to establish contact with the client's emotional memories, and these are filled with sights, sounds, smells, and other felt sensations that are not verbally coded (Greenberg and Paivio, 1997).

Removing Blocks

In the context of EFT-Y, blocks are simply processes that stop us from accessing or expressing emotion. Just as a singer with stage fright would feel their throat tighten up and not be able to access their full voice, emotion blocks cause unnecessary tension in the body—this serves as a block that stops other important impulses from travelling through and becoming expressed. This tension changes the client's voice (pitch, tone, and volume), their breathing, their bodily felt sense, and their movement or action. If the block is not removed, their body cannot express any emotion that they may feel because the block gets in the way. Relaxation allows activated emotions to flow through. The process you use to remove blocks is important—it's not something clients can typically just "will" themselves through. Once they start thinking, it's not possible to be "in the moment"—you are looking either backwards (reflecting) or forwards (anticipating). Neither of these states allows you to be in the moment. After emotion blocks are processed, and tension is released, the intended emotion can be expressed. This is also the way that therapists can be "live" in the moment: present, genuine, and fully there with the client. Putting your activated energy into the here and now allows you to use your energy in the way that will be most authentic and helpful. The self-interruption split process can specifically target blocks and serve to process them.

EFT-Y Process and Chair Work Set Up Guides

Given how complex and multifaceted human emotion can be, any attempt at capturing emotion process through schematics or other logic-based forms of description is not going to result in a one-to-one map of the real-life process for a specific client. However, schematics and set up guides can help us pay attention to critical elements, provide an overview of the process, and provide us with a roadmap for getting started. The dialogue examples and guides provided in this chapter will need to be accompanied by repeated practice and **process supervision**, which involves reviewing and reflecting on video recordings or audiotape of therapy sessions together with an EFT-Y supervisor.

Self-Interruption Split—Two Chair Enactment

Self-Interruption Split is one of the most important and commonly used experiential exercises in EFT-Y. Youth often find it challenging to engage with emotion, and may inadvertently or deliberately employ a variety of responses to interrupt or avoid their own emotion activation or experiencing. These strategies include laughing, dismissing or minimizing their feelings, silence and non-responsiveness, focusing on secondary emotions, indicating annoyance or boredom, or refusing to engage in the experiential task. Of course, there are many other responses or behaviours that can serve to interrupt emotion processing. Regardless of the specific client response, these interruptions can frustrate and confuse therapists and impede the client's progress in therapy. Interruptions are also understandable, self-protective, and worthy of our attention. Addressing them directly may be somewhat awkward at first, but can lead the way to identifying core emotions and strengthening the client-therapist relationship.

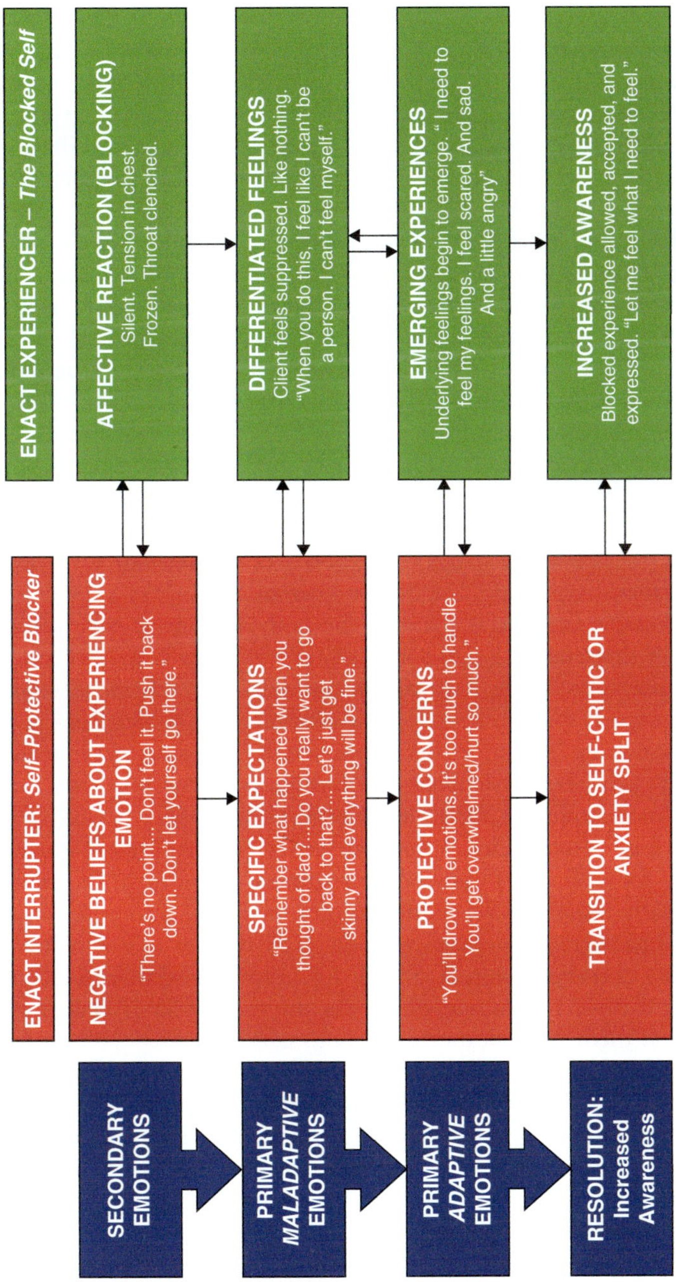

Figure 2.1 Self-Interruption Split Enactment and Dialogue Example.

Empty Chair Tasks: Open for Business (OFB)

While EFT-Y is primarily an individual intervention to be used with youth, the themes and content of therapy that are driven by the youth themself often center around their primary attachment relationships. Involving parents directly in treatment is an option (see Chapters 3 and 4), although not always possible, necessary, or clinically effective. For some youth, there will be little to no actual involvement of a parent in the therapy process. Nevertheless, through the EFT-Y Open for Business (OFB) tasks, youth can attempt to identify, express, and explore what has transpired within their parent–child relationship. Another alternative is to use OFB tasks to access cut-off emotions, express feelings and needs, share upsetting experiences, and generally speak openly without the fear of reprisal or abandonment by the parent. OFB is adapted from Unfinished Business (UFB), which is an empty chair task used in EFT with adults. For youth, OFB offers three levels that are progressively more challenging and emotionally evocative: Level 1, Witness Your Parent; Level 2, Parent as Witness, and Level 3, Open for Business.

What Happens Next? Debrief and Ending an EFT-Y Session

As EFT-Y therapists, we spend the majority of our sessions focused on our client's expressed, emerging, and disowned emotions. Just as a client receiving massage therapy on painful parts of the body may experience soreness or fatigue after the session, a client in psychotherapy that is focused on painful emotions may experience residual, breakthrough, or otherwise unexpected emotional experiences after session. Adolescents can be particularly vulnerable to emotion dysregulation. Before the youth leave a session in which they engaged in chair work, save about 10–15 minutes to check in with them and ask about their current emotional experience. What do they notice? How does their body feel? What emotions can they identify in their present state? Check specifically for feelings of vulnerability, sadness, resentment, or grief. It can be particularly important to debrief painful or overwhelming feelings if the youth will be returning to school, attending activities, or seeing their caregiver immediately after the session. Acknowledge, affirm, and clarify all feelings that are present. Check if there is anything else the youth would like to share with you. Remind them that unexpected feelings may arise over the next few days and plan for self-care and support. You may wish to provide them with a way to reach you, should they become distressed and feel that they cannot regulate their emotions as well as they are used to doing. Finally, it's good to let youth know what to expect in terms of follow-up care and any contact with you directly or indirectly between sessions, and to discuss the separation between in-therapy conversations and the communication that they will have outside therapy. For example, even if they engaged in OFB with their imagined parent in the chair, the real-life experience of speaking with their parent may not

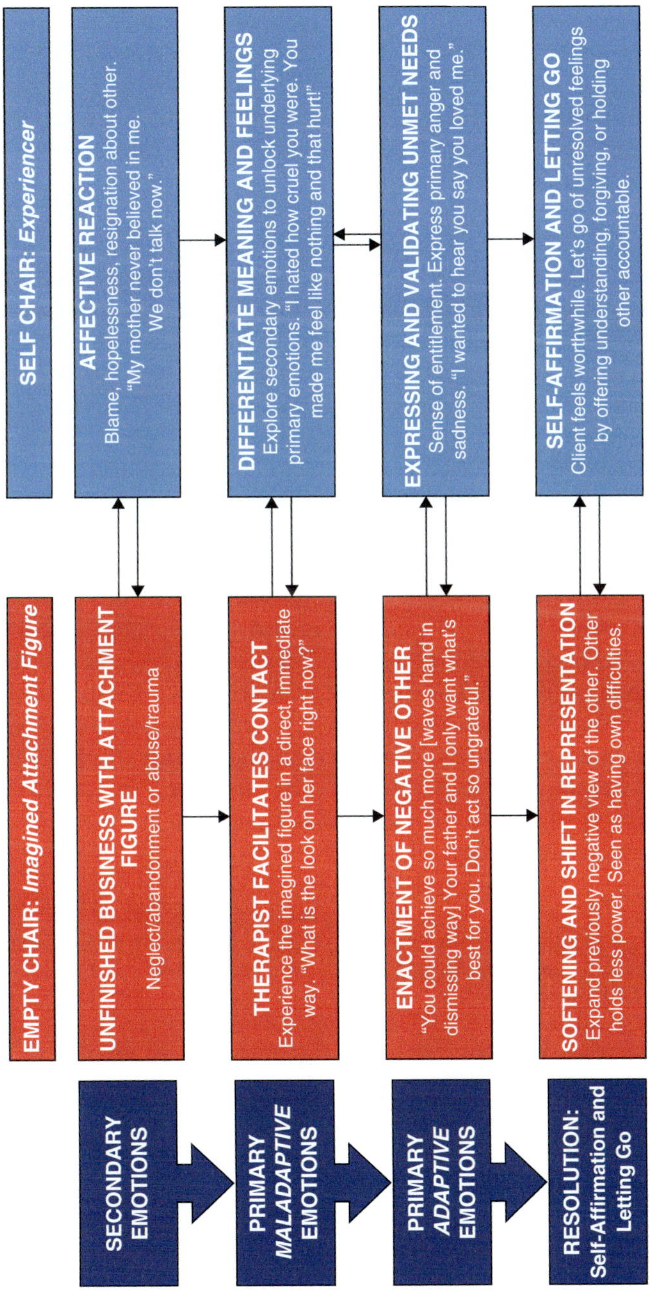

Figure 2.2 Open for Business Process.

proceed in the same way. Prepare your client for this and help them think through the pros and cons of sharing any feelings or reflections with their family or friends outside therapy. In general, when in doubt, it's best not to share the therapy process or things that they realized while in therapy with family members outside therapy. Of course, there are exceptions, and there may be other options, such as joint or separate sessions with the caregivers directly, which can be explored with your client.

Conclusion

Emotion focused therapy offers youth an alternative to traditional individual therapies. For many youth, the lack of homework, the humanistic, non-judgemental stance, and the emphasis on powerful emotional processes make EFT an engaging approach that feels authentic to them. Sometimes, after months of talk therapy, the experiential tasks within EFT provide immediate relief, self-knowledge, and contact with a part of themselves that they were not able to access before. As a therapist, it can feel quite liberating not to have to "convince" a young client to express themselves authentically, challenge unhelpful thoughts, or realize the power that they have to make healthy choices; once core maladaptive emotions are transformed, these positive outcomes in motivation, thought, behaviour, and narrative can occur organically. In other words, our job as EFT therapists is to help youth feel what they feel, which allows their feelings to lead them to what they need—and what they need to do to ensure that their needs are met. Most importantly, when youth are deciding for themselves to make changes for the better, they can take ownership of the changes rather than seeing therapy as a place in which an adult tells them what to do. Just as it has for so many adults, EFT can support youth to experience meaningful, lasting gains in their psychological health and overall well-being.

References

Barlow, D. H., Farchione, T. J., Sauer-Zavala, S., Latin, H., Ellard, K. K., Bullis, J., et al. (2017). *Unified protocol for transdiagnostic treatment of emotional disorders: Therapist guide.* Oxford University Press.

Bohart, A. C., & Greenberg, L. S. (Eds.). (1997). *Empathy reconsidered: New directions in psychotherapy.* American Psychological Association. https://doi.org/10.1037/10226-000

Elliott, R. (2012). Emotion-focused therapy. In P. Sanders (Ed.), *The tribes of the person-centred nation* (pp. 103–130). Ross-on-Wye.

Elliott, R., & Greenberg, L. S. (2021). *Emotion-focused counselling in action.* Sage.

Elliott R., Watson, J. C., Goldman, R. N., & Greenberg, L. S. (2004). *Learning emotion-focused therapy: The process-experiential approach to change.* American Psychological Association. https://doi.org/10.1037/10725-010

Ginott, H. G., Ginott, A., & Goddard, H. W. (2009). *Between parent and child: The best-selling classic* that *revolutionized parent-child communication.* Harmony.

Greenberg, L. (2010). Emotion-focused therapy: A clinical synthesis. *The Journal of Lifelong Learning in Psychiatry*, *8*(1), 32–42. https://doi.org/10.1176/foc.8.1.foc32

Greenberg, L. (2021). *Emotion Focused Therapy Level 3 Institute* [PowerPoint slides]. York University, Toronto, Ontario.

Greenberg, L. & Pascual-Leone, A. (2022). *Productive emotional processing in psychotherapy: Targeted interventions to facilitate emotional change* [PowerPoint slides]. Centre for Psychology and Emotional Health, Toronto, Ontario.

Greenberg, L. S. (2017). Emotion-focused therapy for depression. *Person-Centred & Experiential* Psychotherapies, *16*(2), 106–117. https://doi.org/10.1080/14779757.2017.1330702

Greenberg, L. S., & Paivio, S. C. (1997). *Working with emotions in psychotherapy*. Guildford Press.

Lebow, J. L. (2012 [2005]). *Handbook of clinical family therapy*. John Wiley.

Pearl, S. B., & Norton, P. J. (2017). Transdiagnostic versus diagnosis specific cognitive behavioural therapies for anxiety: A meta-analysis. *Journal of Anxiety Disorders*, *46*, 11–24. https://doi.org/10.1016/j.janxdis.2016.07.004

Pos, A. E., & Greenberg, L. S. (2007). Emotion-focused therapy. The transforming power of affect. *Journal of Contemporary Psychotherapy: On the Cutting Edge of Modern Developments in Psychotherapy*, *37*(1), 25–31. https://doi.org/10.1007/s10879-006-9031-z

Sloan, E., Hall, K., Moulding, R., Bryce, S., Mildred, H., & Staiger, P. K. (2017). Emotion regulation as a transdiagnostic treatment construct across anxiety, depression, substance, eating and borderline personality disorders: A systematic review. *Clinical Psychology Review*, *57*, 141–163. https://doi.org/10.1016/j.cpr.2017.09.002

Timulak, L., & Keogh, D. (2021). *Transdiagnostic emotion-focused therapy: A clinical guide for transforming emotional pain*. American Psychological Association.

3
EMOTION FOCUSED THERAPY FOR PARENTS

Mirisse Foroughe and Angela Ashley

While assisting youth with emotion transformation is at the heart of emotion focused therapy for youth (EFT-Y), we would be wise to remember the relationships that matter most in youth mental health: the relationships with their primary caregivers. Similar to unfinished business in EFT with adults, EFT-Y provides a systematic approach for accessing, experiencing, and working through the emotions that are connected to a youth's relationship with their parents. However, when working with youth, it sometimes makes therapeutic sense to also provide therapy directly to their parents—either in support of a child's therapy or in place of it. Over the past 50 years, therapeutic interventions that excluded or involved the parental support system have, at best, considered parents on the periphery of the therapeutic process. More recently, we have seen a rise in empirical support for engaging parents and caregivers centrally in therapy with youth. Even when parents are involved, however, their emotional experiences are not typically addressed. In EFT for parents, we apply emotion focused principles and processes to work with parents for the purpose of increasing adaptive emotions, decreasing treatment interference, and facilitating the family's overall well-being.

 DOI: 10.4324/9781003218968-3

Individual child therapists may not require, encourage, consider, or even allow parents to be involved in their child's therapeutic process (Baker-Ericzén et al., 2013; Burke & Loeber, 2015; Foroughe, 2010; Foroughe et al., 2018; Grave et al., 2019; McCauley et al., 2018; Rienecke et al., 2016). Sometimes, this makes sense therapeutically, and we can advance youth mental health with an individual therapy approach. In other cases, however, we may need to allow parents a voice, consider whether their involvement addresses a child's unmet needs, and encourage parents to attend a session even when they don't see how it could help. We strongly believe that therapists should have the opportunity to choose the best course of therapy for their client, and should be given the therapeutic tools to use if they decide that a child would benefit from their parent receiving emotional support. This chapter is written to support therapists to navigate the relatively unchartered waters of parent therapy.

In a review of therapist, youth, and child feedback about treatment barriers within the context of community outpatient mental health services, youth acknowledged that their parents' involvement was beneficial for them and expressed that *the therapist should actively ask parents about their own difficulties in the process, owing to the reciprocal influence that parent–child challenges have on one another* (Baker-Ericzén et al., 2013).

Case Vignette: You're Too Enmeshed with Your Daughter

To help us consider if, and when, parent therapy may be helpful, and how parents may feel about it, it is useful to begin by considering the situation from the parent's perspective. Consider the following case vignette for Sheena and notice the role that her mother was forced into in the process:

My (Mirisse's) best friend in high school had an eating disorder. Although it began precariously, by Grade 12 it was obvious that she was struggling to eat. Even a handful of popcorn would take hours for Sheena to ingest—she would take tiny bites from the flowers of the kernel, one at a time, and then put the popcorn away in her bag for hours before eating again. Like many youth with eating disorders, Sheena thought about food all day. At age 16, she did her own grocery shopping and cooked delicious meals for us, her friends, to eat while refusing to eat the food herself. She also didn't eat much of what her mother, a single working mom, would cook for her. I loved her so much, but I didn't know how to help her. Neither did her mother, a wonderful, intelligent, capable woman who had raised her daughter on her own for all of Sheena's life. Nevertheless, in the grip of the eating disorder, Sheena kept wasting away.

After getting down to a life-threatening 50 pounds, she was admitted to hospital. This started a treatment process with a revolving door, with Sheena being medically stabilized and released, just to relapse. It's arguable if she was ever really "treated" at all. I would learn after my best friend's death that not one of the many doctors, nurses, or therapists offered Sheena's mother any tangible parent support. She was not taught how to help her daughter eat the food that was essentially her medicine, and she was not provided with strategies to deal with Sheena's avoidance. Some of them went so far as to discourage Sheena's mother from trying to help her at all. Like many hospitals at the time, the inpatient units did not allow communication between parent and child during the child's stay. Even as an outpatient, Sheena's therapy records were confidential, and her therapist did not work with parents. By age 22, Sheena was dead. She died alone, in an apartment that her mother rented for her after one of several health practitioners at the hospital claimed that Sheena and her mother were too "enmeshed," and that Sheena would be better off living apart from her mother.

Although the word was never explicitly used, the approach that many health practitioners used in Sheena's case is not so far from the concept of a **parentectomy**: the intentional removal of parent interaction from the therapeutic process so experts can take "better" care of the child without interference (Vandereycken et al., 1989).

The Parentectomy Approach

As therapists, whether we agree with it or not, we can acknowledge the past messaging that parents have received from the health care system—and from society at large—about their potentially negative influence on their child's therapeutic process. Within North America in particular, there is a history of parent exclusion that has functioned both overtly and more subtly over the

Figure 3.1 A Visualization of the "Parentectomy" Approach in Practice.

past many decades (e.g., Bateson et al., 1956; Kinter et al., 1981; Rushton & Kraft, 2013). Even now, many parents of youth share ways in which they have received similar exclusionary messages from health professionals. The following story is from 2021:

> It started right when we showed up for the first meeting—the staff just spoke directly to my daughter and didn't even look at me, like I was invisible. I wasn't invited to join the initial consultation, and nobody set up a separate parent interview with me. I had been taking care of my child for 15 years, but nothing I knew, or understood, or felt was important to the treatment team. All they wanted from me was to pay for the sessions. When I called and left messages because I was concerned about what I was seeing at home, nobody returned my messages for weeks. When I was finally given a few minutes at the end of my child's session, my knowledge and insight wasn't on the agenda—they just wanted to tell me what they knew after seeing my kid for a total of four hours and then sent me on my way. They really thought they knew my kid and our situation better than I did. It was worse than the lack of support from my own family and all the criticism I had been receiving from family members about my child because I expected more understanding from health professionals. It would've helped from the beginning to know what I should or shouldn't expect and why, and to be given a chance to provide my input. If they at least acknowledged me, I would be fine with them deciding what the best approach would be for my child's circumstances. Instead, I felt disrespected by the professionals and useless to my child.
>
> (Laurie, mother of a 15-year-old with generalized anxiety disorder)

Parents on the Sidelines

While our appreciation for family-focused care has moved us away from explicitly blaming parents for their child's mental health struggles, the new role that parents have been given over the past few decades is often one of being "on the sidelines." If you have ever received psychological services yourself as a child, you may have experienced the memorable, and slightly awkward, experience of having a parent drop you off for your sessions and pick you up afterwards. They may have sat with you in silence, wished you well upon entering, or asked afterwards: "Did you have a good session?" As a child, you may have responded with minimal information about the therapy session, what you talked about with your therapist, or that one of the things you talked about was your parents and family life. As mental health care for children and teens has become more common over the past four decades (Barrett, 2019; Gandhi et al., 2016; Gardner et al., 2019; Naveed et al., 2017; Wiens et al., 2020), parents have often watched the therapeutic process from the sidelines, providing only peripheral support to their child's therapy—helping make appointments, driving youth to their sessions, and paying for therapy in some cases. Within this "child-centred" model, the child's therapist may allow them five to ten minutes at the end of the child's session to speak, providing a brief, often vague, "update" and limited time to hear important concerns, address parental fears, or empower parents to play a central role in their child's progress. To be fair, as child therapists, we learn the importance of upholding the child's right to privacy. As well, we do not often learn how to deal with parents, especially those whom we find dismissive, intimidating, or demanding. From the parent's perspective, being kept on the sidelines of a child's therapy can reinforce feelings of guilt, helplessness, and incompetence with respect to knowing what is going on for their child and being able to meet their child's needs. Additionally, when parents are not prepared for the changes they will see in their child, this can lead to further relationship strain and their viewing the child's expressed emotion as a negative outcome of therapy. This was the case for one father who, after eight sessions of EFT-Y for his daughter had resulted in significantly improved clinical outcomes as reported by the youth and their therapist, reported on the parent feedback form that his daughter's symptoms had actually worsened:

> Not seeing any improvement in behaviour. She is a little more moody and irritable since she started therapy. Comes home from therapy with a chip on her shoulder, blames us for things. We think this entitlement and self-indulgence comes from the therapy. Believe a more medical approach would be better—have put her on the wait list at a hospital mental health program.
>
> (Father of a 14-year-old girl with OCD, SAD, and depression)

Parents' Emotional Experience of Child Therapy

Another consideration is how a child's therapy makes parents feel. Of course, a good individual child therapist will naturally be "allied" with their own client, believing them, validating them, and seeing the world from their client's perspective. For a parent, the idea of having another adult connect so intimately with their child and, potentially, with their child's critical or negative views about their parenting or family life can also be highly threatening. To hear a therapist speak from the child's perspective, as if everything the child says is an accurate representation of what happens dynamically and relationally between parent and child, can be very upsetting. As a result, the parent may feel and express anger, dismissiveness, and avoidance towards their child, their child's therapist, or the therapy itself. The parent may wonder what their child actually says about them when alone in therapy, what the therapist must think of them as a parent, and whether the therapist blames them for their child's problems. Guilt, shame, helplessness, fear, and avoidance of emotional pain may be powerful forces, opposing the parent's natural instinct and desire to support their child and be involved in their care. With these considerations in mind, who should be the one to address such concerns when it comes to the impact of child therapy on parents? Should we refer parents for individual adult therapy?

Who Should Provide Parent Therapy?

If we agree that parents sometimes need their own therapy, how do we know which type of therapist a caregiver should see? Adult or child? While some therapists hold competencies across the lifespan of a client and can work with children and adults, many do not. Even those with individual adult competency do not necessarily have training and experience working specifically with parent concerns, which we have found may require a different therapeutic approach than working with individual adults. Working with one person (a parent) in the service of another person's mental health (a child) is not something that most therapists are specifically trained to do. We believe that parent therapy should be considered a separate and unique area of competency, and that therapists should be provided with training and support in order to practise effectively in this area. However, until such a time that graduate training programs and governing bodies regulating the practice of therapy make this change, we need to consider how best to provide parent therapy within the current landscape.

Adult Therapists Should Provide Parent Therapy

The conventional wisdom taught to us as therapists working with children, youth, and families was to refer parents to adult therapists if we were finding them difficult to deal with, we were not sure how to engage them, or we could see that their reactions to their child's mental health needs were sub-optimal. Of course, it was also difficult to assess whether a particular parent's demeanour and behaviour were due to a separate, adult mental health issue or a response to the psychological and practical strain of having a child with mental health challenges—or both. The tricky issue involved here, from our perspective as child and family therapists, is that individual adult therapy does not tend to focus on the adult's role as a parent or take child development into account—and rightly so. Parents undergoing individual therapy will not necessarily receive any support in understanding their child's needs, identifying what they can do to facilitate therapy, or strengthening their relationship with their child. Understandably, individual adult therapists are even less likely than child and youth therapists to work within a **family systems perspective**. They are more likely to focus on the needs of their adult client, see the world from their client's perspective, and ally with their client against the seemingly exhausting or unfair behaviour of the child. Even without speaking against the child or giving parenting advice, individual therapists naturally reinforce the individual adult's needs and perspectives, as they should. Parents may feel appropriately validated as individuals but still not have any support in handling their role as a parent with a child struggling through mental health challenges.

Child Therapists Should Provide Parent Therapy

Child and family therapists, on the other hand, obviously have much practice in putting themselves in the child's place, moment by moment. They often go beyond verbalizations that the child makes and pay close attention to their nonverbal communication, using reflective functioning to surmise what the child may be feeling and not saying—in other words, their **lived experience** rather than their **told experience**. Child and family therapists are also more likely to have training and experience in working from a systems perspective, collecting information from collateral sources beyond their individual client and viewing their client within the larger context of their familial, social, educational, cultural, and historical lives. Even individual child therapists without a background in family therapy rarely do their work without coming into contact with parents, while individual adult therapists rarely meet the children of their clients. The interaction between parent and child is a place that child therapists often find themselves observing and using as a source of information. While all of these points about child therapists suggest that they are in the best position to provide parent therapy, there are some vulnerabilities that child therapists may have and should be considered. First, child therapists are at risk of overidentifying with the child's perspective, including the child's way of viewing the parent–child dynamic. It can be hard to see things from the perspective of the parent, and therefore learning EFT for parents requires us to gain knowledge and practice in doing so. Second, many child therapists feel intimidated or frustrated by parents and avoid engaging with them as a result. The antidote to these negative feelings can sometimes be understanding the underlying function of the parent's attitude or behaviour and perhaps even making connections to the parent's own emotional and relationship history. When we understand where parents are coming from, what their own growing-up years were like, and how they may be feeling now as they face their child's emotions and behaviours, we can respond with empathy and targeted support (Dolhanty & Lafrance, 2019; Foroughe & Goldstein, 2018; Lafrance et al., 2020b). Other times, making connections to our own emotional and relationship history can also be helpful in avoiding emotional blocks that can interfere with our ability to work effectively with parents (Greenberg & Vrana, 2018; Lafrance et al., 2020c; Dolhanty & Lafrance, 2019).

A Caring Stance

It can be helpful to take a deliberate stance of caring for the parent whom we want to engage. While this may seem obvious, the truth is that, when we do invite parents into their child's therapy process, it's typically for the sake of the child. While we will surely have many goals for the parent session that relate back to their child's feelings and needs, it is the feelings of the parent in front of us that we need to genuinely attend to as the initial focus of parent EFT sessions. In doing so, we can be in a better position to facilitate emotion transformation for the parent in ways that will ultimately benefit the child's therapy. As a therapist, if you feel that parent behaviours, the parent–child dynamics, or family issues at home are getting in the way of treatment progress, parent EFT can help—but only if parents feel safe enough to partake. We can start by arranging a meeting with the parent and acknowledging their genuine desire to help their child, as well as how difficult a child's mental health struggles can be for the whole family. As therapists, we know that caring, acknowledgement, and validation are half the battle. Now for the other half.

Changing the Process

From initial contact onwards, there are changes that can be made to our process that will facilitate parental involvement. The following list may be helpful in considering changes when starting to incorporate parent EFT into your practice or program:

- Create a separate clinical chart for parents.
- Consider holding a parent background interview prior to meeting their child, allowing you to strategize precisely if, when, and how to involve them in therapy.
- Invite parents to join the initial consult if appropriate (typical for youth 12 and under; the time can be split for youth 13 and up or those preferring time alone).
- If youth prefer not to have parents at the consult at all, invite parents for a separate parent interview after the consult (of course, let the youth know you will do so).
- Negotiate confidentiality with youth and parents to have a clear agreement on what you will and will not share—this need not be limited to mandatory reporting obligations.

In addition to these practical adaptations to the clinical process, the overriding impression that should be present throughout our communication with parents is unconditional positive regard (Rogers, 1957), to the same degree that we offer their child in session. We need to explicitly convey to parents that their role in their child's recovery is "critical, necessary, and powerful" (Foroughe, 2018b, p. xv), and we, as therapists, believe in their dedication to and love for their child. Sometimes, this messaging alone can overturn a parent's assumption that you were just going to "fix the child" without their involvement.

Building Capacity in Ourselves

Perhaps the most powerful way to support parents emotionally is to convey that you are comfortable working with them, despite any challenges that may arise. This is much easier said than done. Some parents are very challenging to work with. Just when we think we have seen everything a parent can throw at us, another curve ball laced with shame or fear may be tossed our way. To dodge dealing with these difficult emotions, we may feel pulled to say, "I don't work with parents."

If we believe the parent is so difficult to talk to, involve, and work with, we can imagine how difficult it feels for the child of that parent. Our relationship with these figures can be helpful or unhelpful, but it is a relationship just the same—regardless of whether we allow them into the therapeutic space. The aim of EFT for parents is to leverage this relationship for adaptive and healthy ends. If we know that it is not appropriate for us to work with a particular parent directly, we can have a network of referral options in place and foster collaborative communication with other therapists, benefitting our respective child and parent clients. If we believe that changes in the parent's responses will contribute substantially to positive outcomes for a child, we can build the capacity both within ourselves and within parents to move past any historical or current barriers that they are facing to support their child's recovery.

Preparing Parents for Changes in Child Emotion and Emotional Expression

Some of the therapeutic exercises in EFT for youth may bring to light intense, painful emotions that leak outside of sessions and into interactions

Figure 3.2 "I Don't Work with Parents."

with others in day-to-day life. This new, yet heightened, emotionality within their child can make parents think their child's symptoms are getting worse, leading to the parent withdrawing them from services (Foroughe, 2018a). In EFT for parents, the therapist works to reduce this misattunement between parent and child by *providing the parent with information about the emotional processing they can expect*. For example, a child may attempt to use assertive anger towards their parent as an adaptive way to address their unmet needs. However, if the parent is not part of this process themselves, or is not practising it for their own benefit, the child may express this assertive anger and be met with a misattuned response, such as the parent becoming defensive or punitive (Foroughe, 2018a). By involving parents in the emotion focused change process within their own sessions, parents become better equipped to deal with both their child's emotion processing and their own. Consider the following quote from a father reflecting on the eight sessions of EFT-Y his daughter had completed:

> The therapy taught her a lot of things—she shared with me that she was scared to show her feelings before and didn't want to upset people. I encouraged her to advocate for herself and am very pleased to see this starting to happen. Teacher conference meeting was positive—she is more confident at school and "not being a doormat."
>
> (Father of a 16-year-old girl with social anxiety)

A child may also have a difficult time refraining from sharing what they have learned about family dynamics within their sessions (Foroughe, 2018a). For example, a child may return home after a productive therapy session, finally feeling free from self-blame, and state, "it's all your fault! I'm not the problem, you were parenting me wrong!" If a parent is unprepared for this abrupt change in their child's emotional awareness, this interaction may lead to the child feeling strongly invalidated. To avoid this, we can prepare parents to anticipate the multitude of emotional reactions that a child may have to their therapy, including crying more; blaming others; being irritable or overly sensitive; responding to parents' efforts at relationship discussions with silence, angry blasts or dismissiveness; and much more. Preparing parents to manage their own emotional reactions regardless of their child's reactions is the most foolproof way to provide support and to allow the child's emotion transformation process to continue.

Reducing Parental Fear and Increasing Self-Efficacy

It is important to consider the different levels of emotional arousal and confidence parents display upon engaging in their child's treatment process. Research suggests that, if parents experience high stress and low self-efficacy (e.g., confidence in functioning in a primary support role for their child) when supporting their children with their mental health issues, this impedes treatment outcomes and can lead to early termination of services by parents (Foroughe et al., 2018; Heath et al., 2015; Nock & Kazdin, 2001). Those who are highly emotionally aroused, fearful, or engaging in self-blame may lose their ability to think rationally or clearly, be unable to apply previously learned skills, and engage in behaviours that accommodate and reinforce their child's illness (Foroughe et al., 2018; Siegel, 2010; Stillar et al., 2016). When EFT is conducted with parents, they are taught to attend to these unprocessed or maladaptive emotions, practise positive parenting behaviours, support their child, and engage with the treatment tasks (Bloomfield & Kendall, 2012; Lafrance Robinson et al., 2014; Foroughe et al., 2018). In addressing parents' maladaptive emotions, the goal is to help parents demonstrate recovery-focused behaviour while supporting their child.

Skills Training

Parents can also be taught skills to support their child using emotion coaching, relationship repair, and recovery coaching strategies (Ansar et al., 2021; Ansar et al., 2022; Hagen et al., 2019; Lafrance et al., 2020a). By engaging in these strategies, parents learn more about how to convey a clear message to their child in both voice and body, while also taking some of the blame and responsibility they feel off the child's shoulders. This is done through an approach known as *body and voice shaping or sculpting*, helping the parent practise empathy and validation by listening to the child attentively, responding in an attuned manner, tolerating negative emotions, and conveying a nonverbal message just as clear as what is being spoken (Foroughe & Goldstein, 2018). We can pay close attention to emotions that may be impacting a caregiver's ability to produce body language, tone, and other paralinguistic and nonverbal behaviours congruent with their intended message (Foroughe & Goldstein, 2018). For example, if a parent is asking their child to wake up and get ready for school in the morning, turning away their body and using a passive tone could convey the message, "I am not confident that you will listen to me, and I am worried that I will upset you." Parents can be provided with repeated practice in sessions and assigned homework outside session to assist this process, such as writing out an apology for a difficult interaction between parent and child (Foroughe, 2018a). Prior to any joint sessions, parents should also be prepared that it may feel like the therapist is "siding" with the child in the session, especially if the parent is used to seeing the therapist alone (Foroughe, 2018a). Skills training allows parents to practise providing emotional support and prepares the parent to focus on their role in facilitating a corrective emotional experience for parent and child.

EFT for Parents

Within individual parent sessions, therapists can support the processing of **emotion blocks** in two core areas: (1) empathic support and guidance inwards and (2) evocative experiences.

Empathic Support

In 1975, child psychoanalyst and social worker Selma Fraiberg shared the story of Mary, a five-and-a-half-month-old infant, and her mother, Mrs. March, who consented to be part of a clinical family study after Mrs. March had wanted to put Mary up for adoption (Fraiberg et al., 1975). First described as a "rejecting mother," Mrs. March suffered from a tragic past of abandonment, poverty, and strained relationships with those closest to her. Mary, who appeared to receive only the basic care necessary for survival, was too quiet and under-stimulated—a baby who had not experienced the socio-emotional exposure needed for healthy development. When Mary cried, Mrs. March appeared distant and unfeeling, making absent gestures to soothe and causing the onlooking staff to question whether Mrs. March heard the baby's cries at all.

Fraiberg described thc phenomenon between Mary and Mrs. March as relating to the "unremembered past of the parents," or *ghosts in the nursery*. These metaphoric ghosts can possess a parent to mimic the abuse or neglect of their own childhood or avoid feelings and experiences that remind them of old feelings. Fraiberg and her colleagues advised that, in order to exorcize these "ghosts," empathy needed to be extended to the parent's feelings and unmet needs. In EFT for parents, empathy is a core intervention that strengthens the therapeutic alliance, guides clients to their internal experience, and can lay the foundation for evocative emotion work.

Empathic Affirmation

Empathic affirmation can be used to assist parents in addressing their underlying maladaptive emotions (Pos & Greenberg, 2007). If a parent shares a deeply personal, perhaps tragic, memory from their past growing up, the therapist must be ready to step in to offer acceptance and validation. For example, if a parent shares that they had been verbally berated as a child any time they had a poor grade in school, an appropriate response from the therapist may be, "That must have hurt you to hear," or, "That must have made you feel like a failure." The goal is to promote awareness and acceptance of disavowed or neglected emotions. In doing so, a parent's primary emotions can begin to be addressed.

Empathic Attunement

Best alluded to as "taking a walk in someone else's shoes," this empathic attunement highlights the importance of responding to a parent in a connected and aligned manner, both verbally and through our nonverbal communication. In other words, therapists should practise awareness of how their voice and body align with those of the parent. Physically leaning into the conversation, reacting with appropriate facial expressions, maintaining eye contact, and mirroring the parent's level of emotional intensity are micro-behaviours that the therapist can engage in to join the parent's experience. For example, if a parent becomes distressed and cries while recounting an instance of sexual abuse from their past, the therapist may lean in closer and offer a tissue, while also expressing genuine facial concern and saying, "There is so much pain." Closely following and mirroring the parent's experience is a core process in empathic attunement.

Validation

This form of empathy is key to the EFT process with parents, because they often fear that their feelings are not valid in the context of their child's mental health struggles. A therapist's expression of validation for a parent in session will create an environment in which they feel their emotions and experiences are normal and they do not have an inherent deficiency as a parent. Validation helps build the therapeutic alliance between the therapist and parent, making them feel more inclined to share their emotional responses and feelings, free from judgement and the need to justify their actions. For instance, a parent may say, "The kids just don't listen to me. I've tried everything. They only listen to their father; I don't know what to do." An appropriate response from the therapist may in turn be, "Yes, that can be extremely frustrating; when you feel like you've tried everything, and the kids still don't listen. It's completely normal to feel unsure of what to do next." When the therapist validates, the parent can have their experience legitimized and their feelings allowed, which is the first step in emotion transformation.

Empathic Conjecture

This approach to empathy consists of the therapist making guesses or hypotheses as to what the parent is thinking or feeling. Often addressing attachment-related fears within themself and to others, the parent is assisted in moving forward with their emerging experiences to find new meaning. By asking "Does that fit?" questions, the therapist can work with the parent to allow them to become more aware of their emotional experience, its meaning, and related action tendencies. For example, if a parent discusses their strained relationship with their own mother, a response emphasizing empathic conjecture from the therapist could be, "It seems that not talking to your mother is causing you some sadness, is that right?" or, "There's a strong wish that your mother was still talking to you, is that right?" In facilitating this dialogue, the therapist can offer supportive insight with a nonauthoritarian approach (Bohart & Greenberg, 1997).

Reflection

Reflection is a key component in client-centred therapies, but is often misconstrued as a verbatim summary of what the client said. As conceptualized by Carl Rogers, reflection should focus on the emotion within the client's response or experiential felt sense as opposed to superficial content (Arnold, 2014). Reflection invites the client to add to and correct the therapist's understanding, based on the match between the therapist's reflection and the client's inner felt experiencing (Elliott, 2012). For example, a parent may express they have never had someone in their life that looked out for them or openly expressed love. In turn, the therapist could respond by saying, "Yeah. You felt like you were alone and no one had your back, right? No one was there to tell you how much you meant to them?" In the process, the therapist reflects the parent's intention back to them in a tentative manner, intentionally leaving room for the client's corrections or further remarks.

Evocative Responding

When a therapist engages in *evocative responding*, they ask a parent when, what, where, and how questions to elicit their primary emotions and gain a deeper understanding of their experiences (Elliott et al., 2004). For example, you might say, "What's happening right now? What's that like for you?" or, "Your face just seemed to change now, can you describe how that just made you feel?" By doing this, we can assist the parent to increase their awareness and help reorganize their experience to make it clearer or encourage exploration.

Empathic Evocation

Empathic evocation involves the therapist's use of dramatic and expressive language, as if they are the parent, to better assist a parent in accessing their experiences, finding meaning, and exploring emotional schemes (Elliott et al., 2004). For example, a parent may express, "It hurts too much to think about my dad. He really hurt me and I just can't go back to that because I won't be able to stop thinking about him." To which you could reply, "Yes, it's sort of like a dark figure that creeps in the shadows and it's frightening to turn on the light and see it." Just as with empathic reflections, empathic evocations are open to revision, correction, and further exploration.

Heightening

Heightening is the process of highlighting, exploring, and focusing on key emotions using imagery, to make the parent's experience more vivid (Elliott et al., 2004). Some examples may include, "You just wish you could disappear. It's so hard to feel all of this, and you just want to go away. It's so much for one person to bear," or, "It's such a heavy weight to carry. It crushes you sometimes and feels impossible to carry on. You just wish you could take all that weight off, but it's so hard to do." It is best to use the client's own remarks as the foundation of heightening, building upon their feelings, experiences, and needs to offer a vivid image or story that can capture an important part of the client's experience.

Reflecting Underlying Emotions

Reflecting underlying emotions involves recognizing and attending to emerging emotions that may not be immediately apparent to the parent and then creating narratives to explain them (Pos & Greenberg, 2007). For instance, the therapist may say, "Of course you yell when you get angry. Because you feel so overwhelmed by what you are feeling that you need to express yourself or you're afraid no one will hear you. Is that right?" Overall, this approach helps to focus the therapy process and clarifies the emotional responses underlying the interactions of the parent.

Reframing

By using *reframing*, we can work with a parent to change or shift their perspective on an emotional issue and alter their behaviour in terms of the wants, needs, and primary emotions informing the parent's position in the parent–child relationship. For example, you might say, "Maybe you are afraid to say no to your son because of the fear of losing the relationship you have with him like you did with your father. Does that sound about right?" Reframing can help shift the meaning of a parent's responses, clarifies their attachment significance, and can foster more positive perceptions of their relationship with their child or own attachment figure.

Enactments

Lastly, *enactments* can be used by a therapist to shape the interaction, whether it be with the other party involved in the room (e.g., child, their own parental figure) or imagined dialogue using tasks such as two-chair dialogue and empty chair work discussed below (Elliott et al., 2004). In these interactions, the therapist will assist in heightening the parent's primary emotions and have them express these emotions to the other involved party to become more aware of their own responses and emotions in the relationship. For example, a parent imagining their mother in the opposite chair to them may be asked, "Okay. So now, can you turn and tell her directly, 'that really hurt me'?" Or, "Can you ask her right here, right now, for what you need most from her?" The parent can then enact what is needed, such as support or validation, to address attachment and emotion concerns (Elliott, 2012). Overall, enactments for parents can help restructure their interactions, creates new responsive dialogue, and introduces bonding events.

Evocative Intervention

Emotion blocks refer to emotional obstacles that get in the way of a parent supporting their child: a parent feeling scared to say "no" to a child's unreasonable request, a parent feeling emotionally triggered by a child's healthy expression of assertive anger, and so on. While blocks can originate within parents from feelings such as shame, fear, helplessness, and hopelessness in their current parenting style, they can also be products of their emotional history and intergenerational patterns of attachment insecurity and trauma. If left unchecked, these blocks can begin to interrupt a child's treatment progress and recovery, resulting in parental **treatment interfering behaviours** (TIBs). These disruptive words and behaviours from the parent can actively work against therapeutic progress and may include anything from invalidating a child's shared, unmet needs to silencing or suppressing a child's assertive anger or even dismissing their own adaptive emotions in session.

In order to reduce the risk of TIBs, a therapist can first address parents' maladaptive emotions or "blocks" by developing an understanding of the *type* of block—whether it be related to setting limits or showing empathy (Foroughe & Goldstein, 2018). For parents who struggle with setting limits, worrying about confrontation and repercussions such as rejection and extreme emotion, the core block tends to be more *fear-based* (Foroughe & Goldstein, 2018). Alternatively, those who struggle to show empathy via validation are concerned about appearing "too soft" or over-empowering their child and may have a more *shame-based* block (Foroughe & Goldstein, 2018). Every TIB has a caregiving interfering emotion (CIE) behind it. While the concept of the "block" refers to the obstacle to progress in therapy, the concept of the CIE reminds us that a parent is struggling and needs our support so that they can be a source of support for their child's treatment. No matter what the CIE happens to be, therapists can attune to these underlying emotions and use EFT chair work to assist the parent in becoming aware of their block, tolerating and regulating the emotion, and transforming it into something more adaptive (e.g., relief, self-compassion; Foroughe & Goldstein, 2018).

Evocative EFT Tasks

With appropriate training and supervision in EFT, therapists can use experiential chair work tasks such as self-interruption split, self-critic split, and unfinished business.

Self-Interruption

As outlined in Chapter 1, self-interruption split chair work is commonly used when a client is stopping themselves from feeling both emotionally and physically (e.g., tensing their muscles, shaking their head) in their parenting role. By having the parent rotate between two chairs, one being the "Interrupter" and one being the "Experiencer," parents can enact what they may do without thinking when shutting down their emotional expression. In doing so, they can become more aware of how they shut themselves down and, in turn, can react to and challenge that part of themselves to access the true, underlying emotions reinforcing this reaction. For example, a parent may express that, any time they ask their child to do something and they are met with opposition, they instantly shut down and stop trying. In this case, they may explain that they feel as though it's not worth it and don't want to get into an argument. The therapist can then facilitate a two-chair dialogue in which the parent can be both the Interrupter, who pushes for the parent to shut down and not continue engaging with the child, and the Experiencer, who responds to how that voice makes them feel. In doing this, the parent may reveal that, perhaps, they were prevented from speaking their mind as a child, that they are fearful and anxious when dealing with conflict owing to their own parents limiting their expression. Overall, the goal is for parents to allow the core emotions bubbling under the surface to rise and become accessible. When they do, the therapist can then decide whether to explore these feelings further using other chair work, including self-critic split or unfinished business.

Self-Critic Split

In the self-critic split chair work, the therapist helps the parent to differentiate between the critical part of themself and the part that is experiencing the criticism. Once the therapist identifies a marker within the parent—for instance, a comment such as, "I'm useless as a mother"—the therapist can help the parent engage in self-critic chair work. The therapist will support the initiation of dialogue between the two selves, encouraging and modelling the self-critic with the goal of supporting the parent in becoming more aware of how they are criticizing themselves. This process evokes feelings and needs in the experiencing chair in which parents can deepen and differentiate their responses to the criticism (Shahar et al., 2011). In turn, the experiencing self begins to learn and become more assertive about their emotional needs. For example, the parent who thinks they are a bad mother may deepen the sadness and fear they feel and, in turn, begin to realize their unmet needs for comfort and acceptance. With a newly discovered sense of entitlement to such needs, the parent can become more assertive in their demands for these needs. With practice and several enactments, the self-critic can soften or the experiencing self can strengthen, or both. For the mother in our example, a "softening" of the self-critic could sound like, "I know you can get through this. Sometimes it will be hard to get the kids to listen to you, but try. You are a good mother and you're doing your best." Alternatively, a strengthening in the experiencing self may sound like, "Stop criticizing me. I can get through this. Sometimes it will be hard to get the kids to listen to me, but I'm a good mother and I'm doing my best." At this point, these two sides or parts within the person can negotiate and integrate, resulting in a transformation of the inner experience for the parent next time they are in the same situation. As in all EFT chair work, there needs to be an adequate degree of emotional activation—not too little and not too much—for adaptive transformation to happen.

Unfinished Business

If past interpersonal experiences are in the way of a parent's ability to support their child, unfinished business chair work may be helpful. This can be an intensely evocative experiential task. While we discuss parent-specific considerations in this chapter, appropriate training and supervision in EFT are necessary to learn and practise experiential exercises and use them responsibly and effectively. In this task, parents will sit across from an empty chair and imagine one of their attachment figures, typically their mother or father, sitting across from them. The therapist can assist the parent in assertively conveying distressing memories, unresolved primary emotions, and unmet needs, with the goal of having an attuned emotional experience and feeling able to let go of the "unfinished business" with their attachment figure. This can be a gradual process over several therapy sessions, although we find that parent EFT can move quickly as compared with typical EFT work with adults.

Adapted from Greenberg and Vrana (2018), we have found that the resolution to the unfinished business task with parents can take many forms:

- Seeing the attachment figure positively and with understanding.
- Seeing the attachment figure as having done their best, despite their limitations.
- Seeing the attachment figure as someone who holds less power.
- Holding the attachment figure accountable for the violation or hurt endured.
- Forgiving the attachment figure for their past violations.
- Forgiving themselves for not living up to the attachment figure's expectations or not knowing how to handle the relationship when they were a child.

Clinical Case

Client: Michael, age 45.
Child: 15-year-old female; borderline personality disorder; eating disordered symptomatology.
Marker: In the parent background interview, Michael shared that he wants to be supportive but finds it difficult to empathize with his daughter because his parents taught him to be "strong."
TIB: Child reports father yells and criticizes her when she expresses vulnerable feelings.
Task: Unfinished Business.

Therapist: So, going back seems like it would be …
Michael: A waste of time! [chuckles]
Therapist: Right, it's hard to imagine that it will help at all, and I really appreciate you being willing to try it out just a few times.
Michael: Yeah, I'm good with trying anything. So, what do you want me to do?
Therapist: Okay—lets try something—just picture your mother in the empty chair here. [Michael is directed to look at chair across from him and allowed a few seconds to make contact.]
Therapist: What happens for you when you imagine your mother? How do you feel?
Michael: Well, right now it's wanting to let her know that I've got things under control with my family. She doesn't need to be concerned. I can handle things no matter what.
Therapist: Tell mom what it's like when she's concerned about you or thinks you can't handle things.
Michael: [5 second pause] Oof. I don't like the sound of that.
Therapist: Tell her what you don't like … what is hard for you to feel?
Therapist: [Five second pause] Well, I don't like her looking down on me or thinking I can't keep my family in line.
Michael: Tell her … mom, I don't like you looking down on me. When you think that I can't handle my family, it makes me feel …
Therapist: This is tough. Wow. Okay, hold on. I can do this. Okay, mom, listen, I got this. This whole thing with Dora is gonna be just fine, don't you worry about me.
Michael: When you worry about me, I feel …
Therapist: Alright, so feelings, feelings … when you worry about me, I feel like I want you to stop. I want you to know that I can take care of my business, like you always taught me to do.

Therapist: I don't want to let you down? It hurts me to think that you're looking down at me or … what's the hardest part of mom being worried about the way things are going for you? Tell her what hurts you …

Michael: It hurts me to know that you don't have confidence in me. Like when you come over and look around the house like you're looking for something to criticize. And the way you look at Dora like she's this messed up kid and it's like I messed up [voice cracks, eyes water, clears throat, looks at the door]. What do you call this? EFT? Like extra f'd up therapy?

Therapist: It makes sense that it's hard because of course you care what your mother's opinion is and how she sees you. She worked so hard to help you get through hard times and achieve what you have in your life. It's like, "You gave me so much and I feel sad and ashamed when I think you are disappointed in me, when you see me as having messed up …?"

Michael: Exactly. I feel a certain sense of failure? Like I am not living up to your expectations. I feel that look and I don't like the way you see me.

Therapist: Come over here and be mom [invites Michael to switch chairs]. Be mom in those moments and look at Michael that way that she looks at him.

Michael: [Enacts his mother, looking dissatisfied and disappointed.]

Therapist: Put into words what her look is conveying. Maybe it's like "Michael, you are a messing up. You are not a good enough parent." Or …

Michael: Son, you're failing. This is bad. In our family, failure is not an option.

Therapist: Switch [invites Michael to switch back to Self chair]. How does it feel to be on the receiving end of mom's look?

Michael: It doesn't feel good. It sucks.

Therapist: What do you notice about this feeling? Where is it in your body?

Michael: My chest. My stomach. My face. I feel hot in my face. Flushed. Like I want to be invisible.

Therapist: Embarrassed … ashamed … or …? Tell mom how it feels when she looks at you that way. When you give me that look, I feel …

Michael: [Ten second pause; tearful] Mom … Mom, when you look at me that way, I feel ashamed. I feel like a failure. And it doesn't help my parenting much. I take it out on Dora and I let her down. I let myself down. I need this to stop. You've always had a way to just cut me down when you look. When I was five years old playing T-Ball and you looked at me like I was the most disappointing kid in the field. It just shot me down like a grenade. I was totalled.

Therapist: Totalled—I had no confidence left? Tell her how it impacted you back then.

Michael: Back then, it just cut me down to size and I lost all of my faith in myself. I was only five years old. I didn't know better. It was always "Be strong. You can do better." And even now, I just lose my faith in myself, in my daughter, in the future.

Therapist: I lose faith and it gets in the way of parenting my daughter. Tell mom what you need instead of disapproval in those moments?

Michael: I need you to see me. I need you to believe in me. Wow. [Sighs, shakes head, puts head in hands]. That's exactly what Dora needs from me in those moments. She needs *me* to believe in her and not see her like this messed up kid. Because if I feel like a failure as a parent, I make her feel like a project that has gone wrong. I need to show her that she's amazing. I need to build up my confidence so that she can build up her confidence.

Therapist: How do you feel as you say that?

Michael: Determined. Clear. Lighter. This is pretty powerful stuff. I still don't know if I like it ... but wow. It feels kind of good.

Therapist: What do you want to do?

Michael: I want to help my daughter see how wonderful she is.

Conclusion

Despite historically being excluded, blamed, or relegated to minor roles in their child's therapy, parents can be central, powerful agents of change in a child's emotional life. When supported and able to access their internal resources, healing a child's emotional wounds is almost always within a parent's scope of ability. As therapists, we can acknowledge that parents may experience significant caregiving interfering emotions that block their ability to support their child emotionally or behaviourally. Parent EFT provides an opportunity to work through CIEs and their associated blocks when you, as a therapist, identify that it may be helpful to do so. EFT for parents and other caregivers can go further than skills-based caregiver interventions and provide an individualized, intensive, process-experiential therapy for a segment of the population that can often feel isolated, unsupported, judged, and under enormous pressure to raise the future generation. Owing to the history of negative messaging, and the tendency to feel guilty and helpless when their child is suffering, parents may need us to invite, encourage, and expect them to be involved in the therapeutic process. With enough empathic, emotion focused support, we can help even the most sceptical or reluctant parent to take one step forward.

Practical Tips

Do:

- Consider your clinical process and everything from frontline staff, forms and documents, charting, scheduling, and confidentiality agreements in order to make parent involvement possible and effective when you decide it may be helpful.

- Meet parents where they are at and take one step forward from there—a phone call or brief meeting may just be a starting point but can provide hope and build trust.
- Invite parents into their child's treatment process and have them play an active role.
- If you are working in a private setting, bill for your parent sessions—this is important self-care for therapists and will help avoid resentment and burnout. Billing for parent sessions also formalizes and legitimizes parent therapy.
- If you are working in a public or highly structured setting in which there are barriers to access for parents needing support, consider raising these issues with clinical management.
- Encourage parents and remind them of the important relationship they hold with their child.
- Acknowledge parents' own trauma and emotions that may be impacting their caregiving role in their child's recovery.
- Offer parent-only sessions to provide empathic support and be free to focus on the parent's emotions.

Don't:

- Blame parents for TIBs or interpret or analyze what went wrong for the parent—help parents achieve their own understanding from the inside out, guided by emotion.
- Condone parentectomies, even in subtle ways. Push back against systemic policies and attitudes that are exclusionary to parents and caregivers.
- Be afraid of working with parents and their presenting concerns. Almost always, they have the child's best intentions in mind and want to work with you.
- Forget the relationship that matters the most to a child's recovery: the one between parent and child.

References

Ansar, N., Lie, H. A. N., Zahl-Olsen, R., Bertelsen, T. B., Elliott, R., & Stiegler, J. R. (2022). Efficacy of emotion-focused parenting programs for children's internalizing and externalizing symptoms: A randomized clinical study. *Journal of Clinical Child & Adolescent Psychology*, 1–17. https://doi.org/10.1080/15374416.2022.2079130

Ansar, N., Hjeltnes, A., Stige, S. H., Binder, P-E., & Stiegler, J. R. (2021). Parenthood—lost and found: Exploring parents' experiences of receiving a program in emotion focused skills training. *Frontiers in Psychology*, *12*, 1–12. https://doi.org/10.3389/fpsyg.2021.559188

Arnold, K. (2014). Behind the mirror: Reflective listening and its tain in the work of Carl Rogers. *The Humanistic Psychologist*, *42*, 354–369.

Baker-Ericzén, M. J., Jenkins, M. M., & Haine-Schlagel, R. (2013). Therapist, parent, and youth perspectives of treatment barriers to family-focused community outpatient mental health services. *Journal of Child and Family Studies*, *22*(6), 854–868. https://doi.org/10.1007/s10826-012-9644-7

Barrett, S. (2019). From adult lunatic asylums to CAMHS community care: The evolution of specialist mental health care for children and adolescents 1948–2018. *French Journal of British Studies*, *XXIV*(3). https://doi.org/10.4000/rfcb.4138

Bateson, G., Jackson, D.D., Haley, J., & Weakland, J. (1956). Towards a theory of schizophrenia. *Behavioural Science*, *1*, 251–264. https://doi.org/10.1002/bs.3830010402

Bloomfield, L., & Kendall, S. (2012). Parenting self-efficacy, parenting stress and child behaviour before and after a parenting programme. *Primary Health Care Research and Development*, *13*(4), 364–372. https://doi.org/doi:10.1017/S1463423612000060

Bohart, A. C., & Greenberg, L. S. (Eds.). (1997). *Empathy reconsidered: New directions in psychotherapy*. American Psychological Association. https://doi.org/10.1037/10226-000

Burke, J. D., & Loeber, R. (2015). The effectiveness of the stop now and plan (SNAP) program for boys at risk for violence and delinquency. *Prevention Science*, *16*, 242–253. https://doi.org/10.1017/S1463423612000060

Dolhanty, J., & Lafrance, A. (2019). Emotion-focused family therapy for eating disorders. In L. S. Greenberg & R. N. Goldman (Eds.), *Clinical handbook of emotion-focused therapy* (pp. 403–423). American Psychological Association.

Elliott, R. (2012). Emotion-focused therapy. In P. Sanders (Ed.), *The tribes of the person-centred nation* (pp. 103–130). Ross-on-Wye.

Elliott R., Watson, J. C., Goldman, R. N., & Greenberg, L. S. (2004). *Learning emotion-focused therapy: The process-experiential approach to change*. American Psychological Association. https://doi.org/10.1037/10725-010

Foroughe, M. F. (2010). *Examining family-based treatment for adolescents with restricting eating disorders* [Doctoral Dissertation, York University]. Library and Archives Canada.

Foroughe, M. (2018a). Emotion-focused therapies for children and adolescents. In M. Foroughe (Ed.), *Emotion focused family therapy with children and caregivers: A trauma-informed approach* (pp. 23–44). Routledge. https://doi.org/10.4324/9781315161105

Foroughe, M. (2018b). Foreword: A caregiver-based intervention. In M. Foroughe (Ed.), *Emotion focused family therapy with children and caregivers: A trauma-informed approach* (pp. ix–xvi). Routledge. https://doi.org/10.4324/9781315161105

Foroughe, M., & Goldstein, L. (2018). Processing parent blocks. In M. Foroughe (Ed.), *Emotion focused family therapy with children and caregivers: A trauma-informed approach* (pp. 80–98). Routledge. https://doi.org/10.4324/9781315161105

Foroughe, M. F., Stillar A., Goldstein, L., Dolhanty, J., Goodcase, E. T., & Lafrance, A. (2018). Brief emotion focused family therapy: An intervention for parents of children and adolescents with mental health issues. *Journal of Marital and Family Therapy*, *43*(3), 410–430. https://doi.org/10.1111/jmft.12351

Fraiberg, S., Adelson, E., & Shapiro, V. (1975). Ghosts in the nursery. A psychoanalytic approach to the problems of impaired infant-mother relationships. *Journal of the American Academy of Child Psychiatry*, *14*(3), 387–421. https://doi.org/10.1016/s0002-7138(09)61442-4

Gandhi, S., Chiu, M., Lam, K., Cairney, J. C., Guttmann, A., & Kurdyak, P. (2016). Mental health service use among children and youth in Ontario: Population-based trends over time. *The Canadian Journal of Psychiatry*, *61*(2), 119–124. https://doi.org/10.1177/0706743715621254

Gardner, W., Pajer, K., Cloutier, P., Zemek, R., Currie, L., Hatcher, S., Colman, I., Bell, D., Gray, C., Cappelli, M., Rodriguez Duque, D., & Lima, I. (2019). Changing rates of self-harm and mental disorders by sex in youths presenting to Ontario emergency departments: Repeated cross-sectional study. *The Canadian Journal of Psychiatry*, *64*(11), 789–797. https://doi.org/10.1177/0706743719854070

Grave, R. D., Eckhardt, S., Calugi, S., & Le Grange, D. (2019). A conceptual comparison of family-based treatment and enhanced cognitive behavior therapy in the treatment of adolescents with eating disorders. *Journal of Eating Disorders*, *42*(7), 1–9. https://doi.org/10.1186/s40337-019-0275-x

Greenberg, L., & Vrana, G. (2018). Overview of emotion-focused therapy. In M. Foroughe (Ed.), *Emotion focused family therapy with children and caregivers: A trauma-informed approach* (pp. 9–10). Routledge. https://doi.org/10.4324/9781315161105

Hagen, A. H. V., Austbø, B., Hjelmseth, V., & Dolhanty, J. (2019). *Emosjonsfokusert ferdighetstrening for foreldre*. Gyldendal.

Heath, C. L., Curtis, D. F., Fan, W., & McPherson, R. (2015). The association between parenting stress, parenting self-efficacy, and the clinical significance of child ADHD symptom change following behaviour therapy. *Child Psychiatry & Human Development*, *46*(1), 118–129. https://doi.org/10.1007/s10578-014-0458-2

Kinter, M., Boss, P. G., & Johnson, N. (1981). The relationship between dysfunctional family environments and family member food intake. *Journal of Marriage and The Family*, *43*(3), 633–641. https://doi.org/10.2307/351764

Lafrance, A., Henderson, K. A., Mayman, S. (2020a). *Emotion-focused family therapy: A transdiagnostic model for caregiver-focused interventions*. American Psychological Association. https://doi.org/10.1037/0000166-000

Lafrance, A., Henderson, K. A., & Mayman, S. (2020b). Working through caregiver blocks. In *Emotion-focused family therapy: A transdiagnostic model for caregiver-focused interventions* (pp. 81–105). American Psychological Association. https://doi.org/10.1037/0000166-000

Lafrance, A., Henderson, K. A., & Mayman, S. (2020c). Working through clinician blocks. In *Emotion-focused family therapy: A transdiagnostic model for caregiver-focused interventions* (pp. 105–119). American Psychological Association. https://doi.org/10.1037/0000166-000

Lafrance Robinson, A., Dolhanty, J., Stillar, A., Henderson, K., & Mayman, S. (2014). Emotion focused family therapy for eating disorders across the lifespan: A pilot study of a 2-day transdiagnostic intervention for parents. *Clinical Psychology & Psychotherapy*, *23*(1), 14–23. https://doi.org/10.1002/cpp.1933

McCauley, E., Berk, M. S., Asarnow, J. R., Adrian M., Cohen, J., Korslund, K., Avina, C., Hughes, J., Harned, M., Gallop, R., & Linehan, M. M. (2018). Efficacy of dialectical behavior therapy for adolescents at high risk for suicide: A randomized clinical trial. *JAMA Psychiatry*, *75*(8), 777–785. https://doi.org/10.1001/jamapsychiatry.2018.1109

Naveed, S., Waqas, A., Majeed, S., Zeshan, M., Jahan, N., & Haaris Sheikh, M. (2017). Child psychiatry: A scientometric analysis 1980–2016. *F1000 Research*, *6*, 1293. https://doi.org/10.12688/f1000research.12069.1

Nock, M. K., & Kazdin, A. E. (2001). Parent expectancies for child therapy: Assessment and relation to participation in treatment. *Journal of Child and Family Studies*, *10*(2), 155–180. https://doi.org/10.1023/A:1016699424731

Pos, A. E., & Greenberg, L. S. (2007). Emotion-focused therapy. The transforming power of affect. *Journal of Contemporary Psychotherapy: On the Cutting Edge of*

Modern Developments in Psychotherapy, *37*(1), 25–31. https://doi.org/10.1007/s10879-006-9031-z

Rienecke, R. D., Accurso, E. C., Lock, J., & Le Grange, D. (2016). Expressed emotion, family functioning, and treatment outcome for adolescents with anorexia nervosa. *European Eating Disorders Review: The Journal of the Eating Disorders Association*, *24*(1), 43–51. https://doi.org/10.1002/erv.2389

Rogers, C. R. (1957). The necessary and sufficient conditions of therapeutic personality change. *Journal of Consulting Psychology*, *21*(2), 95–103. https://doi.org/10.1037/h0045357

Rushton, F. E., & Kraft, C. (2013). Family support in the family-centered medical home: An opportunity for preventing toxic stress and its impact in young children. Child health care providers offer valuable support and connections for families. *Child Abuse & Neglect*, *37*(Supplement), 41–50. https://doi.org/10.1016/j.chiabu.2013.10.029

Shahar, B., Carlin, E. R., Engle, D. E., Hegde, J., Szepsenwol, O., & Arkowitz, H. (2011). A pilot investigation of emotion-focused two-chair dialogue intervention for self-criticism. *Clinical Psychology and Psychotherapy*, *19*(6), 496–507. https://doi.org/10.1002/cpp.762

Siegel, D. J. (2010). *Mindsight*. Bantam Books

Stillar, A., Strahan, E., Nash, P., Files, N., Scarborough, J., Mayman, S., et al. (2016). The influence of carer fear and self-blame when supporting a loved one with an eating disorder. *Eating Disorders*, *24*, 173–185. https://doi.org/10.1080/10640266.2015.1133210

Vandereycken, W., Kog, E., & Vanderlinden, J. (1989). *The family approach to eating disorders: Assessment and treatment of anorexia nervosa and bulimia*. New York: PMA.

Wiens, K., Bhattarai, A., Pedram, P., Dores, A., Williams, J., Bulloch, A., & Patten, S. (2020). A growing need for youth mental health services in Canada: Examining trends in youth mental health from 2011 to 2018. *Epidemiology and Psychiatric Sciences*, *29*, E115. https://dx.doi.org/10.1017%2FS2045796020000281

4
Parent–Youth Dyadic EFT

Mirisse Foroughe and Imayan Neela

When parents seek out therapy for their child, they do not likely know what exactly they are agreeing to and what the other options might be; very few parents are aware that dyadic or triadic therapy is even possible. Why would we, as therapists, want to offer parent involvement as an option? One reason to offer parent involvement is the benefit to the youth's emotion regulation. Research strongly supports the idea that caregivers play an important role as emotion regulators, or "external organizers," for their children (Hughes and Baylin, 2012; Siegel, 2012; Zimmermann et al., 2001). In this role, parents can help children develop their emotion socialization skills, alongside self-regulatory capacities, via direct coaching, guidance, and adjustments in family interactions (Brumariu, 2015; Foroughe et al., 2018; Waters & Cummings, 2000). Second, parents who are not directly involved in the therapy process often have a hard time giving us the space and time that we require as therapists—they may call, email, or approach us with concerns at the end of their child's session. Being "left out" can build suspicion or animosity towards the process, making our job more challenging, stressing out the youth, and putting more strain on the parent–child relationship. In some cases, parents may prematurely remove their child from

DOI: 10.4324/9781003218968-4

treatment if they are feeling uncertain about what takes place during the therapy process. Finally, involving parents takes the sole responsibility for therapeutic progress off the child. Parents can be held accountable to support the process, make some changes themselves, and create an environment that will sustain lasting improvement for the youth. When parents are provided opportunities for appropriate involvement alongside a child's therapy, there are improvements in both therapeutic process and outcome (Diamond et al., 2014; Foroughe & Muller, 2012; Lafrance et al., 2020; Woodfield & Cartwright, 2020).

Dyadic or triadic parent–child therapy can require therapeutic strategies that are different from any other kind of therapy. If the majority of our clinical work involves children, parents, families, and couples on their own, parent–child work can fall outside our everyday experience, training, and skill set. In this chapter, we aim to provide an overarching structure for parent–youth therapy and explore clinical questions as to when to consider this option, to what extent it should be employed, and how to go about doing so effectively within an emotion focused therapy (EFT) framework.

What Exactly Is Parent–Child Therapy?

In contrast to individual EFT, the "client" in parent–child dyadic therapy is the relationship between two people. Broadly speaking, the tasks of dyadic therapy involve exploring feelings and unmet needs, improving communication, and optimizing how the parent–child relationship addresses the emotional and behavioural functioning of the child. Much of the therapeutic time should be spent with parent and child together, although individual "break-out" meetings within the course of a session and the occasional hour-long individual session are common. In fact, the work that helps the parent and child achieve repair can be done in separated or joint dyadic sessions, depending on the clinical presentation and emotional processing style of each member of the dyad. The main distinguishing factor of dyadic therapy is that it aims to facilitate repair within the relationship and provide the parent and child a corrective emotional experience; this focus on repair and corrective experiences within the actual relationship stands in contrast to a child attending therapy on their own and learning to access self-care, grieve unmet needs, and accept their parents' limitations. The corrective emotional experience can take place within the session or within the parent and child's daily life; flexibility is built into the process, and **relational markers** can help therapists guide the dyad along a path of improved communication and emotional engagement. In the context of EFT-Y, relational markers refer to cues within the parent–child interaction that denote the strength of the relationship. For example, relational markers include how comfortable or tense the interaction is, openness to the other person's viewpoint, reflective capacity in relation to the other, ability to speak directly to one another (versus only through the therapist), and willingness to offer forgiveness for past relationship breaches or current limitations. As we observe the dyad, we can note these and other markers that signal how much structure and support the dyad needs in order to productively engage in therapy. If the markers are indicating a highly strained mode of interaction within the dyad, we will need to provide greater structure and support by way of intervening in the communication, reframing, guiding the interaction, and so on.

For many youth, interacting with their parent or caregiver is a daily occurrence outside the therapy session, irrespective of the parent–child interaction being negative or positive. Although individual EFT-Y sessions, and particularly empty-chair work, may help youth address feelings and needs by interacting with internal representations of their parents (Elliott et al., 2004), the real-life relationship with the parent is not addressed through individual therapy. For youth experiencing a strained parent–child relationship and attending individual therapy, change within the parent–child relationship is not likely to occur unless the youth initiates such change. For some youth—especially younger adolescents—it may not be developmentally adaptive to "let go" of unmet needs. Indeed, if a parent can be successfully engaged in dyadic therapy, it may not be in the youth's best interest to let go, move on, and essentially "give up" on the parent–child relationship meeting their emotional needs (Foroughe, 2018). In summary, while individual therapy can help some youth achieve emotion transformation on their own, dyadic EFT allows therapists to have the flexibility to work with parents and children together or in separated sessions towards the same treatment goals: improved communication, more effective emotional expression from the child, attuned responses from the parent, and corrective emotional experiences that provide confidence and hope to parent and child that their own relationship can be a source of strength, support, and growth.

Principals of Parent–Child Therapy

EFT for parents and children draws from core EFT principles as well as other evidence-based therapeutic modalities, emphasizing *emotion processing*, *the primacy of the parent–child relationship in a child's emotion regulation*, and *therapeutic intervention in the interpersonal communication between parent and child.* After providing a brief overview of each modality that has influenced dyadic EFT, we will share the adaptation of EFT for parent–child dyads.

Attachment-Based Family Therapy (ABFT)

The main objectives of ABFT are to help adolescents rebuild protective parent–child relationships and communication patterns by developing a better understanding of how they perceive their relationship inadequacies (Diamond et al., 2014). These objectives are achieved through the therapist bringing focus to interpersonal family processes that may cause or contribute to mental health

Table 4.1 Attachment-Based Family Therapy Process Overview.

Task	*Process Goal*
Task 1: Relational reframe	Transform how members within the family frame problems and solutions
Task 2: Adolescent alliance	Gain a better understanding of attachment narratives from the adolescent's perspective
Task 3: Parent alliance	Reframe the parents' working model of the adolescent and their role as parents
Task 4: Healing	Engage in conversations geared towards processing and healing attachment ruptures
Task 5: Security	Support parents to address challenges youth are facing in their lives outside of the family. By the end of the last task, parents should be able to facilitate change through improved attachment security

challenges in youth. Communication is paramount and allows for the sharing of previously unexpressed primary emotions and unmet needs; these feelings and needs are communicated directly while the therapist facilitates secure attachment between parent and child (Diamond et al., 2010, 2014). Parents are guided to arrive at an understanding of how their current challenges, in tandem with their relationship history, impact their parenting. Once both parties are well prepared and feel supported in their understanding of their relationships, they are brought together to begin conversations with emotionally productive outcomes. During these dyadic sessions, a translation model of change is utilized for creating corrective attachment experiences where the youth can express vulnerable feelings or needs, and parents can respond with sensitivity and availability (Diamond, Shahar et al., 2016). The therapist monitors the emotional tone and depth of conversation and supports the youth in translating emotions into words, differentiating, accepting contrasting feelings, and improving emotion regulation capacity instead of defaulting to silence or blasts (Tsvieli et al., 2020). Spanning approximately 14–20 sessions, ABFT has five tasks—each with both a process and an outcome goal (Diamond, Russon et al., 2016). While outcome goals differ for each dyad, process goals remain the same (see Table 4.1).

Emotion Focused Family Therapy (EFFT) and Emotion Focused Skills Training (EFST)

Dyadic EFT utilizes intervention strategies from caregiver-based interventions, particularly when conducting separate parent sessions or meetings. Emotion focused family therapy and emotion focused skills training for families were founded based on the core principle that the efficacy of caregivers, especially in response to the need to support their child's health, is the best source of support for the child's recovery (Lafrance Robinson & Dolhanty, 2013; Foroughe, 2018; Foroughe et al., 2019; Lafrance et al., 2020). The primary mechanism of supporting caregivers to overcome emotion blocks and strengthen their self-efficacy is EFT's transformation process of changing emotion with emotion. The core components of this modality include coaching parents to provide therapeutic apologies, strengthen or repair the parent–child relationship, and provide their child with behavioural and emotional support. Behavioural support may include interrupting maladaptive symptoms, correcting problematic behaviours, and challenging anxiety to engage in new behaviours. Emotional support begins with caregivers receiving psychoeducation regarding emotion processing and its role in youth mental health, followed by having caregivers explore and practise the responses necessary to provide emotion coaching to their child "in the moment." Caregiver behaviours such as denial, over-control, criticism, and enabling problematic symptoms are normalized and understood as functions of the caregiver's underlying emotions, such as fear, anger, and shame. By working through these feelings and practising a new way of responding to their child's needs, caregivers are empowered to overcome emotion blocks and get on with the tasks at hand. When supporting caregivers, therapists aim to involve and empower without judging or blaming: caregivers are viewed as the solution and not the problem. A critical consideration for therapists in this modality is the importance of addressing their own emotion blocks in the process of supporting others to do the same.

Dyadic Emotionally Focused Family Therapy[1]

Although our dyadic approach to EFT for youth and parents or for co-parents is grounded in Greenberg's EFT model, we acknowledge that Johnson's EFT model has been applied to dyads and families and bears some similarities as an attachment and emotion focused intervention. The tasks of emotionally focused family therapy are to support parents in their understanding of their children by cultivating nurturing and attuned responsiveness while helping the child accept nurturing from the parents (Johnson, 2018). This takes place in three primary stages over the course of 10–12 sessions. Stabilization, the first stage, is centred around the de-escalation of negative interaction cycles. Emotional responses are reframed as part of a dynamic system that is driven by primary emotions. During this initial stage, the therapist forms an alliance and assesses the family. The therapist is then guided by access points; for example, within the second access point, termed securing parental investment, the therapist obtains parent consent and establishes their engagement in the process (Furrow et al., 2019). The second stage, restructuring attachment, includes a focus on interactions that address attachment wounds, triggers, fears, and needs. The facilitation of bonding between parent and child is the key objective of this stage. In the third stage, consolidation, changes are made to narratives of family problems, and repairs are implemented. In this stage, the therapist has two main objectives: (1) the unravelling and restructuring of attachment emotions and responses and (2) the restructuring of the key patterns of interaction to create bonding opportunities and achieve a secure connection. Emotionally focused family therapy aims to transform the unhealthy cycles of interaction that form or perpetuate attachment insecurity within the family, while strengthening interactions that provide attachment bonding opportunities.

Parent–Child Interaction Therapy (PCIT)

PCIT is a dyadic therapy based on social learning principles and designed for parents and young children (age 2–7) with externalizing disorders (Timmer et al., 2005), but we have found parents with a child of any age can benefit from the modelling and direct guidance that are part of this approach. The goal of the intervention is to transform how parents interact with their children in order to address child behavioural challenges. The process occurs in a live session where the therapist guides parents away from dysfunctional interactions and towards positive parenting. According to Woodfield and Cartwright (2020), PCIT has two core components: child-directed interaction (CDI) and parent-directed interaction (PDI). Each component begins with an hour of didactic training, followed by the therapist observing parents while they play with their children and providing coaching and feedback. During the first phase, the goal is to create or reinforce existing mutually rewarding interactions. The PDI component of this phase begins with a parent-only session for skills building. The goal in this phase is for parents to learn effective child behaviour management skills. A consistent rhythm of parents giving commands, ensuring the child complies with those demands, and providing praise to the child for their compliance is established by the end of the process. While this approach may seem a simplistic way to support parents with adolescent children, it can actually be incredibly useful and practical when incorporated in addition to the relationship building and emotional support tasks that are part of dyadic EFT. While some parents can readily infer or intuit the behavioural approaches that will work for their child, other parents struggle more, and having concrete examples, modelling, and direct support to implement changes can provide much-needed relief.

Emotion Focused Couples Therapy (EFT-C)

While EFT-C is a therapeutic intervention for couples, there are key processes that we have found useful to apply to dyadic parent–child therapy as well as co-parent EFT sessions. Problems in couples begin to form when attachment, identity, and affection needs are unmet (Greenberg, 2015; Greenberg & Goldman, 2008). Problems also arise when there is inability to face separation, and this inability gives way to anger, depression, or distancing. When attachment needs are not met, a pattern of interaction, or *cycle*, forms between the dyad. There are four types of cycle identified, and, while each of them can be useful when applied to dyadic EFT for parents and children, the first is a cycle that we see very commonly in practice. The pursue–distance cycle occurs when one partner pursues the other for more intimacy. For example, one partner may feel lonely and abandoned and so they struggle for more contact with the other partner. This struggle might be expressed in complaint, blame, and criticism. The other partner may then feel inadequate, incompetent, and ashamed at repeatedly "failing" their partner, resulting in retreat and distancing behaviours that further drive the lonely partner to continue expressing feeling abandoned and expressing criticism. The cycle is self-reinforcing because, the more the first partner criticizes when they feel lonely, the more the other partner will feel inadequate and pull away, which only increases the feelings of loneliness in the first partner. Some parents seeking therapy for their child's mental health difficulties present with interaction patterns in their *couple* or *co-parent* relationship that resemble the pursue–distance type. Often, the partner in support of therapy is the "pursuer," while the "distancer" is more likely to be sceptical of any co-parent or family-based approach and may disengage from therapy overtly (refusing to attend) or covertly (attending sessions but criticizing or derailing the process, deactivating emotions to avoid meaningful engagement, etc.). The pursue–distance interaction cycle also presents within parent–child dyads and can lead to attachment ruptures and painful unmet needs for youth as well as strong feelings of frustration and shame for parents.

Other interaction cycles identified in EFT-C may also be applicable to parent–child relationships; certainly, they are relevant for co-parent relationships.

The dominant–submissive cycle refers to an interaction pattern in which one partner takes on more tasks in the relationship and functions relatively well, while the other partner "gives up" and under-functions. Often, this pattern begins with one of the partners being more adept at stating their needs and wants as well as being quicker to make decisions.

The blame–withdraw cycle describes a pattern in which one partner's feelings are not heard or their needs are not met. This brews feelings of insecurity or loneliness that are not expressed, but the partner hopes that the other will sense this need. When the other partner does not seem to sense and respond to the need, this results in the first partner feeling neglected or unloved. Eventually, the neglected partner progresses to blaming and criticizing the other. When faced with criticism and blame, the other partner withdraws.

The shame–rage cycle occurs when one partner feels humiliated, which leads to intense anger. The anger can lead to violence in the couple. The shame is often rooted in vulnerability, powerlessness, or abandonment with a poorly developed ability to share vulnerable feelings.

While all of the negative interaction cycles identified in EFT-C emerge from unexpressed primary emotions and needs, they are maintained by the expression of secondary emotions such as resentment, criticism, anger, or blame. When parents display negative secondary emotions, the therapist may also feel targeted and react to these secondary emotions. All of us can relate to strong feelings of frustration towards a particular parent in our practice—and an equally strong desire not to work with them at all! Training in EFT-C can help us recognize these interaction patterns when they occur, allowing us to notice when parents are stuck in a self-reinforcing cycle so that we are less likely to take their behaviour personally or have strong emotional reactions that pull us into an unhelpful cycle along with the parent–child dyad.

Dyadic EFT with Co-Parents

Admittedly, engaging one parent in the therapeutic process for their child can be a challenging task—when and why would we want to engage two parents? Just as parent–child relational challenges may call for dyadic sessions to support the EFT process, co-parent EFT is called for when challenges within the co-parenting relationship are in the way of therapeutic progress. Examples include:

1. One parent supports therapy, while the other opposes it.
2. Each parent has different goals for the child's therapy, and these goals contradict one another.
3. Parenting styles are in conflict.
4. One parent has a much stronger relationship with the child, while the other has a strained relationship.
5. One parent is highly engaged in therapy, and the other has distanced themself from it.
6. The child is sufficiently unwell that you feel the parents will need to assume a large role in the therapeutic process.

In addition to individual EFT for parents, co-parenting EFT sessions are often implemented to support the relationship between parents and provide the child with a cohesive and positive image of both parents in support of their recovery (Foroughe, 2018). In co-parenting EFT sessions, despite the circumstances of their relationship (i.e., together, separated, divorced), both parents are engaged to work in two main areas: (1) processing their secondary and core maladaptive emotions that are triggered within the co-parenting relationship and impeding therapeutic progress; and (2) building each other up through forgiveness and support, as relevant, to allow both parents to play a strong role in supporting their child's journey to recovery (Foroughe, 2018). In session, parents provide input and explore strategies towards the treatment plan, while the therapist assesses the co-parenting dynamic, uses empathic responding, and supports the processing of emotional blocks to treatment-supportive behaviours.

Attending to the Co-Parenting Relationship

There are several approaches to support therapists when they are attempting to bring the co-parenting relationship into clearer focus. One approach is to use a formal questionnaire that each parent completes separately, which can then be used as a springboard for further reflection and discussion. The McHale Co-Parenting Scale (McHale, 1997) consists of questions about the communication, support, and responsiveness between co-parents and how they speak to and treat one another in the presence of the child. Another approach is to use a paradoxical intervention,[2] such as the "And that's half you" activity. A paradoxical intervention is one that disrupts the status quo, making the client uncomfortable by engaging in a task that is the opposite of what they would normally do. For example, most parents would not directly say anything disparaging about their child. However, many parents sometimes communicate negative messages indirectly, by criticizing the other parent. In this case, a paradoxical intervention would have the parent put the unspoken message into words—without the child there to hear it, of course—so that the parent can directly experience the messaging in an emotionally evocative manner.

By having parents put indirect verbal or nonverbal messages into direct phrasing, our goal is to reconnect parents with their desire to protect their child from negative or hurtful messaging (Foroughe, 2018). Another co-parenting intervention is to practise building the other parent "up." Although it can be challenging for a parent to reorient themselves to say positive things about the other parent, EFT can help with empathic responses that validate the parent's

Table 4.2 And That's Half You Activity Examples.

And That's Half You Activity	
If the parent says or implies this:	*Ask them to say it like this:*
Dad is lazy and does not do anything to help	"Your dad is lazy and does not want to help me, *and that's half you.*"
Mum is overbearing and controlling	"Your mum is overbearing and controlling, *and that's half you.*"

experience as well as chair work to help process strong negative emotions. The greater the strain between parents, the more important it may be to spend time in separated parent sessions. Separated sessions, or parts of sessions, can have dyadic, co-parenting goals while allowing each parent a safe space to work through conflicted feelings and access their own desire to reduce suffering for their child (Foroughe, 2018).

Parent–Youth EFT

In dyadic parent–youth EFT, we borrow specific intervention strategies from the aforementioned approaches to dyadic therapy: a gradual approach to preparing the child and parent for joint sessions (EFFT/ABFT), didactic coaching and practice, often including review of video recordings (PCIT), facilitating and emphasizing direct communication between the dyad (ABFT), a de-blaming and empowering approach to caregivers (EFFT/EFST), as well as drawing from Greenberg's EFT model to track moment-by-moment emotion process, deepen expressed empathy, and support the experiential processing of emotion blocks. The integration of these approaches results in a dynamic intervention that is malleable to the needs and circumstances of each parent and child.

Preparing Youth and Parents: Separated Dyadic Therapy

When Youth Are Not Ready for Joint Sessions

When youth refuse to allow parent involvement in their sessions, even for a few minutes, separated dyadic therapy can be a helpful starting point. In our experience, the child's refusal is driven by strong feelings of fear about what might go wrong if they are sitting in a joint session with their parent. Remember, a child knows what it's like to try and interact with their parent. They may have had countless interactions that went very wrong. Their defences and their reluctance are there for a reason. The Witness your Parent, Parent as Witness, and Open for Business experiential tasks, reviewed in Chapter 2, can be particularly helpful in accessing and clarifying the youth's feelings and needs without requiring them to participate in joint sessions with their parent. Often, through these experiential tasks, youth come to realize that they need their parent's support and that not having this need met is an obstacle to their current mental health, their relationships, and even their academic or workplace success. Still, many youth will refuse to allow their parent to be involved in the process while continuing to spend much of the therapy session talking about the parent or the parent–child relationship. This approach-avoidance paradox does not have to stop therapy from progressing. As EFT-Y therapists, we can provide separated parent and child sessions that work towards common goals. After all, it's much easier for us to support youth in giving their parent another chance when we are working to prepare the parent to respond differently the next chance they have.

The approach of using separated sessions to prepare youth and parents for dyadic therapeutic communication has also been found to be successful for young adults and their parents (Diamond, Russon et al., 2016). In ABFT, a critical point in the therapeutic process occurs during Task 4, when the family converges for the joint session. Before doing so, youth and the parents are prepared in Task 2 and Task 3, respectively. During Task 2, the therapist and adolescent meet alone to explore the damaged trust, and relationship ruptures, in addition to the youth's strengths and interests. Specifically, the therapist aids in the youth's development of an attachment rupture narrative, which explores how the attachment ruptures worsen their challenges and pose obstacles when the youth turn to their parents for support. The main outcome of this task is for the youth to be able to express their feelings in a coherent, regulated manner. During Task 3, the therapist explores the current challenges that parents are facing, including vocational or financial difficulties, problems within their couple relationship, each parent's own history of attachment ruptures, as well as mental health challenges. The goal is for parents to become better listeners to the concerns of their youth, but the process includes understanding the parents' lived experience, unique circumstances, and personal strengths that can be drawn upon to support the parent–child relationship.

When Parents Are Not Ready for Joint Sessions.
There are certainly times when we see a parent and child together in session, often in an initial consultation, and immediately feel a need to separate the dyad. Often, there is intense anger or criticism being expressed about the child, and we want to protect the child from hearing negative things about themself (e.g., "He is a violent, aggressive child without any remorse"). Sometimes, the parent is expressing hopelessness or helplessness through self-deprecating comments (e.g., "I never should've been a parent. I have no idea how to deal with this"), and we sense that the parent certainly needs support but that the child should not be witness to their parent's lack of self-efficacy. The assessment of parent "readiness" may also be one that the parent makes about the communication between parent and child, through comments such as: "I don't know how to talk to my daughter. I think she needs to talk to someone else." In each of these cases, time-limited parent sessions can allow the therapist to focus on the parent's feelings, provide empathic support, and work towards removing the blocks to the parent's self-efficacy, their compassion for the child, and their compassion for themself. Within the separated dyadic therapy, parents can be supported to develop their own empathic and validating responses when their child shares their pain or unmet needs—whether the child's expression

happens in a joint session or outside therapy (Diamond, Russon et al., 2016). Specifically, parents can access their ability to remain non-defensive, empathic, and curious in order to successfully encourage their children to further elaborate on their feelings. When helping a child access and express previously unexpressed primary emotions such as fear, shame, assertive anger, and grief, the parent's empathic response to these emotions can propel therapeutic progress.

Parental involvement in therapy will have a better chance of facilitating breakthroughs if the parents are prepared for what to expect, supported in processing their own emotional reactions, and have an opportunity to uncover a new way of responding that they can use the next time they are in a challenging situation with their child. Process research in emotion focused therapy has demonstrated that a profound and meaningful apology can have a strong impact on therapeutic progress when there has been a breach in a relationship (Greenberg et al., 2010). We can help parents to think through, prepare, and practise such an apology, as well as let their children know exactly how things are going to be different from now on—they need not promise huge changes, but specific and manageable modifications to their interactions, reactions, or even the rules of the house.

Overall, the involvement of parents in separated sessions can establish their alliance with the therapist, allow parents to access their self-efficacy, and improve their understanding of the child's challenges. This is especially important when parents emphasize only the individual-level factors involved in their child's mental health difficulties, such as the child's oversensitivity, defiance, or poor genetics. In dyadic EFT, a multidimensional perspective of youth mental health is emphasized early in the process in much the same way as it is in EFFT (Foroughe, 2018). When this multidimensional perspective is shared with parents in tandem with an invitation to join the treatment process, it can be a great opportunity to de-blame caregivers and empower them to take an active role in their children's therapeutic progress.

What if a Therapist Is "Not Ready" for Joint Sessions?

In some cases, it is clear to us that the caregiver and child are not ready for joint dyadic sessions. In other cases, we may acknowledge to ourselves that we are not feeling ready to move forward and hold joint sessions. It can be helpful to reflect on the source of our reservations—do we feel intimidated? Are we concerned that a joint session may activate emotions too much and be unmanageable? Are we worried about how we will manage the feelings, behaviour, and needs of more than one client at a time? Many psychotherapists, in their training, focused on either children or adults; unfortunately, the artificial separation between a child and their parents is often built into graduate school and clinical training of the therapist. For those therapists fortunate enough to have received training in both child and adult therapy, or even marital and family therapy, it can still be a challenge to balance the needs of each person in the dyad or family. To a greater or lesser extent, almost all of us can benefit from clinical training in the area of parent–child and family therapy. It is also possible to have different therapists for the separated sessions and the joint dyadic therapy, allowing therapists working as part of a team to collaborate or create a virtual team with an external therapist. While having a different therapist take on the joint sessions can allow us to engage someone with more experience or comfort with dyadic therapy, it also requires greater communication between the two therapists (or three therapists, if the parent also has their own therapist) to work together successfully.

Triadic EFT

There are many reasons to go beyond the dyad and engage both caregivers in a therapy session with the youth. This is most common early on in therapy, to assess the relationship dynamic, share your case formulation, and set goals. In some cases, parents may be very well aligned with one another but both seem to be misaligned with the youth or with the goals of therapy in some way. You may want to have the youth and parents together in the session, at least for part of the time, so that you can work through misalignment, misunderstandings, or parent–child conflict. For example:

- The youth would benefit from having the opportunity to express themself and be heard in a safe space, with your support and facilitation of the communication.
- You would like the youth and both parents to hear the same information at the same time.
- Therapy goals, as set by the youth, are not supported by their parents or are in opposition to the parents' understanding of what is important to focus on. You want to find a compromise and bring everyone on the same page.

Prior to a triadic session, it can be helpful to prepare each client and strategize how best they can communicate their feelings and needs. It may be necessary to set boundaries around what will be communicated in the triadic session, especially if the youth is experiencing moderate to severe mental health difficulties or is particularly vulnerable. Youth also benefit from practising what they are going to say prior to a session involving their parents—this practice can be done effectively using the empty-chair exercise, where they picture their parents and then share what they want to say. It can feel very different to say something to you as the therapist, such as, "I'm so hurt that my mother ignores me," than to say the same thing in empty-chair work with the imagined parent: "It hurts me so much that you ignore me."

Tasks and Processes in Parent–Child EFT

In addition to establishing a strong therapeutic bond, agreeing on therapeutic goals, and using empathic responding (detailed in Chapter 2), there are specific intervention strategies that work well for youth and parents in dyadic sessions, as follows:

Reframing

Reframing involves changing or shifting the perspective on a behaviour or relational dynamic. The therapist can reframe each person's behaviour or the parent–child interaction in terms of the underlying primary emotion of each person. In this segment, the EFT-Y therapist reframes a parent's tendency to explode and become harshly critical of their child:

Parent: I just don't recognize her. When she behaves that way, I don't even like her. My heart starts racing and I get so angry. It's like she's not my kid and I don't want her around.

Therapist: It sounds like maybe you panic because there's fear that you are losing control, and she's going down the wrong path? Is that sort of how it feels?

Parent: Sort of, but I'm not panicked. I just hate myself and her in those moments because it's such an insult, so humiliating—after everything I've tried to do, everything I've sacrificed. It's like everything is falling apart for the kids and I can't stop it.

Therapist: Right, I understand—so it's more like you explode when there's shame about not being in control of the household, a sense of failing the kids?

Parent: Yeah, I think so ... and then I become so overcontrolling and they hate me for it.

Therapist: And you overcontrol because you care so much about their future, not because you want to control them or hurt them. Your love and concern for them doesn't get through to them in those moments.

Reframing shifts the meaning of specific interactions and behaviours, clarifies their relational significance, and fosters more positive perceptions of the self and the other person in the dyad. Traditionally, reframing has been a therapeutic strategy in family therapy, but EFT-Y therapists can also use it when working individually with youth or a parent, in preparation for relationship changes in the dyad in joint sessions or outside therapy. In dyadic therapy, the other person in the parent–child relationship is always present in the therapy room, even when they are not physically there. Whether the dyad is in session together or individually, it is important to integrate reframing with validating the emotional experience of the individual, so that we are not taking either person's side but framing each person's behaviours in the best light possible and interpreting their significance based on underlying primary emotions.

Empty-Chair Work with Parents or Youth

Imagine your mother in this chair. This prompt, revised according to the significant other being imagined, can be the starting point for emotion processing: *How do you feel when you see her?* An opportunity to experience expressing feelings and needs out loud for the first time might be: *Tell your mother how you've been feeling since your parent's divorce.* Or enact the significant other in an imagined two-way dialogue: *Be your mother and respond as she would.* Parents and children can be engaged in chair work during separate sessions, often in preparation for dialogue that will take place between them. Having the opportunity to access, explore, and clarify one's feelings before having the actual conversation can help determine exactly what they wish to express as well as how to express it. Experiential practice allows for heightening or softening of intensity, contact with the primary emotion, and the opportunity to work through the process with the therapist's empathic support before attempting to share painful feelings directly with a loved one. Even small changes in these areas can lead to significant improvements in the way conversations turn out between parent and child.

Accessing Adaptive Emotions

Perhaps the most transformative aspect of chair work tasks in dyadic therapy is the opportunity to access adaptive emotions. When youth first engage in empty-chair work, they often report or show that they are feeling awkward, embarrassed, and uncomfortable. Once youth are supported through the social awkwardness and unfamiliarity of EFT chair work, many find that chair work offers them a powerful portal to connecting with the feelings that they need. This can seem like a strange concept at first, but adaptive feelings are simply the feelings that are most useful in a given situation: assertive anger when we need to set a limit, compassion when we need to forgive someone or ourselves, sadness when we need to reach out for support to help us through pain—being able to access the right feeling for the circumstances is exactly how EFT reduces suffering and supports our overall adjustment to our lives.

When there has been a period of conflict, a need to cover up core feelings, or other obstacles to contacting our adaptive emotions, our reactions can lead us to more pain. For example, a parent may want to improve their relationship with their teen daughter after years of strain and enter dyadic therapy with this goal in mind. However, when the teen begins expressing their anger and pain, the parent's initial reaction is not likely going to be the emotionally attuned response that the relationship needs. Chair work with parents can help them access the emotion that they need to feel more of (e.g., loving compassion towards a sad or lonely child) in order to provide their child with a corrective emotional experience. This experience does not need to stop at having the child's unmet emotional needs addressed but can extend to having unmet practical needs met, such as having the parent commit to spending more time together, criticizing the youth less, or providing practical support to the therapeutic process by ensuring that a self-harming youth is supervised closely.

Restructuring Interactions

Through restructuring interactions, the therapist offers an empathic response, reflection, or task for the parent–child relationship. The purpose of restructuring is to facilitate a new perspective or a new emotional experience or elicit a new response. This shift challenges old relationship patterns and links the intrapersonal therapeutic work that was completed in individual sessions to behaviour change in the interpersonal space. Restructuring can include tracking communication, reflecting feelings, or guiding interactions. For example, in speaking to the parent in a dyad, a therapist might say:

> Something important just happened. It seemed like you moved away from your anger, mom, just for a moment and appealed to Joey from a more vulnerable place … maybe from a place of sadness and longing, or …? [Therapist now turned to the youth] But Joey, I wonder if you were still paying attention to the anger and didn't notice that mom was showing her sadness, so you kept going with defending yourself, and were surprised when mom started to become tearful?

The main function is to slow down and clarify steps in the interpersonal transaction or back-and-forth, allowing the dyad to pay attention to neglected emotions, consider deeper meanings, and notice even the smallest opportunity to connect and support one another. The therapist can also steer attention away from one person's faults, focusing instead on their emotions, values, or needs (Johnson, 2007). This has a humanizing impact and encourages the other person to see their loved one through a caring and understanding lens. Restructuring interactions can also occur through facilitating behavioural tasks within the session; examples of these tasks include: (1) allowing youth to share a painful emotion or unmet need in the session with their parent and then asking the parent to summarize what they heard, reflect on the underlying emotion, or directly validate what they just heard; (2) having each member of the dyad list what they wish the other would start doing, stop doing, and continue to do more; and (3) placing one person in an imaginary "soundproof booth" while we support the other through a difficult emotion, allowing the process to be an opportunity for modelling, for building compassion, or for reducing fear and avoidance of each other's emotions.

Sharing Feedback, Formulation, and Plan

When parents are aware of what their child is in therapy for and how we as therapists are formulating the issues, they have a much better chance of being part of the solution. While some parents may be resistant or disagree with our formulation, many of them will be open and appreciative as well as happy to be involved. Inviting parents into a feedback, formulation, and treatment planning session is an opportunity for us as therapists to tell the dyad or family what our impressions are, what we plan to do, and what to expect about the process. Compared with the initial sessions before this feedback or the therapy session after it, the feedback meeting can be the best time for the therapist to take the floor and develop agreement on goals and tasks, making the process clearer for everyone so that each person knows what we are planning to do (for now; this can change, of course) and how they can contribute to the success of the treatment. A somewhat formal, precise, and structured approach to this meeting can be particularly helpful in orienting clients because EFT does not typically provide them with handouts or worksheets to follow. In some cases, the information shared during this feedback meeting can be further formalized in a brief report or through a treatment contract that everyone signs.

Identifying and Externalizing Cycles

A powerful tool for the dyadic/triadic therapist, borrowed from EFT-C, is the identification of relationship problems in terms of a cycle. This cycle should summarize key elements of what each party has shared with us about what happens for them emotionally and behaviourally, how these feelings and behaviours show up in the relationship, and how the resulting negative interactions between them fuel a cycle that takes on a life of its own. The cycle is thereby externalized and becomes the *common enemy* that hurts everyone involved (Denton et al., 2009). An example of a dyadic cycle is presented in Table 4.3, based on a case of a 17-year-old, Julie, in their first year of university and presenting to therapy with depression. Their mother, Ashraf, was engaged in dyadic sessions after it became apparent that there were relationship dynamics that were maintaining Julie's self-criticism, self-isolation, and depression.

After we have "zoomed in" on each person's experience, fleshed out how they feel, and possibly connected their sensitivities to their life experience, their values, or characteristics that they identify in themselves, we can share our understanding of the cycle. In identifying this cycle for the parent and child, the therapist might summarize the dyadic process in a manner that touches on

Table 4.3 Example of a Dyadic Cycle.

	Primary Emotion	*Behaviour*	*Emotional Impact*	*Physical Sensations*	*Behavioural Impact*
Parent (Ashraf)	Loneliness/abandonment	Calling and texting repeatedly; criticism and complaint	Parent feels more abandoned, lonely, and rejected	Tension in chest; throat activated; Sinking feeling and butterflies in stomach	Increased tension; parent seeks more contact and/or criticizes child
Child (Julie)	Shame/inadequacy	Avoiding contact; shutting down	Child feels criticized, not good enough, overwhelmed	Face feels flushed; wanting to hide or run away; fatigue	Conflict and tension in relationship; child withdraws further

each individual's experience as well as how feelings, behaviours, and reactions are linked. For example, in Julie and Ashraf's case, we might say:

> Okay, so mom when Julie went off to university, there was this feeling of being lonely, missing her, and wanting to connect. This sometimes felt very intense, and you noticed that you were on the verge of tears, your throat was swollen, and you felt this sinking feeling in your stomach. When you felt this way, you usually called or texted Julie and sometimes criticized her for not being in touch and complained that she was neglecting you; Julie, when mom reached out to you and shared her feelings, you felt criticized and like you would never be good enough as a daughter, and you just wanted to get away from the conversation because you were feeling really down on yourself and starting to criticize yourself. So you pulled away, contacted mom less frequently, sometimes didn't reply to her messages, and spent more time alone. Ashraf, when Julie pulled away, you felt even more concerned about the relationship, even more lonely and abandoned, and you started sending longer messages explaining how you were feeling and how she was letting you down. The more mom expressed herself, the more you felt criticized and down, Julie; the more you felt down and pulled away, the more you felt lonely and abandoned, Ashraf. Does that seem like the cycle that has been going on between you?

If the dyad agrees that the identified cycle is accurate for them, we can continue to externalize this cycle, framing it as separate from them as individuals or as a dyad, and develop their motivation and agency in transforming the cycle.

Enactments

The most emotionally evocative interventions in EFT, as applied to dyadic sessions, are enactments. Enactments can include directing a client to express certain feelings and needs, heightening primary emotions and expressing them to the other, individual role play with the other as witness, and dyadic role play. Enactments involve the therapist heightening one person's primary emotions, facilitating the exploration or expression of these emotions, and involving the other partner in the interaction (Johnson, 2007). In other words, an enactment allows one to talk to the other within a prescribed role or on specific directions (Denton et al., 2009). Parent and child have an opportunity to engage in a structured interaction and become more aware of their emotions and responses within the relationship, with the therapist focusing on empathy throughout the process (Elliott et al., 2011, 2018; Johnson, 2007; Rankin et al., 2006). Examples of therapist prompts that encourage direct expression include: "Can you turn and tell him directly how much this hurts you?" or "Can you ask her right now for what you need?"

The main function of restructuring the interaction using enactments is that it supports the dyad to engage in sharing of previously withheld feelings, vulnerabilities, and needs in a new way.

Conclusion

Dyadic EFT-Y encourages flexibility in the therapeutic process involving youth. Whether for a few minutes of a session or for the entirety of every session, or even with separated sessions working towards the same goals, it can be useful to have guiding principles and practical tools to work with parent–child or co-parent dyads. Where we may have felt before that we could not see two members of the same family, we may see why and when a dyadic approach may be exactly what is needed. Furthermore, when we observe that a parent's individual therapy seems to be at odds with our therapeutic goals for the child and family, we can invite a parent into our process, strengthen our alliance with them, and even collaborate with their individual therapist to ensure that we are working towards common purposes.

Notes

1 Based on Sue Johnson's emotionally focused therapy model.
2 Paradoxical interventions were first introduced by Minuchin in structural family therapy.

References

Brumariu, L. E. (2015). Parent–child attachment and emotion regulation. *New Directions for Child and Adolescent Development*, *2015*(148), 31–45. https://doi.org/10.1002/cad.20098

Denton, W. H., Johnson, S. M., & Burleson, B. R. (2009). Emotion-focused therapy–therapist fidelity scale (EFT-TFS): Conceptual development and content validity. *Journal of Couple & Relationship Therapy*, *8*(3), 226–246. https://doi.org/10.1080/15332690903048820

Diamond, G. M., Rochman, D., & Amir, O. (2010). Arousing primary vulnerable emotions in the context of unresolved anger: "Speaking about" versus "speaking to." *Journal of Counseling Psychology*, *57*(4), 402–410. https://doi.org/10.1037/a0021115

Diamond, G., Russon, J., & Levy, S. (2016). Attachment-based family therapy: A review of the empirical support. *Family Process*, *55*(3), 595–610. https://doi.org/10.1111/famp.12241

Diamond, G. M., Shahar, B., Sabo, D., & Tsvieli, N. (2016). Attachment-based family therapy and emotion-focused therapy for unresolved anger: The role of productive emotional processing. *Psychotherapy*, *53*(1), 34–44. https://doi.org/10.1037/pst0000025

Diamond, G. S., Diamond, G. M., & Levy, S. A. (2014). *Attachment-based family therapy for depressed adolescents*. American Psychological Association. https://doi.org/10.1037/14296-000

Elliott, R., Bohart, A. C., Watson, J. C., & Greenberg, L. S. (2011). Empathy. *Psychotherapy*, *48*(1), 43–49. https://doi.org/10.1037/a0022187

Elliott, R., Bohart, A. C., Watson, J. C., & Murphy, D. (2018). Therapist empathy and client outcome: An updated meta-analysis. *Psychotherapy*, *55*(4), 399–410. https://doi.org/10.1037/pst0000175

Elliott, R., Watson, J. C., Goldman, R. N., & Greenberg, L. S. (2004). Empty chair work for unfinished interpersonal issues. In R. Elliott, J. C. Watson, R. N. Goldman, & L. S. Greenberg, *Learning emotion-focused therapy: The process-experiential approach to change* (pp. 243–265). American Psychological Association. https://doi.org/10.1037/10725-012

Foroughe, M. (Ed.). (2018). *Emotion focused family therapy with children and caregivers: A trauma-informed approach* (1st ed.). Routledge. https://doi.org/10.4324/9781315161105

Foroughe, M., & Muller, R. T. (2012). Dismissing (avoidant) attachment and trauma in dyadic parent–child psychotherapy. *Psychological Trauma: Theory, Research, Practice, and Policy*, *4*(2), 229. https://doi.org/10.1037/a0023061

Foroughe, M., Stillar, A., Goldstein, L., Dolhanty, J., Goodcase, E. T., & Lafrance, A. (2018). Brief emotion focused family therapy: An intervention for parents of children and adolescents with mental health issues. *Journal of Marital and Family Therapy*, *45*(3), 410–430. https://doi.org/10.1111/jmft.12351

Foroughe, M., Stillar, A., Goldstein, L., Dolhanty, J., Goodcase, E. T., & Lafrance, A. (2019). Brief emotion focused family therapy: An intervention for parents of children and adolescents with mental health issues. *Journal of Marital and Family Therapy*, *45*(3), 410–430. https://doi.org/10.1111/jmft.12351

Furrow, J. L., Palmer, G., Johnson, S. M., Faller, G., & Palmer-Olsen, L. (2019). *Emotionally focused family therapy: Restoring connection and promoting resilience.* Routledge.

Greenberg, L. S. (2015). *Emotion-focused therapy: Coaching clients to work through their feelings* (2nd ed.). American Psychological Association. https://doi.org/10.1037/14692-000

Greenberg, L. S., & Goldman, R. N. (2008). *Emotion-focused couples therapy: The dynamics of emotion, love, and power.* American Psychological Association.

Greenberg, L., Warwar, S., & Malcolm, W. (2010). Emotion-focused couples therapy and the facilitation of forgiveness. *Journal of Marital and Family Therapy*, *36*(1), 28–42. https://doi.org/10.1111/j.1752-0606.2009.00185.x

Hughes, D. A., & Baylin, J. (2012). *Brain-based parenting: The neuroscience of caregiving for healthy attachment.* W. W. Norton.

Johnson, S. M. (2007). The contribution of emotionally focused couples therapy. *Journal of Contemporary Psychotherapy*, *37*(1), 47–52. https://doi.org/10.1007/s10879-006-9034-9

Johnson, S. M. (2018). *Attachment theory in practice: Emotionally focused therapy (EFT) with individuals, couples, and families.* Guilford Press.

Lafrance, A., Henderson, K. A., & Mayman, S. (2020). *Emotion-focused family therapy: A transdiagnostic model for caregiver-focused interventions.* American Psychological Association.

Lafrance Robinson, A., & Dolhanty, J. (2013). Emotion-focused family therapy for eating disorders across the lifespan. *National Eating Disorder Information Bulletin*, *28*(3).

McHale, J. P. (1997). Overt and covert coparenting processes in the family. *Family Process*, *36*(2), 183–201. https://doi.org/10.1111/j.1545-5300.1997.00183.x

Rankin, K. P., Gorno-Tempini, M. L., Allison, S. C., Stanley, C. M., Glenn, S., Weiner, M. W., & Miller, B. L. (2006). Structural anatomy of empathy in neurodegenerative disease. *Brain: A Journal of Neurology*, *129* (11), 2945–2956. https://doi.org/10.1093/brain/awl254

Siegel, D. J. (2012). *The developing mind.* Guilford Press.

Timmer, S. G., Urquiza, A. J., Zebell, N. M., & McGrath, J. M. (2005). Parent–child interaction therapy: Application to maltreating parent–child dyads. *Child Abuse & Neglect*, *29*(7), 825–842. https://doi.org/10.1016/j.chiabu.2005.01.003

Tsvieli, N., Nir-Gottlieb, O., Lifshitz, C., Diamond, G. S., Kobak, R., & Diamond, G. M. (2020). Therapist interventions associated with productive emotional processing in the context of attachment-based family therapy for depressed and suicidal adolescents. *Family Process*, *59*(2), 428–444. https://doi.org/10.1111/famp.12445

Waters, E., & Cummings, E. M. (2000). A secure base from which to explore close relationships. *Child Development*, *71*(1), 164–172. https://doi.org/10.1111/1467-8624.00130

Woodfield, M. J., & Cartwright, C. (2020). Parent–child interaction therapy from the parents' perspective. *Journal of Child and Family Studies*, *29*(3), 632–647. https://doi.org/10.1007/s10826-019-01611-5

Zimmermann, P., Maier, M. A., Winter, M., & Grossmann, K. E. (2001). Attachment and adolescents' emotion regulation during a joint problem-solving task with a friend. *International Journal of Behavioral Development*, *25*(4), 331–343. https://doi.org/10.1080/01650250143000157

5

Emotion Focused Therapy for Youth with Anxiety

Mirisse Foroughe, Angela Ashley, and Imayan Neela

Fear is a normal, useful emotion in everyday functioning and can act as a warning for threats to our safety (Adolphs, 2013; Timulak, 2018). However, if an individual feels that they do not have support and protection from these "threats," they can become hypervigilant and insecure and internalize a sense of being unsafe that may progress to clinical levels of anxiety (Watson & Greenberg, 2017). Generalized anxiety disorder (GAD) can cause serious impairment in daily functioning as well as significant social and economic consequences (American Psychiatric Association, 2013). Social anxiety disorder (SAD), characterized as a fear of social situations and discomfort around other people, has been shown to affect up to 12% of individuals during their lifetime (Elliott & Shahar, 2017; Kessler et al., 2005). Research shows that anxiety often begins in early childhood and impacts a wide sociodemographic range of youth. For individuals aged 3–17, anxiety is the most prevalent of mental health disorders, affecting approximately 9.4% or 1 in 11 youth (Bitsko, 2022). Prevalence rates among youth also increase with age, reaching 13.7% for 17-year-olds. This means that nearly one out of every six youth experience anxiety disorders,

DOI: 10.4324/9781003218968-5

placing them at elevated risk for other psychological disorders, physical illness, academic difficulties, and negative impacts on their familial relationships (Bitsko, 2022). Research also indicates that at least 40.7% of youth with anxiety are untreated, and that anxiety often has to reach severe levels before youth are provided with treatment (Ghandour et al., 2019).

Although research supports the use of cognitive therapies for individuals with anxiety, these do not work for everyone, and some people are considered "treatment-resistant" (Borkovec et al., 2002; Hanrahan et al., 2013). For those with social anxiety disorder, treatments have focused mainly on cognitive and behavioural, interpersonal, and psychodynamic approaches (Acarturk et al., 2009; Shahar et al., 2017). However, many individuals do not respond well to CBT, still experiencing symptoms by the end of therapy and, minimally, up to two years later (Davidson et al., 2004; Elliott & Shahar, 2017; Haberman et al., 2019; Leichsenring et al., 2013, 2014; Moscovitch, 2009; Shahar et al., 2017). With room for improvement, emotion focused therapy for youth (EFT-Y) serves as a brief intervention that engages youth in treatment without the requirement of homework outside sessions. Among adult populations, EFT is an empirically supported treatment for anxiety (Greenberg & Goldman, 2019; O'Connell Kent et al., 2021), including GAD specifically (Elliott, 2013; Elliott et al., 2014; Timulak et al., 2017) as well as social anxiety (Shahar, 2014; Shahar et al., 2017). This chapter will share EFT's conceptualization of anxiety, describe core intervention strategies, and outline specific adaptations to best support youth.

EFT's Conceptualization of Anxiety

Although we often hear people say that they are "feeling anxious," anxiety is not technically considered an emotion; anxiety is an emotion-avoidance system. Fear, and sometimes disgust, typically drive this anxious avoidance, and EFT conceptualizes anxiety as feelings of fear and vulnerability originating from negative, painful, or overwhelming experiences during which a person felt they lacked proper protection and support (O'Brien et al., 2019). As a result, individuals may experience decreased self-regulation and weakened coping skills, leading to feelings of invalidation, silencing of their feelings, and viewing themselves as unsafe in the world or unworthy of love and support. Memories of feeling intense pain or being overwhelmed may have consolidated from early experiences of neglect, rejection, or a general lack of caregiver attunement to the youth's needs (Watson & Greenberg, 2017). This does not mean that caregivers were abusive or neglectful; it may have been the child who was unusually sensitive and simply needing more security and support than their environment provided. The reason for looking back through an individual's memories of their early experiences is to better understand the primary emotions that underlie their struggles with anxiety, not to lay blame on either the child or the parent. One way to help families try to avoid blaming and finger-pointing is to simply acknowledge that the caregiver's resources and the child's needs may simply have been mismatched. For the child, being unable to protect or soothe themselves during and after painful or overwhelming experiences can contribute to a sense of vulnerability and fear. This fear reinforces anxiety-based responses which parents can be helped to identify, including anxious avoidance ("I can't go to school today"), over-controlling ("I can only go to school if I have my red shirt on), and irritability ("Leave me alone!"). Again, in speaking to caregivers, it is important to note that the feelings of not being protected or cared for are from the child's perspective and do not necessarily reflect the parent's perceptions or "truth" but the child's internal experience.

Over time, worry and anxiety may function as the Self's misguided attempts to protect from overwhelming painful memories and emotion (Watson & Greenberg, 2017) and lead to a self-reinforcing cycle of perceived vulnerability, fear, and avoidance. In the following case example, we are introduced to Angie, a 10-year-old girl, presenting to therapy after several years of perceived vulnerability and fear that maintained her anxiety symptoms.

Case Example

Client details: Angie, Age 10

Diagnoses/presenting concerns: generalized anxiety disorder, separation anxiety, school refusal

Identifying a marker: Angie had missed four months of school when she presented for therapy. She experienced intense fear and frequent panic attacks upon separation from her parents and several weeks of night waking as a result of anxious thoughts, and she had persistent feelings that something terrible was going to happen to her family. In this excerpt, Angie was engaged in her first chair work exercise. The dialogue begins in the "anxiety split" chair, facing her "Self" chair.

Therapist: Okay, so in this chair, be the part that makes you scared. It can be anything. Just, scare yourself, and then get yourself feeling all tense and worried.

Angie: There's someone trying to hurt our family and we can't get away. [Turns to look at therapist]

Therapist: Okay, face yourself. There's someone trying to hurt your family and you can't get away. Be more specific. What's the person trying to do?

Angie: When you're walking, like, to school, or from school, or something like that, or at the mall, or something, they'll shoot you.

Therapist: Yeah, and something terrible is going to happen to you, right? And what else, tell me more things you can use to worry about. In school, school's really hard, it's EQAO, it's going to be so hard.

Angie: Yeah, it's going to be so hard, and I'm going to be failing, and it's going to get so bad. I'm scared.

Therapist: Yeah. So, school's going to be hard and someone's trying to get you and you're not safe. You're not safe, and what else?

Angie: I'm not safe.

Therapist: You're not safe.

Angie: The world just doesn't like us and our family.

Therapist: And say it in second person: "The world doesn't like *your* family."

Angie: The world doesn't like *your* family. Bad things are gonna happen to us, just because.

Therapist: Bad things are just gonna happen, right, and make her worry more. Tell her the worst thing that will happen.

Angie: There's danger everywhere. You have to keep worrying, or really bad things will happen …

Therapist: Now change. [Angie switches seats and sighs heavily, as if catching her breath]

Therapist: That was a lot. Tell her what it's like when she does this. How does it make you feel?

Angie: It makes me feel so worried inside and then I don't get to sleep because I am constantly thinking about, like, how do you stop this and blah, blah, blah, and then I get up in the morning after trying to fall asleep all night, and then I'm still so worried, and I drive my mom crazy because I need to follow her around, and I drive my father crazy because I am following my mother around. So I just …

Therapist: So, tell her. How is this affecting your life and your family? You are making things …

Angie: You are making my life really difficult! You are driving me crazy!

Therapist: Yeah. And it's been going on for a long time. Tell her what it's like, to live with her in your ear for so many years.

Angie: Um … it's … I don't know how to say it. Sometimes, there's a good, like, "Don't do this, you might choke," or like, "If you jump off of a bridge, you could die."

Therapist: Okay, so I appreciate when you save my life.

Angie: Yeah, I appreciate that. But otherwise, you don't need to worry me so much because then I worry every day, and it's not good.

Therapist: It's not good how? Tell her the impact on you.

Angie: Every time I do something, I will worry like crazy, and it stops me from doing what I'm doing. It's so stressful for me.

Therapist: Just one more time, come back here [therapist motions to the other chair, and Angie switches seats]

Therapist: Respond. Be the worried part again and respond.

Angie: But if I don't worry you, bad things will happen. I have to worry you. That's my job. Like, my job is to worry you.

Therapist: Okay, right, that's what I'm supposed to do, is worry you. And then, so this part just repeats the message, right? Do it some more, scare yourself again.

Angie: So, I just have to keep worrying you, because something is gonna happen or something …

Therapist: Make it the scariest thing it could be.

Angie: Someone's gonna break into your house and just kill all of your family.

Therapist: Switch. [Angie switches seats, looks visibly tense and shaken]

Therapist: And so, tell me, what does it feel like when you hear all that?

Angie: It makes me really nervous because then I'll be, like, out on the streets or something, and then I'll see this guy who's like, walking towards me, and he was just gonna like, pass the road or something, but he is walking towards me and I would freak out like he would come and kill me.

Therapist: Yeah, yeah. So, what does it feel like in your body?

Angie: I get like … I get an imbalanced energy. And it's like … [motions to her stomach]

Therapist: Your tummy hurts?

Angie: Yeah, and I can't breathe.

Therapist: Ok, so we can take a little breath right now. Soft breath … How are you doing?

Angie: Yeah, I'm okay, just feeling …

Therapist: Alright, tell her [motions to empty chair]. What are the feelings? Speak them out, please.

Angie: It feels really hard. It makes me angry. It just makes me …

Therapist: Yes … angry because?

Angie: Angry because I'm suffering. I don't want to feel this way anymore.

Therapist: Say it again.

Angie: I don't want to feel this way anymore.

Therapist: What do need when you feel this way? What do you need from her?

Angie: I need you to worry a little bit less. Or a lot less. So I can actually sleep through the night without waking up. Like, I think the longest I've slept in a row in the last three weeks is probably an hour, because then I wake up and my shoulders are so tight and my neck hurts. Every hour I'll wake up because I get worried.

Therapist: You keep coming up when it's my turn to sleep. Tell her what you need her to do instead. What would help?

Angie: I need you to only worry me, like if I'm gonna do something really … I don't know how to explain it.

Therapist: If there's actually something dangerous?

Angie: Yeah. If there's actually something dangerous, then you can worry me and I won't do it.

Therapist: It can't be an emergency all the time, right? It's tiring. So, can you just say in one sentence what you need her to do instead? So, worry me only when it's dangerous. And the rest of the time?

Angie: And the rest of the time … let me sleep! Because I'd have a lot more energy if I slept. And let me just be a normal Grade 5 kid. Give me some peace.

Therapist: How does it feel when you're asking her that?

Angie: It feels good … like I feel lighter in my shoulders and like something lifted off my chest. It actually feels like I can sleep if I want to. But as soon as I say that, I'm also a bit scared. But not as scared as before.

Therapist: So part of you feels relieved, like "Okay, yes, this is what I want," but then, on this side, there's the anxiety part saying "Oh no!"?

Angie: Yeah, exactly, but it's farther way, like it's quieter.

Therapist: Quieter than before or quieter than the other part?

Angie: Both. Like I, me, I feel stronger than that part now. But she's still there.

Therapist: Alright. Is it okay to stop here? And this is something we can work on again. We don't have to do the chairs every time, just when it seems like a good idea.

Angie: Okay, yeah.

In her first chair work exercise, Angie's therapist supports her through the following process: (1) enact the anxiety split; (2) scare herself with the specific fear that she can respond to; (3) express how this feels directly to the anxiety split imagined in the other chair; (4) respond as the anxiety split and repeat the fear-inducing message as intensely as possible; (5) switch to experience her emotions and felt sense when scared; (6) express this feeling, its impact, and what she needs instead of feeling this way. At some point between the fifth and sixth segment of this process, Angie spontaneously accesses assertive anger, which serves to undo some of her fear and provide her with some hope and relief. For many youth with GAD, performance anxiety, and separation anxiety, EFT-Y can help access adaptive emotions that interrupt symptoms and drive behavioural change.

Early emotional memories of being shamed or bullied by others may also contribute to the development of social anxiety (Elliott & Shahar, 2017). Growing up, these feelings may arise if youth experience impactful instances of interpersonal mistreatment, such as bullying that they feel unable to handle assertively, cruel comments that bring about shame, or abuse in the face of helplessness. In each of these situations, for one reason or another, the young person did not perceive that they had access to adequate support in the form of love, validation, or protection from a primary attachment figure (Elliott & Shahar, 2017; Shahar, 2014; Shahar et al., 2017). Fear is also not the only emotion that can underlie anxiety. Adhering to the *social degradation* model, repeated negative interpersonal experiences of degradation can ultimately result in traumatic emotional pain, presenting as primary shame or sadness (Elliott & Shahar, 2017). These maladaptive emotions may continue to be perpetuated by an *anxious internal critic* that actively reinforces this shame, in a self-perpetuating cycle, while trying to monitor for "dangerous" situations it must protect the vulnerable Self from (Elliott & Shahar, 2017). Although youth may only display the *secondary* emotions of reactive fear and behaviour in anxious-avoidant (e.g., refusing school) or over-controlling (e.g., obsessing over their homework) ways, the anxiety is understood to be disguising, and protecting against, the painful shame underneath (Shahar et al., 2017; Elliott & Shahar, 2017).

The Five Phases of EFT for Anxiety Disorders

When EFT was first attempted with youth in our centre, clinical implementation began with children and teens in therapy for anxiety-based difficulties. Following phases used in EFT for adults with anxiety closely (Watson & Greenberg, 2017; O'Brien et al., 2019; Elliott & Shahar, 2017), we developed clinical adaptations and practical tips for the use of EFT with younger clients. For the majority of clients between 9 and 17 years of age, an eight-session model was associated with significant clinical improvement. For youth with greater chronicity of anxiety disorders or lower tolerance for working with emotions, there are several options to allow for a more gradual approach at the start of therapy and greater depth of emotional processing throughout: (1) EFT-Y for eight sessions plus the option of "add-on" booster sessions that may be spaced out as bi-monthly or monthly meetings; (2) an additional eight sessions, resulting in a 16-session model that more closely follows the pace of EFT with adults; (3) a two-phase approach, beginning with a coping-based intervention (e.g., CBT) and moving to emotion work afterwards. The model we share here is the standard eight-session version of EFT-Y.

Phase One: Therapeutic Alliance and Emotion Assessment (Sessions 1 and 2)

What to Do

As is the case with all EFT therapists, we begin therapy with youth by becoming attuned and attentive to their experience within the therapeutic space, helping them feel safe, and providing a sense of acceptance. For those with social anxiety, building a healing, therapeutic alliance may require our focused attention and additional time owing to their interpersonal sensitivity. In this initial phase, we aim to provide empathically attuned responses to the youth's experiences as we concurrently conduct the emotion assessment. In practice, sessions focus on listening to the client's story and gently connecting what they share with relevant emotional and physical experiences. Often, youth with anxiety have received too little or too much protection during painful, frightening, or overwhelming experiences. When feelings become clearer and more specific, they may feel fear of embarrassment, sadness, shame, or worry about losing control. Common symptoms include worried thoughts, over-controlling of situations, rituals, and avoidance behaviours. In EFT-Y formulation, youth develop GAD symptoms in order to protect themselves from the situations, people, places, or interactions that they fear will evoke painful, frightening, or overwhelming feelings. Clinically, these youth present with (and referral reasons often list) low self-confidence, low self-esteem, risk avoidance, performance fears, and a sense of being weak or unworthy compared with their peers. The youth's initial narrative may be full of negative self-references but often lacks a coherent story of what exactly happened or is happening. In cases of social anxiety, our empathic prompts and responses can help youth access the sadness and loneliness they feel as a result of avoiding social situations and relationships, preparing for the upcoming **anxiety split** chair work. The foundational work conducted in Phase One begins with the therapeutic bond but goes beyond this bond to include an emerging agreement on the role of emotion in the maladaptive process and, consequently, the importance of emotional change in the attainment of treatment goals; we refer to this as *bond plus agreement on tasks and goals* (Greenberg, 2021).

How to Do It

Empathic affirmation, resonance, validation, and attunement (see Chapter 2 for a detailed overview of empathic responding) can be particularly helpful in this phase, as is a general focus on the youth's physical felt sense and the nonverbal behaviour that you notice throughout the session. At times, there may be a high level of congruence between what you observe and what they report feeling—for example, you may see them slump their shoulders and drop their head, and they may report feeling dejected and sad. Other times, youth may struggle to contact their physical sensations or connect these with emotion words that seem to match. Encourage youth to attend to feelings and elaborate on the anxiety emotion schemes that spontaneously arise while they are sharing their story. For example, when they look tense, pause, or swallow while relaying something that has happened for them, we can pause their narrative for a moment and check in on how they are feeling as they talk to us, what physical sensations they notice in their body, and how these feelings and sensations change as they begin to pay direct attention to them. Socializing youth to notice and attend to live emotion can be an excellent method of acclimatizing them to EFT right from the first session. Given that connecting with feelings and sensations appears to come readily for many youth, we can often go further to explore the meaning and impact of these feelings on their daily life (What does it mean to you that this fear is so big in your life? How does it affect you each day?); what role fear and anxiety play in their behaviour and inner experience (What do you avoid so you don't have to feel this way? How do you cope? What has it been like to live with this fear?); and what action tendencies are associated with those feelings (When you feel this way, what do you notice in your body? What do you want to do right now?). This gentle but persistent guidance to attend to the moment, focusing on their physical and emotional experiences, and explore the meaning and impact of their feelings throughout the telling of the "anxiety story" will engage them in developing a **collaborative case formulation**. Youth often appreciate having the therapist join them in this shared understanding of how anxiety "works" in their unique situation. Often, they collect information throughout the week to share in-session, sometimes enjoying drawing or mapping out the process, intuitively capturing aspects of the emotion schemes that EFT researchers use.

Phase Two: Secondary Emotion Processing and Beginning Chair Work (Sessions 2 and 3)

What to Do

In this second phase, youth can begin working through core emotion schemes using experiential tasks that are common to adult EFT (Greenberg et al., 1993). We found that children and young adolescents are able to engage in this phase by Session 2, or at the latest in Session 3, in either the 8- or 16-session course of therapy. In the anxiety split two-chair dialogue presented in Angie's session transcript above, the anxiety-producing part of the Self is imagined to be sitting across from the **Experiencing Self**. Just as in the Witness Your Parent experiential exercise, some youth find it sufficiently evocative just to imagine the anxiety split part of themselves. Youth can begin to identify the feelings, emotional experience, physical sensations, and both the day-to-day and cumulative impact of the anxiety split on the Experiencing Self. Some youth spontaneously access feelings of anger and irritation towards the anxiety split, pushing or kicking the empty chair back, expressing their assertive anger, or sharing deep hurt and sadness towards the anxiety split. One of the most empowering aspects of the anxiety split chair exercise is that the youth begin to see that it is a part of themselves that is impacting their experienced anxiety. Instead of continuing to do so, they feel inspired and hopeful that they can impact themselves in a healthier way and work towards greater self-acceptance, affirmation, and support. There are several useful EFT experiential exercises that can be used during Phase Two: anxiety split, current interpersonal conflict, self-critic, self-interruption, and the three levels of EFT Unfinished Business adapted for youth: Witness Your Parent, Parent as Witness, and Open for Business.

How to Do It

As EFT therapists, we can help facilitate this work on emotion regulation. If the youth starts to engage in emotional or behavioural avoidance, we can use some additional empathic affirmation, breathing exercises, or mindfulness strategies to help reduce the overwhelming anxiety. For example, we could say, "This is really overwhelming for you. It must be so scary to talk about, and you can feel yourself getting anxious, right?" In doing so, we can start to normalize the youth's experience, validating their emotional reactions to continue encouraging their emotional expression. If a youth is over-regulated, feeling numb, or lacking emotional expression, continuing the use of chair work to help heighten the experience of anxiety (e.g., more anxious criticism during the anxiety split) may help to elicit an emotional reaction. For instance, the youth's anxiety producer might say, "You can't do anything! You are always too anxious and scared to get anything done. You'll never change." With an emotion focused lens, this may provoke painful primary emotions, such as fear and shame, to awaken within the youth, increasing their awareness of what triggers their anxiety in preparation for deeper processing.

Chair Work

Anxiety markers: Before beginning any chair work, we can use **emotion markers**; these markers are indicators of the youth's emotional state and help determine the task that is appropriate for the youth's presenting concerns. For example, if the youth expressed statements starting with the words "I worry so much" or "I feel so anxious," a worry dialogue using an anxiety split may help the youth address these worries by bringing together the part of the Self that worries and the part of the Self that experiences the impact of these worries (Watson & Greenberg, 2017). Alternatively, if the youth is critiquing or making shameful, negative comments about themselves, this may be a marker to use a self-critic split so that a youth can explore and reach a point of self-compassion and reduce their negative self-treatment (Watson & Greenberg, 2017). Lastly, if the youth expresses vulnerability and perceived attachment-related injuries, this may be a marker to try Open for Business empty-chair work to address their unmet needs and developmental origins of their maladaptive anxiety responses. The Open for Business task and its less intensive variations are adaptations of EFT's Unfinished Business task (Watson & Greenberg, 2017).

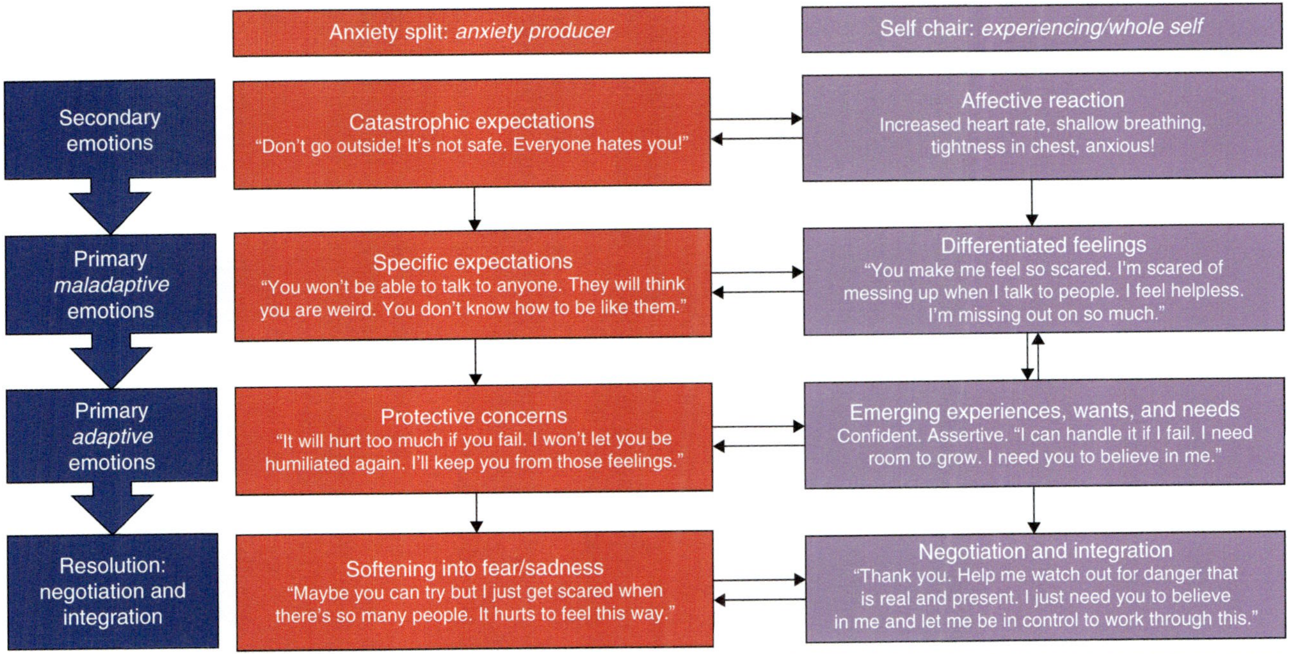

Figure 5.1 Anxiety Split Chair Work.

Note: The figure depicts an example of a youth struggling with social anxiety and how an anxiety split can be carried out. Note that this process is not always linear. Back and forth movement between each step of the process is common before achieving a healthy resolution.

Anxiety split: Also known as a worry split, this two-chair dialogue differentiates the Anxiety Producer part from the Experiencing Self. The function of the Anxiety Producer is typically to protect against painful or overwhelming emotion—most often fear, sadness, disgust, or shame (Watson & Greenberg, 2017).

The anxiety-split task process is as follows:

1. The task begins with the Anxiety Producer expressing catastrophic expectations that increase the Self's anxiety symptoms (e.g., avoidance, over-controlling, overthinking, worrying) and affect-based bodily reactions (e.g., tension, increased heart rate, shaking, upset stomach). For example, in Figure 5.1, the Anxiety Producer for a youth experiencing social anxiety says, "Don't go outside! It's not safe! Everyone hates you!" Someone without social anxiety may hear this as a gross overestimate of danger, but for youth with SAD the effect can be increased anxiousness and, eventually, exhaustion and hopelessness from the constant need to be on high alert.
2. The EFT therapist seeks to deepen and evoke the experience of emotion by asking the youth to express very specific worst-case expectations as the Anxiety Producer. What is the worst that could happen if they took the chance and went out to engage socially with others?
3. As the Experiencing Self, the youth will be supported to fully access the fear, shame, or sadness that the Anxiety Producer is warning them about. Once they are in contact with the emotion, their experience can be further explored, and the immediate and long-term physiological, psychological, social, and performance impact of being made to feel this way can be expressed.
4. Switching back to the Anxiety Producer role, the youth can notice if there is any spontaneous softening that occurs. If so, they can express it to the Self (e.g., "Okay, go ahead and try to make friends, we'll see how it goes, and I won't stop you from trying"). If not, they can continue to warn of threat and identify the protective function of the anxiety split ("It's going to hurt too much if you fail! I can't let that happen").
5. At this stage, a negotiation takes place between the Anxiety Producer and the whole Self. These parts are engaged in a zero-sum game: if one side strengthens, the other necessarily loses ground. If the youth spontaneously asserts their needs using primary adaptive anger, this new emotion can transform the original emotion activated by the Anxiety Producer (e.g., shame, fear, etc.). Some youth express compassion for the Anxiety Producer and recognize its genesis in their early childhood experiences; youth can realize that the Anxiety Producer is merely a split-off part of the Self that is trying to protect them because of memories of past pain or feeling overwhelmed. This softening process furthers possibilities of

negotiation and integration between the two sides to come to a new place of acceptance and self-compassion.

While it's best to follow the youth's lead with respect to adaptive emotion that will be part of their transformation (i.e., self-compassion vs. adaptive anger), therapists may have to support the youth to access these adaptive emotions through empathic responding ("Maybe it was quite painful for your younger self to go through that embarrassment and she had to come up with some way not to feel that again?") or further evocative tasks ("Picture yourself at age six, when you remember feeling so embarrassed. How do you feel towards that six-year-old right now? What do you want to say to her?"). Sometimes, anxiety split work can help resolve symptoms and provide enough relief that more intrusive work is not necessary. Other times, if the young client is not experiencing adequate relief, other chair work tasks (e.g., one of the three levels of Open for Business) may identify and address unresolved relationship-related injuries. Another possible obstacle to resolving an anxiety split is if we are inadvertently working with a Coach Critic instead of the Anxiety Producer. Figure 5.2 differentiates the functions of the Anxiety Producer and the Coach Critic.

 **Anxious Critic**	**Coach Critic** 
"You don't know what to do!"	"You worry too much."
"You're going to fail!"	"Other people can handle more."
"Everything is going to go wrong!"	"You should be able to do this."
"Everyone is going to laugh at you."	"Don't be so anxious"
"You're gonna fall apart."	"People would like you more if you were confident!"

Figure 5.2 Anxious Critic versus Coach Critic.

Anxious Critic versus Coach Critic: The anxious critic is direct in its criticism, causing fear, panic, and excessive worrying within the Experiencing Self. As depicted in Figure 5.2, the anxious critic may say things such as, "You're gonna fall apart," "You're going to fail," and other catastrophizing statements. On the other hand, the coach critic may take a more subtle approach, putting the Experiencing Self down by dismissing their efforts or suffering, comparing them with others, or empty cheerleading. As seen in Figure 5.2, this may include phrases such as, "You worry too much," "Don't be so anxious," and similarly unhelpful "encouragement."

Self-critic split: If the youth demonstrates markers of a harsh critical voice, this suggests that the self-critic split task may be appropriate (Watson et al., 2019). Instead of expressing catastrophic expectations as the Anxiety Producer does, the self-critic process emphasizes critical statements that result in feelings of deep shame and failure. These self-statements often attack a person's character, capability, and personal qualities. Chapter 6 provides more in-depth coverage of this task.

Empty-chair work: For youth with anxiety, empty-chair experiential tasks can be used to address a history of perceived mistreatment, misattunement, or just a mismatch between their needs and their environment or their caregiver's resources. Youth often do not expect that empty-chair exercises will be as evocative as they are. They may contact deep feelings of loss, sadness, and grief. They may remember past experiences, unlocking emotional memories that can lead them to new resolutions. Of course, a child's relationship with their primary caregivers is still very much "in process," and some modifications are needed in order to successfully adapt EFT Unfinished Business (e.g., Watson & Greenberg, 2017) to this population. In the EFT-Y model, there are three levels of the empty-chair task that have been applied successfully to youth:

Level 1 is Witness Your Parent (WYP): In this intervention, youth simply imagine their parent or caregiver in the empty chair across from them. They are then guided to focus inwards and access the physical sensations, emotions, and action tendencies that they notice. They speak only to you, the therapist, rather than directly to their caregiver. In symbolizing their experience, youth are sometimes able to gain clarity, acceptance, and relief. Many youth will experience strong emotions through the WYP task, and it's a good idea to leave at least a third of the session to debrief. Prepare youth that they may feel tired later and may have unexpected feelings come up. When starting empty-chair work with youth, it's best not to rush into the more intensive tasks in Levels 2 and 3. Allow for a session or two to evaluate the impact of the task before returning to deepen it. Your evaluation should include several key questions:

1. Was the task adequately evocative to increase the level of emotion arousal and bring the youth into contact with their emotions, as relevant to the therapeutic process? If so, the WYP task can be repeated to access, clarify, and transform emotion without moving to more intensive levels.
2. Were the emotional sequelae manageable for the youth outside the session? What came up for them during the week between sessions, and can any increase in distress be safely managed?
3. Did the youth feel the urge to share information from their experience of the task with their caregivers, and, if so, how did this impact the parent–child relationship? Was there any cause for concern? Should support for parents be considered? (See Chapters 3 and 4.)
4. Considering the answers to questions 1–3 above, is further deepening or arousal of emotion required?

Level 2 is Parent as Witness (PAW): In the Parent as Witness task, the youth sits across from the empty chair and pictures their parent, but this time they are prompted to speak directly to them and share how they are feeling. The parent is imagined witnessing the youth's emotions and struggles through therapist prompts such as, "Imagine your dad was here, listening to you. Tell dad how hard it has been for you with this anxiety." The therapist can support the youth to fulsomely share their feelings, painful memories, experiences, concerns, and needs directly with the parent. If the youth begins to share with the therapist instead, they are gently redirected to return to the conversation with their parent: "Tell them what hurt the most," or "Tell them what would help you."

Throughout the process, numerous times, youth should also be prompted to check in on their bodily felt sense in the moment, their feelings, and what it's like to be sharing with their parent. Towards the conclusion of the task, youth are directed to tell the therapist how they imagine their parent might respond to what has been shared. As an alternative, if youth are engaged in the dialogue with the parent and emotion processing is productive, some youth benefit from sharing their expected parental response directly with the parent, allowing youth to also tell the parent how they feel about the expected parent response. In summary, the sequence of therapist prompts can include variations of the following suggestions:

1. Imagine your parent in the empty chair, witnessing what you are sharing. Tell them what you are feeling and how hard things have been for you.
2. How do you feel as you say this to your mother/father? What is happening now for you? What do you notice in your body? What feelings are coming up? Where do you feel them? What are the feelings telling you? Share them with your mother/father.

3. How do you imagine your mother/father might respond if they were here? What would they say? What might they feel but not necessarily say? What would be happening for them?
4. a. Tell your mother/father how you feel about the response they would likely have. Where does that leave you? b. Tell them, when you respond like that, I feel ... Tell them what you need instead. How do you feel as you say that?

To conclude the PAW task, we can support youth to explore what they need when they feel this way and what they want to do about that. We can help youth to determine the action tendency associated with their needs, whether they feel like speaking directly to their parent in reality or would allow us to reach out to their parent and offer parent sessions to prepare for a dyadic conversation in or outside therapy. They may be able to make a plan for self-care or accept that their parent would not respond in an optimal way but that another caregiver would be an alternative source of support, such as the other parent, a grandparent, or other family member. Again, in the debrief, we can prepare youth for feelings of sadness, anger, or even fatigue that may come as a result of an intensive, experiential task. We can also evaluate the level of emotion activation and processing, as well as the practical possibilities or limitations of working with their parent(s), working with the youth to expand their circle of support, and so on. We can also determine if the youth may benefit from the more evocative Open for Business chair work task, which allows for the opportunity to enact their parent's responses.

Level 3 is Open for Business.

The marker: The youth has a lingering unresolved feeling about a primary attachment figure or the earlier levels, WYP and PAW, were productive but did not allow for fulsome resolution and the actual parent is not available to engage in parent sessions or dyadic work with their child.

The task: Open for Business. This task is most analogous to the Unfinished Business chair work in EFT for adults, with adaptations for youth as well as the alternative, to invite the parent into a future session if the youth and therapist agree that this may lead to a corrective emotional experience (see Chapters 3 and 4 for options to involve parents in solo, separated, or joint sessions).

Phase Three: Primary Emotion Processing (Sessions 3–6)

With the support of their EFT therapist, youth at this stage can begin to dive into their underlying primary maladaptive emotion schemes driving their secondary anxiety. For GAD, this can be any combination of fear, sadness, or shame, while those with social anxiety may address underlying sadness and shame. Youth can sometimes struggle to stay with these powerful emotion states and become extremely vulnerable. As EFT therapists, we can continue to monitor them, demonstrating empathic affirmation and unconditional positive regard while working through their secondary reactions to get to their core emotional pain. This may require a significant amount of courage and perseverance from both the youth and within ourselves, taking a two steps forward, one step back approach in support of their emotion transformation. Once oriented to their underlying primary emotion(s), we can use corresponding chair work that reflects their underlying emotional needs. For example, if the youth expresses markers of negative self-treatment, you may introduce the self-critic split chair work. In GAD, this voice shames the person with criticism and contempt to make them feel defective or broken. For example, the critic might say, "Nobody likes you, you're such a loser. You should just stay home." For someone with social anxiety, this may activate their shame emotion scheme, which the opposite, experiencing chair can react to. At this point, more adaptive responses, including sadness, anger, and self-compassion (Shahar, 2014), may emerge, and we, armed with our EFT knowledge, can key into them both verbally and nonverbally to support the youth in generating additional dialogue and address their unmet needs. In GAD, by using two-chair dialogues between the Self that is responsible for the suppression of emotional experience and the part of the Self that is responsible for blame and neglect, the youth can learn to better address and regulate these voices. In doing so, a union can be formed between the critic and the Experiencing Self, helping the youth achieve a better sense of self-compassion and self-acceptance.

Phase Four: Emotional Change and Repairing Sources of Anxiety (Sessions 4–7)

At this stage, youth can access deeper emotions related to their anxiety by continuing to use two-chair dialogues, including anxiety splits, self-critic splits, and empty-chair work, as described in the Phase Three description. "Over-practising" can help youth feel more comfortable with uncomfortable feelings and can reinforce the new and emerging emotion schemes. Many youth have specific fears or tasks that they would like to practise through in-session exposures, and this can be an effective way to bridge the emotional transformation to a practical one. Some youth will spontaneously begin internalizing the chair work process and using aspects of the dialogue outside session, in their day-to-day lives:

> It was so cool! I was standing in front of the class, about to do my presentation, and I was so scared. Suddenly, I just started doing the chair work but in my head. I said "Stop making me worry all the time! I need to feel calm. Please support me." And then I imagined myself at, like, age 4 and so little and scared. And I just started giving myself support, like at my

> age now and taking care of the little scared person. It was so fast—I just all of a sudden felt different. My stomach even stopped hurting and I did my whole presentation smiling.
>
> (Jayden, age 12)

At this stage, it can also be especially important to use empty-chair work to facilitate emotion transformation and address developmental sources of anxiety to reduce their influence on the youth as their treatment progresses. In social anxiety, these unexpressed feelings and unmet needs may surround attachment relationships that often emerge from complex trauma (Paivio & Pascual-Leone, 2010). Beyond the empty-chair work presented here, more details about addressing histories of complex trauma among youth can be found in Chapter 8.

With social anxiety, by using either empty-chair or self-critic chair work, another round of emotional deepening can be explored to address unresolved, secondary feelings towards their perceived interpersonal mistreatment to fully understand the root cause of their traumatic pain. This core pain is often presented in three forms: feeling fragile or exposed, feeling violated or injured, or (most commonly) feeling abandoned or rejected by others. After acknowledging these feelings, we can use our EFT lens to support youth in using adaptive emotions and **transformative self-soothing** as resources to cope, helping them accept and identify their unmet needs, such as the need for protection, boundaries, or self-compassion. Imaginal restructuring can also be used by imagining oneself in the painful memory and practising self-soothing (Elliott & Shahar, 2017; Lane et al., 2015). For example, a youth with social anxiety may go back to the time when they were in a busy supermarket, feeling anxious and alone in a crowd of people and trying to buy something. Looking back, the current Self can recall this experience and offer care and guidance, responding in a more emotionally attuned and self-compassionate way by saying, "You can do this. I know it's scary. No one is staring at you, even though I know you feel like it. I'm here with you. We will get through this." In the process, not only does the past Self feel validated, but the current Self can transform and reconsolidate the shame emotion scheme into one of self-compassion and confidence in social settings (Elliott & Shahar, 2017).

Phase Five: Consolidation and End of Therapy (Sessions 5–8)

Towards the end of the EFT treatment, depending on the progress made, we as therapists can support the youth in taking what they have learned forward. Considering that maladaptive coping strategies and avoidance may have been ingrained in a youth for a long time, supporting each youth in bringing forward and consolidating the changes they have made in session is essential to overcoming these old habits. In social anxiety, this could include challenging

avoidant processes and reclaiming one's belonging in social contexts. For those with GAD, self-soothing strategies can be further practised and reinforced. This transition away from therapy can also take time, during which the youth and EFT therapist may reduce the frequency of their sessions to help ease the impact of the transition on the youth. This time can also be spent addressing any setbacks that require additional two-chair dialogue to provide additional reassurance and emotional transformation opportunities for the youth.

Parent Involvement in EFT for Anxiety

As emphasized in Chapter 3, parents can be important partners in their child's treatment process, and involving them can reduce the risk of treatment-interfering behaviours (TIBs). In the treatment of anxiety, parent TIBS can include: not supporting exposure tasks/not challenging anxiety symptoms, providing youth with too much reassurance, using fear or shame to try and "motivate" the child, modelling anxiety-based responses, and shutting down the expression of primary emotions. In these and similar cases, we can engage parents in the process and provide them with the psychoeducation, support, and emotion processing that they may need to help their child overcome anxiety.

Conclusion

Anxiety is a coping mechanism covering an underlying fear of facing difficult emotions. It can present as avoidance, over-control of the environment, or simply irritability and distress. EFT can be extremely efficient and effective for youth experiencing anxiety, whether symptoms represent generalized or social anxiety disorder. Children as young as 9 years old were able to grasp the concept of Self versus Anxiety Producer and engage in two-chair work. While the majority of youth will respond to cognitive-behavioural approaches for the treatment of anxiety, EFT can serve as an adjunct to exposure-based therapies, particularly when youth do not seem to have awareness or access to their self-critical or anxiety-producing thoughts. EFT-Y is also an alternative therapy to consider when traditional approaches fail or if youth do not adequately engage in a behavioural approach that relies on out-of-session homework exercises.

Practical Tips

Do:

- Look out for nonverbal behaviours and verbal markers of anxiety in your client so that you can time your interventions when fear is activated.
- Bring the youth's attention to physical sensations in their body, especially when they have difficulty using emotion words—for example, "Where do you feel the panic in your body?"

- Allow extra time to build a therapeutic alliance with your client with social anxiety, taking into consideration their high interpersonal sensitivity.

Don't:

- Expect that every client with anxiety will benefit from the same process or pace. Consider the suggested phases and experiential tasks as a guide, paying close attention to client emotion markers and individual progress. Empathic attunement is your compass.
- Forget to highlight and consolidate what was learned and practised within session. While EFT-Y does not include a homework or workbook component, you can bring the youth's attention to what they experienced emotionally in the session, what they feel like doing next, and what plans they want to make—particularly after they have asserted their needs or resolved an anxiety-split. Having the chance to put their plans into words while they are experiencing a new feeling can be very powerful and clarifying.

References

Adolphs, R. (2013). The biology of fear. *Current biology*, *23*(2), R79–R93. https://doi.org/10.1016/j.cub.2012.11.055

Acarturk, C., Cuijpers, P., Van Straten, A., & De Graaf, R. (2009). Psychological treatment of social anxiety disorder: A meta-analysis. *Psychological Medicine*, *39*(2), 241–254. https://doi.org/10.1017/s0033291708003590

American Psychiatric Association (Ed.). (2013). *Diagnostic and statistical manual of mental disorders: DSM-5 (5th ed.)*. American Psychiatric Association.

Bitsko, R. H. (2022). Mental health surveillance among children—United States, 2013–2019. *MMWR Supplements*, *71*. https://doi.org/10.15585/mmwr.su7102a1

Borkovec, T. D., Newman, M. G., Pincus, A. L., & Lytle, R. (2002). A component analysis of cognitive-behavioral therapy for generalized anxiety disorder and the role of interpersonal problems. *Journal of Consulting and Clinical Psychology*, *70*(2), 288.

Davidson, J. R., Foa, E. B., Huppert, J. D., Keefe, F. J., Franklin, M. E., Compton, J. S., Zhao, N., Connor, K., Lynch, T. R., & Kishore, G. (2004). Fluoxetine, comprehensive cognitive behavioural therapy, and placebo in generalized social phobia. *Archives of General Psychiatry*, *61*, 1005–1013. https://doi.org/10.1001/archpsyc.61.10.1005

Elliott, R. (2013). Person-centered-experiential psychotherapy for anxiety difficulties: Theory, research and practice. *Person-Centered and Experiential Psychotherapies*, *12*(1), 16–32. https://doi.org/10.1080/14779757.2013.767750

Elliott, R., Rodgers, B., & Stephen, S. (2014, June). The outcomes of person-centred and emotion focused therapy for social anxiety: An update. Paper presented at conference of the Society for Psychotherapy Research, Copenhagen, Denmark.

Elliott, R., & Shahar, B. (2017). Emotion-focused therapy for social anxiety (EFT-SA). *Person-Centered & Experiential Psychotherapies*, *16*(2), 140–158. https://doi.org/10.1080/14779757.2017.1330701

Ghandour, R. M., Sherman, L. J., Vladutiu, C. J., Ali, M. M., Lynch, S. E., Bitsko, R. H., & Blumberg, S. J. (2019). Prevalence and treatment of depression, anxiety, and conduct problems in US children. *The Journal of Pediatrics*, *206*, 256–267.e3. https://doi.org/10.1016/j.jpeds.2018.09.021

Greenberg, L. (2021). *Emotion Focused Therapy Level 3*, York University, Toronto, Ontario.
Greenberg, L. S., & Goldman, R. N. (Eds.). (2019). *Clinical handbook of emotion-focused therapy*. American Psychological Association. https://doi.org/10.1037/0000112-000
Greenberg, L. S., Rice, L. N., & Elliott, R. (1993). *Facilitating emotional change: The moment-by-moment process. Process.* Guilford Press.
Haberman, A., Shahar, B., Bar-Kalifa, E., Zilcha-Mano, S., & Diamond, G. M. (2019). Exploring the process of change in emotion-focused therapy for social anxiety. *Psychotherapy Research*, *29*(7), 908–918. https://doi.org/10.1080/10503307.2018.1426896
Hanrahan, F., Field, A. P., Jones, F. W., & Davey, G. C. (2013). A meta-analysis of cognitive therapy for worry in generalized anxiety disorder. *Clinical Psychology Review*, *33*(1), 120–132. https://doi.org/10.1016/j.cpr.2012.10.008
Kessler, R. C., Berglund, P., Demler, O., Jin, R., Merikangas, K. R., & Walters, E. E. (2005). Lifetime prevalence and age-of-onset distributions of DSM-IV disorders in the national comorbidity survey replication. *Archives of General Psychiatry*, *62*(6), 593–602. https://doi.org/10.1001/archpsyc.62.6.593
Lane, R. D., Ryan, L., Nadel, L., & Greenberg, L. (2015). Memory reconsolidation, emotional arousal, and the process of change in psychotherapy: New insights from brain science. *Behavioral & Brain Sciences*, *38*(e1), 19. https://doi.org/10.1017/s0140525x14000041
Leichsenring, F., Salzer, S., Beutel, M. E., Herpertz, S., Hiller, W., Hoyer, J., Huesing, J., Joraschky, P., Nolting, B., Poehlmann, K., Ritter, V., Strangier, U., Strauss, B., Stuhldreher, N., Tefikow, S., Teismann T., Willutzki, U., Wiltink, J., & Leibing, E. (2013). Psychodynamic therapy and cognitive-behavioral therapy in social anxiety disorder: A multicenter randomized controlled trial. *The American Journal of Psychiatry*, *170*(7), 759–767. https://doi.org/10.1176/appi.ajp.2013.12081125
Leichsenring, F., Salzer, S., Beutel, M. E., Herpertz, S., Hiller, W., Hoyer, J., Huesing, J., Joraschky, P., Nolting, B., Poehlmann, K., Ritter, V., Strangier, U., Strauss, B., Tefikow, S., Teismann T., Willutzki, U., Wiltink, J., & Leibing, E. (2014). Long-term outcome of psychodynamic therapy and cognitive-behavioral therapy in social anxiety disorder. *The American Journal of Psychiatry*, *171*(10), 1074–1082. https://doi.org/10.1176/appi.ajp.2014.13111514
Moscovitch, D. A. (2009). What is the core fear in social phobia? A new model to facilitate individualized case conceptualization and treatment. *Cognitive and Behavioral Practice*, *16*(2), 123–134. https://doi.org/10.1016/j.cbpra.2008.04.002
O'Brien, K., O'Keeffe, N., Cullen, H., Durcan, A., Timulak, L., & McElvaney, J. (2019). Emotion-focused perspective on generalized anxiety disorder: A qualitative analysis of clients' in-session presentations. *Psychotherapy Research*, *29*(4), 524–540. https://doi.org/10.1080/10503307.2017.1373206
O'Connell Kent, J. A., Jackson, A., Robinson, M., Rashleigh, C., & Timulak, L. (2021). Emotion-focused therapy for symptoms of generalised anxiety in a student population: An exploratory study. *Counselling and Psychotherapy Research*, *21*(2), 260–268. https://doi.org/10.1002/capr.12346
Paivio, S. C., & Pascual-Leone, A. (2010). *Emotion-focused therapy for complex trauma.* Washington, DC: APA.
Shahar, B. (2014). Emotion-focused therapy for the treatment of social anxiety: An overview of the model and a case description. *Clinical Psychology & Psychotherapy*, *21*(6), 536–547. https://doi.org/10.1002/cpp.1853

Shahar, B., Bar-Kalifa, E., & Alon, E. (2017). Emotion-focused therapy for social anxiety disorder: Results from a multiple-baseline study. *Journal of Consulting and Clinical Psychology, 85*(3), 238–249. http://dx.doi.org/10.1037/ccp0000166

Timulak, L., McElvaney, J., Keogh, D., Martin, E., Clare, P., Chepukova, E., & Greenberg, L. S. (2017). Emotion-focused therapy for generalized anxiety disorder: An exploratory study. *Psychotherapy, 54*(4), 361–366. https://doi.org/10.1037/pst0000128

Timulak, L. (2018). *Transforming generalized anxiety: An emotion-focused approach* (1st ed.). Routledge. https://doi.org/10.4324/9781315527253

Watson, J. C., & Greenberg, L. S. (2017). *Emotion-focused therapy for generalized anxiety.* American Psychological Association.

Watson, J., Timulak, L., & Greenberg, L. S. (2019). Emotion-focused therapy for generalized anxiety disorder. In L. S. Greenberg & R. N. Goldman (Eds.), *Clinical handbook of emotion-focused therapy* (pp. 315–336). American Psychological Association. https://doi.org/10.1037/0000112-014

6

Emotion Focused Therapy for Youth with Depression

Mirisse Foroughe and Serena Darking

Clinical depression affects approximately 280 million people worldwide and is a leading contributor to the global burden of disease (World Health Organization, 2013). According to the *Diagnostic and Statistical Manual of Mental Disorders* (5th edition), depressive disorders are characterized by persistent depressed mood and/or a loss of interest or pleasure in daily activities. Depression is typically accompanied by symptoms such as weight or appetite loss or gain, insomnia or hypersomnia, psychomotor agitation or retardation, loss of energy, feelings of worthlessness or guilt, concentration difficulties, and suicidal ideation (American Psychiatric Association, 2013). While depression has been primarily viewed as an adult mental illness, current developmental studies highlight that depression often begins during childhood and adolescence (Solmi et al., 2022). Frequently, untreated youth depression increases the risk of a range of adverse outcomes later in life if left untreated (Maughan et al., 2013; Thapar et al., 2012), such as worsening depression (Baez & Heller, 2020; Korczak & Goldstein, 2009), higher rates of comorbid Axis I and II disorders, medication use, and emergency department visits (Korczak & Goldstein,

DOI: 10.4324/9781003218968-6

2009). Depression in youth also has immediate risks and consequences including decreased educational attainment (Wickersham et al., 2021), social isolation (Segrin, 2000), maladaptive emotion regulation strategies (Joormann & Stanton, 2016; Schäfer et al., 2017), and suicidality (Spirito et al., 2011).

In an emotion focused therapy (EFT) conceptualization, the onset of depression occurs when the Self is no longer able to productively connect to its emotions and inner needs (Greenberg & Watson, 2006). For youth seen at our centre, factors such as family bereavement, child maltreatment, intergenerational trauma (see Chapter 8), loss, peer conflict and rejection, bullying, unforeseen illness, and societal pressures can lead to difficult emotional experiences that feel overwhelming. When these emotional experiences are not fully processed and are instead avoided, dismissed, ignored, or otherwise "blocked" from progressing through an emotion transformation process, problematic personal narratives can develop (Angus, 2012). Within these narratives are core depressive experiences that can manifest as self-criticisms, anxious dependencies, or feelings of isolation (Greenberg & Watson, 2006; Kramer & Pascual-Leone, 2016; Salgado et al., 2019). Self-criticism may resemble something like, "I will amount to nothing" or "I am unlovable." With anxious dependencies, the youth may say or think, "I am helpless" or "I am incompetent." Additional statements such as, "I am sad" or "I am lonely" may highlight feelings of isolation.

EFT for Depression: An Evidence-Based Treatment Model

EFT is an empirically supported treatment model for adults with depression (American Psychological Association Presidential Task Force on Evidence-Based Practice, 2006). Over the past few decades, EFT for depression has been widely studied, and clinical trials have supported its theoretical and practical implications across Canada and internationally. For example, the York I Depression Study, a pilot study conducted by Greenberg and Watson (1998), compared EFT with client-centred therapy in the outcomes of 34 adult clients with clinical depression. Clients in the EFT condition had greater short-term and long-term improvements in self-esteem, interpersonal functioning, depressive symptoms, and overall levels of symptom distress compared with clients in the client-centred therapy condition. The York II Depression Study, conducted by Goldman et al. (2006), replicated all findings from the pilot study, highlighting the reliability and effectiveness of EFT for treating clinical depression.

Lafrance Robinson and colleagues (2014) applied the EFT model for depression within a group therapy setting of ten adult clients. Not only did they find clinically significant improvements in areas of functioning and emotional regulation, but they also gathered highly positive testimonials from clients related to their experiences of EFT. Clients overall felt the approach is non-judgemental, accepting, and emotionally moving. These testimonials speak to clients' subjective experience and how they feel during and after the process of therapy, which is arguably the target of all therapy. In other words, people seek therapy to *feel* better, not just to score lower or higher on certain outcome scales. Given the importance of emotional functioning and regulation in young people, EFT can likely impact youth in the same way.

Depression in Youth

Depression in youth is more common than many people realize. Approximately 13% of depressive disorders begin before the age of 18 (Solmi et al., 2022), with major depressive disorder being the third most burdensome condition among youth (Abate et al., 2018). Despite the impact depression has on youth, many resist or avoid treatment (Mental Health Commission of Canada, 2015), for reasons such as stigma (Chandra & Minkovitz, 2006), family conflict, abuse, or comorbidities (Maalouf et al., 2011). Youth depression most often co-occurs with attention deficit hyperactivity disorder, dysthymic disorder, anxiety disorders, and substance abuse (Birmaher et al., 2007; Lewinsohn et al., 2003). The prevalence of youth depression places a burden on society in multiple ways, with suicidality being just one example. Depression can be debilitating and exhausting, reducing participation and attendance in school and the workplace, and can lead to increasing delinquency, psychosomatic complaints, engagement in unprotected sex (Birmaher et al., 2007), and health care consumption (Bodden et al., 2018). As such, it is helpful for therapists to know the impact depression has on youth to better understand their young client.

Depression is often marked by maladaptive emotion schemes such as worthlessness, hopelessness, and powerlessness (Greenberg, 2017). One of the aims of EFT is for you as a therapist to transform these maladaptive schemes, given that they are likely contributors to your client's major depression (Choi et al., 2015; Greenberg et al., 1990; Kramer & Pascual-Leone, 2016; Whelton & Greenberg, 2005). While maladaptive emotion schemes associated with depression often emerge during an individual's formative years, there are no existing research studies that include younger populations in the evaluation of EFT for depression. In this chapter, we discuss the delivery of EFT for depressive disorders and inform clinical adaptations and considerations of this model when treating our youth clients.

EFT for Youth with Depression

The findings from the Youth Emotion Transformation study increase our confidence that EFT-Y is an efficacious treatment for youth depression (Foroughe et al., 2023). Compared with youth who did not complete the EFT-Y treatment, those who did complete the treatment had lower symptoms of depression by the end of their sessions and up to four months after. There is also notable evidence that many of the youth with depression experienced **sudden gains**, which are rapid improvements in symptoms, about halfway through their treatment. Mirroring the adult EFT process (Singh et al., 2021), these sudden gains overwhelmingly occurred within sessions rather than between sessions, even with a shorter timeline of eight sessions. About half of the sample of youth in the study had depression, and so these findings can help lay the groundwork for future research on EFT-Y specifically for depression.

Uses of Empathy in EFT-Y for Depression

There are three core modes of intervention in EFT-Y for depression: (1) empathic support, (2) guiding attention, and (3) evocative experiences. **Empathic support** begins in the very first moments of contact with our client, as it supports the forming of a therapeutic bond and opens the door to further exploration of the youth's feelings as treatment progresses. Empathic support includes all uses of empathy highlighted in Chapter 3, including empathic affirmation and empathic attunement. Empathic affirmation is instrumental for youth with depression as it directly supports the identification and symbolization of their vulnerable emotions—often shame and sadness, but also loneliness and fear of shame. Through validation, we ally with the compassionate part of the youth and meet their need to be recognized and cared for. **Guiding attention** includes directing youth to their experiential felt sense, their internal experiences, and what their body cues are telling them. **Evocative experiences** include the various chair work interventions, which are designed to evoke and activate emotion and are described in greater detail throughout the chapter.

Phases of Treatment in EFT-Y for Depression

Common maladaptive feelings associated with depression such as hopelessness, fear, shame, worthlessness, abandonment, and invalidation are accessed throughout the EFT-Y therapeutic process. By addressing these maladaptive feelings, the youth may process their emotional experiences and move towards adaptive emotion responses instead. EFT-Y utilizes several therapeutic techniques within EFT's three-phase model to treat depression.

Phase I: Bonding and Awareness

The first phase of EFT used to treat depression in youth is called the *bonding and awareness phase* and focuses on establishing the therapeutic relationship, promoting the youth's emotional awareness, and collaborating on treatment goals (Greenberg, 2017). A strong therapeutic alliance founded on empathy, unconditional positive regard, and congruency (Rogers, 1957) is fundamental in EFT-Y. For child and adolescent therapists, this client-centred foundation may be familiar. However, therapists with a more behavioural background focused on teaching or guiding youth with structured treatment plans, as is the case with cognitive behavioural therapy or dialectical behaviour therapy, may find it helpful to spend some time on EFT deliberate practice (DP) exercises related to empathy (Goldman et al., 2021).

When we respond to youth's emotional needs in an empathic, non-judgemental, and compassionate way, they are provided with the psychological space to reflect on their own feelings. Of course, the experiences that youth have in relation to us as therapists are analogous to the parent–child relationship. In adult therapy, the therapeutic relationship between client and therapist is essential for therapeutic change (Rogers, 1957) and fosters a sense of safety and security in the client in EFT (Greenberg, 2014; Weerasekera et al., 2001). With empathy and a safety net in place, the client can move towards self-acceptance and begin coping with their pain (Stern, 1985)—simply put, they can internalize self-soothing abilities that would otherwise be nonexistent without a validating and empathic environment. For youth with depression, it is very important to pay attention to the parallel between the therapist–client relationship and their own parent–child relationship. It is likely that, as you establish a relationship grounded in empathy and bonding, the young client is comparing this therapeutic relationship with their parent–child relationship. They are also likely comparing *you* with their own parents. Do they feel like you understand them more than their parents do? Do they wish one of their parents was more like you? Are there ways in which you remind them of their parents, which may or may not be helpful in the therapeutic process? All of these and similar questions can be essential to ask yourself in this phase of treatment.

To set up the core work that EFT-Y will involve, this first phase also calls for the therapist and youth to establish a rationale for targeting emotions and how this will help them reach their treatment goals. The specific rationale is unique to each youth and may include getting in touch with certain emotions, learning more about their own reaction to specific situations, recognizing a particular emotion as the main source of their distress, or finding ways to deal with emotions in a healthier way (Greenberg, 2017). Therapists may find it helpful to support youth in acknowledging for themselves the connection between their feelings and their goals. A motivational interviewing (MI) approach (Dean et al., 2016; Gayes & Steele, 2014; Miller & Rollnick, 2013) can be helpful in this aspect of Phase I. The more the emotion work is tied to the therapeutic goals that the youth has identified, the more agreement there will be that the tasks of EFT-Y are relevant for them.

Phase II: Evocation and Exploration

The second treatment phase of EFT-Y is the *evocation and exploration phase*, which allows the youth to access and process their maladaptive emotion schemes and vulnerable experiences (Greenberg, 2017). Rather than over-arousing negative feelings, the goal of this phase is to modify under-regulated emotions often seen in youth with depression (Greenberg, 2014), including irritability and anger. The EFT therapist first assesses whether the youth is ready to evoke these difficult feelings by observing their emotional processing style and overall capacity for emotional experiencing. For instance, a therapist may want to consider the youth's ability to safely cope with and express their feelings before moving on to this phase. As well, the youth and therapist will establish and practise ways to promote a sense of connection with the present moment before evoking painful emotions. This might include deep breathing, making eye contact with the clinician, describing their surroundings, imagining their safe place, or any other technique that can channel their own internal support. For youth with depression, who may also suffer from risk of suicide or self-harm, trauma, or abuse, more time should be spent fostering the therapeutic relationship and building awareness, with emotion evocation as a longer-term treatment goal (Greenberg, 2017).

Youth with depressive symptoms may also interrupt or block the experiencing of primary emotions. These blocks likely arise from fear of pain or overwhelm associated with recognizing and experiencing these painful feelings (Greenberg, 2017). Blocks may present as dissociating, changing the topic of conversation, irritability, blanking, or complete numbness as primary emotions are closely approached. In EFT-Y, the therapeutic relationship is crucial in helping youth overcome these blocks. Empathic attunement paired with a therapist's appropriate timing and nonverbal cues (e.g., tone of voice, facial expressions, mannerisms, and gestures) allows for the difficult emotions that are currently felt by the youth to be captured and validated by the therapist (Greenberg, 2017).

Phase III: Generating Alternative Emotions and Creating New Narratives

The third and final EFT phase for the treatment of depression has two major components: (1) *generating alternative emotions* and (2) *creating new narratives* (Greenberg, 2017). Alternative emotions can be generated once maladaptive feelings are evoked and validated by the therapist. Validation is pivotal in regulating affect and strengthening the youth's sense of self, especially for underregulated secondary emotions, such as hopelessness, or primary emotions, such as shame and feelings of worthlessness, which are often seen among clients with depression (Greenberg, 2014; Schore, 2003). Once these feelings are validated, they can be transformed into one or more of the following new adaptive emotions: (1) adaptive anger, which helps the youth set healthy boundaries and overcome obstacles; (2) adaptive sadness, which helps the youth reach out for emotional support from others; and (3) self-compassion, which helps the youth overcome feelings of helplessness or self-criticism (Greenberg, 2017). These transformations promote the creation of new narratives for the youth's experiences that acknowledge avoided feelings, resolve maladaptive emotions, recognize unmet needs, and forgive others or hold them accountable for things

Table 6.1 Six Therapeutic Tasks in EFT for Depression.

Marker	*Task*	*End-State*
Vulnerability	Empathic affirmation	Self-affirmation
Problematic reaction point (self-understanding problem)	Systematic evocative unfolding	New view of self-in-the-world functioning
Absent/unclear felt sense	Experiential focusing	Symbolization of felt sense; productive experiential processing
Self-evaluative split (self-criticism)	Two-chair dialogue	Self-acceptance, integration
Self-interruption split	Two-chair enactment	Self-expression, empowerment
Unfinished Business	Empty-chair work	Forgive others, hold others accountable, affirm self

Adapted from Greenberg et al. (1993).

that may have happened in the past (Greenberg & Watson, 2006). The main goals of this phase are to build and strengthen the youth's regulation in the face of strong emotions and to create a more accepting, resilient sense of self by integrating all parts of their experiences.

Therapeutic Tasks in EFT for Depression

EFT for depression is guided by six therapeutic interventions, or *tasks*, that can be introduced by the therapist throughout Phases II and III to facilitate a client's recovery journey as certain themes, or **markers**, related to primary depressive feelings arise (see Table 6.1).

Systematic Evocative Unfolding

Systematic evocative unfolding is used when a client is perplexed or puzzled by sudden episodes of unwanted, dysregulated, and often overreactive emotions related to a specific situation (Greenberg et al., 1993). For example, this can look something like the youth being confused about why their annoyance when their sibling walks into a room. When a youth reaches a **problematic reaction point**, the therapist encourages them to retell their personal narrative to explore and reprocess what may have led to the emotional reaction. A useful metaphor is: "Emotions are like a red light on the dashboard of a car. When it lights up, it is telling you something important and you best look into your engine to see what is happening" (Greenberg, 2017, pp. 111–112). Similarly, the youth's problematic reaction point(s) signals that there are specific, important triggers that require attention. Youth often re-experience the same reaction when retelling their story, and the therapist encourages them in an experiential search for these specific triggers (Elliott, 2012). Once the exact moment of the reaction and its trigger are identified, the youth can begin to positively shift their self-view with a sense of empowerment to make life changes consistent with this new view (Elliott, 2012).

Experiential Focusing

Therapists apply **experiential focusing** to help a client deepen their level of experiencing by going below the surface emotions to allow for accurate **felt sense**, or internal bodily awareness, to take place (Elliott, 2012; Gendlin, 1996). Youth with depression may find themselves speaking in an overly logical, intellectual, or dismissive manner to avoid accessing painful primary emotions. Sometimes, they are just not sure how to identify or label their emotions. In these instances, it is important for the therapist to gently guide the youth towards a more emotionally productive conversation. For example, where a youth might say, "I don't really know what I'm experiencing right now," the therapist could respond with, "See if you can look inside, and ask yourself, 'What's going on with me right now?' and see what comes to you" (Elliott, 2012). When a youth achieves this clear felt sense, their new-found understanding and symbolization of their experiences can be carried beyond the therapy session and integrated into their daily life. This felt sense can help the youth clearly communicate their needs to others around them, especially their caregivers, without being defensive, dismissive, or dysregulated.

Chair Work for Youth with Depression

The EFT interventions that were successfully adapted for youth presenting with depression are self-critic split, self-interruption, and the EFT-Y adaptations for **Unfinished Business**: Witness Your Parent, Parent as Witness, and Open for Business. See Chapter 3 for a more fulsome description of these EFT-Y tasks.

Two-Chair Dialogue: What to Do

The **two-chair dialogue** is one of the most complex tasks in EFT and is primarily used when a client presents with a **conflict split** (Greenberg & Watson, 2006). These splits can present themselves in many ways; however, clients with depression often face a self-criticism split, where a client harshly and punitively judges and criticizes an aspect of their inner self, blocking the experiences and needs of the other parts of the Self (Shahar et al., 2011). Self-criticism has been shown to predict the onset and severity of depression and has become a fundamental treatment target for many clients with depressive disorders (Choi et al., 2015; Sherry et al., 2014; Zuroff et al., 1990). Primary feelings such as worthlessness, helplessness, and anger are often explored during this task.

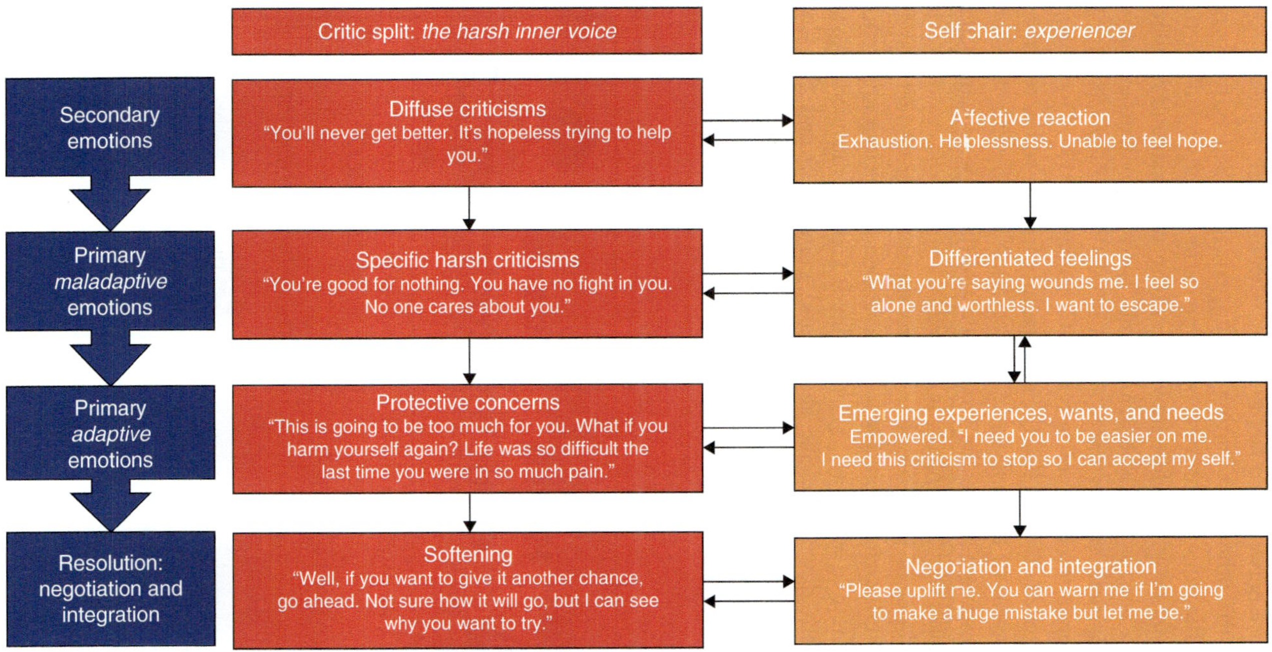

Figure 6.1 Self-Critic Split.

Note: The figure demonstrates a youth experiencing a self-criticism split. As with the anxiety split, this process is not linear. Instead, the process is often cyclical until a healthy resolution is arrived at.

In practice, the therapist begins two-chair dialogue by encouraging the youth to physically move between two facing chairs, with one chair representing the *inner critic* and the other representing the Experiencing Self (Greenberg & Watson, 2006). The young client starts by sitting in the first chair and enacting a dialogue as their inner critic before moving to the second chair and responding to these self-criticisms as the Experiencing Self. The youth will experience secondary feelings initially, such as fear or shame, in relation to their self-criticisms before more primary feelings are activated (Greenberg, 2017). Once primary feelings are triggered, a youth has the opportunity for: (1) self-acceptance by re-owning all aspects of the Self; and (2) integration by achieving an internal, mutual understanding between the inner critic and the Experiencing Self in a soft, compassionate way (Greenberg et al., 1993).

Self-critic split chair work is utilized when the therapist notices that their client is harshly criticizing themselves. As described in previous chapters, the Critic can manifest in two ways: (1) the **Harsh Critic**, who works towards putting the youth down to evoke shame and sadness (2) and the **Coach Critic**, who tries to encourage the client to feel better but instead makes the client feel guilty about their shame and sadness, perpetuating their depression (see Figure 6.2 for examples). After identifying the youth's critical voice,

 **Harsh Critic**	**Coach Critic** 
"You can't do anything right!" "You're such a failure!" "There's something wrong with you." "You're a loser!" "Not one person cares about you."	"Come on, you could have done better." "Just try harder next time!" "Get over it already." "Don't be so depressed!" "Nobody will like you unless you cheer up."

Figure 6.2 Harsh Critic versus Coach Critic.

the therapist asks them to sit in one chair and put the part of themselves that makes them feel worthless, sad, or ashamed in that chair. Next, the youth is asked to move to a second chair where they are the harsh inner voice. Here, they are asked to *be* their harshest critic. This is where the therapist should work with the youth to heighten their feelings and act as the part that makes them feel ashamed and sad. Once the feelings are deeply evoked in the youth, they can move back to the Experiencing Self chair and explain what is happening for them in that moment. With encouragement and gentle coaching, the youth client has the space to describe what they are feeling physically, any memories that are arising, and the specific emotions they are feeling in response to the Critic. Afterward, the youth can go back to the Harsh Critic chair and respond to the Experiencing Self's expressed feelings and needs. The therapist can make note of any softening or lack thereof in the Critic. The youth engages in this exchange until they reach a place of **emotion transformation** and assertively express their needs, often leading to a softening in the Critic along with access to feelings of self-compassion.

Case Example

Client: Erik, 10
Diagnoses: performance anxiety, early signs of depression
Other presenting concerns: school disengagement; low confidence
Identified marker: In the first few minutes of the session, Erik looked discouraged and sat with his head down. He shared that he has not been keeping his grades up at school and he has stopped doing things that he used to do, such as going out for the soccer team, participating in games on his street, and spending time with friends. He expressed concern about not being able to perform well in front of other people or at scheduled events, although he used to have the skills. He has not been sleeping well, is starting to feel sad unexpectedly, and has had very low energy.

Therapist: Be the part of yourself that makes you feel down on yourself and worried about how you are doing. Shame yourself.
Erik: This keeps on happening. This is all your fault.
Therapist: Do it some more.
Erik: You should've worked hard earlier. It's your fault that this is happening.
Therapist: It's your fault because …
Erik: You're paying for it now because you didn't focus earlier.
Therapist: Tell him what he lacks—you lack focus?
Erik: Yeah, you lack focus, you can't stop getting distracted.

Therapist: What does that mean about him? What's the biggest issue with him?

Erik: You're not trying hard enough. [Therapist identifies "Coach Critic" voice]

Therapist: Right … but why isn't he trying? What is it about it?

Erik: You're lazy. You're stupid. You're not a good person. You're a failure.

Therapist: Say that again.

Erik: You're a failure.

Therapist: Switch. [Motions to Self chair]

Therapist: What happens for you here?

Erik: I feel really bad, feel helpless. It's really negative, one-sided, doesn't allow me to think about what's good for me.

Therapist: Tell the critical part of you. When you do this, I feel …

Erik: When you do this, I feel worse.

Therapist: Right, tell him what it's like. Worse than …

Erik: It makes me more like what you are telling me I am.

Therapist: You're making me feel more like this … what's the feeling?

Erik: You're making me feel … [looks at therapist] he causes me to end up more like that.

Therapist: Face him. Tell him what his criticism causes you to end up feeling.

Erik: You're telling me there's no point in trying.

Therapist: You're making me feel helpless? Or discouraged?

Erik: You make it feel more helpless.

Therapist: Helpless. Where do you feel it right now, in your body?

Erik: I feel it in my whole body, like a weight, like a ball and chain. And like a dark cloud hanging over my head no matter where I go. Wow. [Shaking out body, as if overcome with how negative it feels] It's awful.

Therapist: Tell him. When you do this to me, I feel awful everywhere. Speak from the helplessness.

Erik: I feel awful, I feel so heavy, I feel like I can't do anything, I feel stuck in mud, and I feel just … like … I'll never be free, nothing will ever work out for me.

Therapist: That is very heavy … it's a lot to deal with … it must have been so hard to get anything done feeling this way …

Erik: Exactly. [Tearing up]

Therapist: What do you feel right now? There's a sadness or …

Erik: Yeah … I … [crying quietly].

Therapist: It's important, this sadness, and the tears are important. Can you speak from the tears? What are they saying?

Erik: I need to feel better. Like I deserve to not feel this way.

Therapist: What do you need to help you feel better? What would help?

Erik: Just even a more realistic view, unbiased view.

Therapist: Tell him [motioning to the self-critic chair]

Erik: I need you to stop making me feel like crap. [Louder voice, sitting up straight] I need self-awareness that is more realistic.

Therapist: Say that again, stop making me feel like crap.

Erik: Just stop! [Kicked at the self-critic chair]. Sorry, it just makes me mad you know? Like I always stand up for everyone but me.

Therapist: Go ahead and stand up if you feel like it. Either with your body or your voice—stand up for what you need.

Erik: [Sitting up straight, leaning forward, strong voice] I need you to be fair. Not just this one-sided view. You're always telling me everything I did wrong. You never look at things I actually did do. From now on, I want you to calm down a bit. Think about what you're telling me. Think about what will help me. Instead of beating me up, help me a bit. That's your job. You're supposed to help me actually become better.

Therapist: How do you feel right now? How does it feel as you say that?

Erik: Good. It feels really good. Like a weight off me. Like really light. Relieved or whatever. Less annoyed by him. I think he will listen to me. I feel good standing up for myself. I don't think he's a bully, I think he just wants to help me, so I told him how to do it.

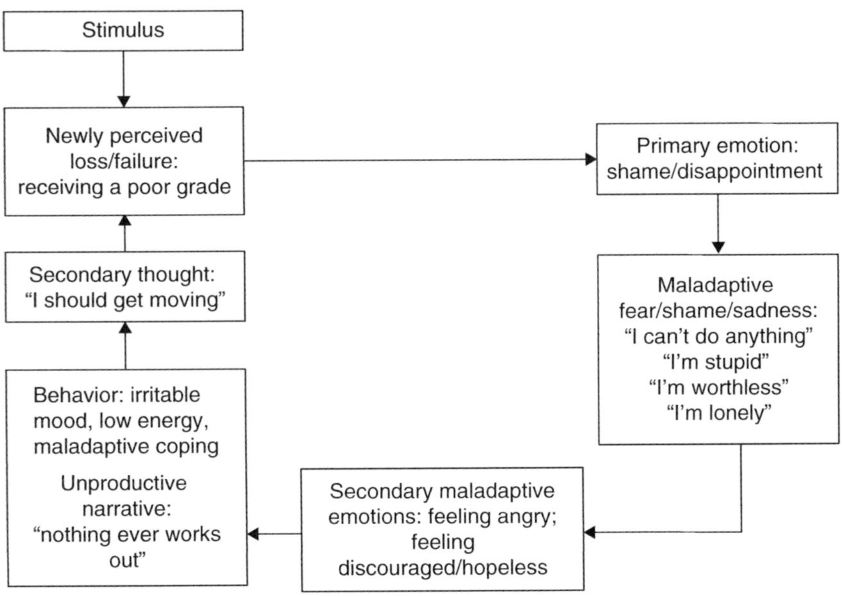

Figure 6.3 Emotion Schematic Cycle of Responses.

Adapted from Greenberg and Watson (2005), p. 54.

Self-Interruption: Two-Chair Enactment

Two-chair enactment is also used when the youth is emotionally distant or avoidant during a therapy session, indicating **self-interruption** (Elliott et al., 2004). Self-interruptions arise when a youth begins to feel or do something during the therapeutic session before relinquishing the process verbally (e.g., makes statements of resignation, reports feeling weighted down) or non-verbally (e.g., clenches fists, holds back tears, reports physical discomfort such as a headache, freezes; Elliott, 2012). For youth with depression, self-neglect is often the root of self-interruption (Salgado et al., 2019). The two-chair enactment task aims to address emotional blocks and feelings of "stuckness" when these self-interruptions occur.

A youth's feeling of stuckness can be the result of split between the emotional, Experiencing Self and the intellectual, distancing Self (Elliott, 2012). The therapist introduces the two-chair enactment by having their client re-enact their own process of self-interruption. Throughout the process, the client is encouraged to direct their attention to their own verbal or nonverbal interruptions as they occur. The initial goal of the self-interruption task for clients with depression is to become contactfully aware of their own avoidant patterns that prevent painful emotional experiences from occurring. Once these interruptions are acknowledged by the client, the therapist can utilize their empathic attunement to help their client explore the impact and unmet internal needs resulting from their self-neglect. This task offers additional awareness to the client about how the process of self-interruption occurs and how it can be undone, offering an opportunity for self-empowerment (Salgado et al., 2019). According to Robert Elliott, all this is to say, "You cannot leave an emotion until you arrive at it" (The Counselling Channel, 2016, 2:19).

Empty-Chair Work

Empty-chair work is used to help clients fully express, and resolve suppressed, primary negative feelings towards others and explore the implicit meaning of past events with them (Greenberg, 2017; Pos & Greenberg, 2007). The Unfinished Business (UFB) task has been found to be highly effective in the treatment of depressive disorders (Greenberg et al., 2008; Paivio & Greenberg, 1995). Empty-chair work begins with the therapist suggesting that the client imagine the significant other in an empty chair in front of them and discuss any unexpressed or unresolved feelings (e.g., sadness, anger, hurt, etc.) towards them, leading to the expression of a client's unmet needs. For youth, the imagined other is almost always a parent or caregiver. It can be extremely painful and sometimes overwhelming for a young client to speak to the imaginary other, and it is therefore important for the therapist to maintain consistent empathic attunement to their client's level of emotional arousal (Elliott, 2012; Paivio & Greenberg, 1995). In addition, the adaptations of UFB—detailed in Chapter 2—allow the therapist to scaffold the task for youth so that it is tolerable and productive, leading to the expression of feelings and needs. Once all unmet needs have been expressed, the therapist has the client take on the perspective of the other to access an alternative view (Greenberg et al., 2008). This view is often more positive and allows the client to: (1) understand/forgive the other and let go, (2) hold the other accountable for their actions, and/or (3) accept and affirm the Self (Greenberg, 2017; Greenberg et al., 2008; Angus et al., 2008).

Clinical Considerations: Impact of Youth Depression on Caregivers

Youth depend on their caregivers for security, support, and emotion regulation. When working with youth experiencing depression, a therapist may ask themself, "Do the parents know how to respond to my client's emotions?" It is possible that the youth's sadness may evoke upsetting memories for their parents whose own cries for help were not addressed during their childhood. Instead of knowing how to respond to the youth, the caregiver may feel helpless and freeze in fear of repeating the unhelpful behaviour of their own caregivers. Another caregiver may react with rage or try to shut down their child's expressions of sadness. Understandably, this unresponsiveness and invalidation from the caregiver may interfere with a youth's treatment and strain the parent–child relationship. Parent or dyadic EFT (see Chapters 3 and 4) can provide much-needed support if parents are struggling to effectively support their child through depression.

Conclusion

Through EFT-Y, therapists can utilize empathic responses to follow their client's hurt as well as activate strategies to help youth in identifying their heartfelt needs when they feel emotional pain or overwhelm. This transformative experience can help undo the cycle of harsh self-criticism, often exacerbated by unhelpful Coach Critic judgements, instead activating a new emotion scheme of self-compassion and self-soothing. Alternatively, many youth find that assertive anger supports their ability to strengthen the Self, stand up for what they need, and feel a healthy sense of entitlement. This activation of primary adaptive anger, an energized and powerful emotion, can be immensely helpful for depression, both psychologically and physiologically. For youth demonstrating reluctance or treatment-resistance towards traditional cognitive-behavioural therapies for depression, the in-session experience of EFT-Y can provide emotional activation that bypasses rational thought and allows for the much-needed expedition inwards.

Practical Tips

Do:

- Pace yourself intentionally slower than you usually would to create discrepancy and motivate the client to want to go forward faster. Youth with depression often find parents, teachers, and other adults try to "push" them too much and too quickly. Your slower rate of speech and attention to speaking on the youth's down breath (as they are breathing out) will also help with overall attunement and empathic receptivity.
- Use emotion focused interventions to draw attention to "process" within the "content" (e.g., "How do you feel as you say this?" and "What do you notice in your body now?").
- Pay close attention to the client's "blocks" as these can prevent them from accessing or expressing emotion. Help the client work through the blocks using the self-interruption split before trying other chair tasks.

Don't:

- Be afraid to jump between the phases of the EFT-Y treatment for depression, as the process is rarely linear. What's important is building the therapeutic alliance and following the client's lead with your emotion compass.
- Try to change the client's Coach Critic voice. Simply acknowledge that the Coach is there and focus your attention on helping the client work with the Harsh Critic instead.
- Forget to build your own tolerance for strong negative emotion. When your client becomes highly activated, or even dysregulated, show them that you can handle their feelings.

References

Abate, K. H., Abebe, Z., Abil, O. Z., Afshin, A., Ahmed, M. B., Alahdab, F., Alam, K., Alavian, S. M., Alkerwi, A., Alla, F., Amoako, Y. A., Anber, N. H., Animut, M. D., Armoon, B., Badali, H., Baune, B. T., Cercy, K. M., Chaiah, Y., Charlson, F. J., … Zucker, I. (2018). Global, regional, and national incidence, prevalence, and years lived with disability for 354 diseases and injuries for 195 countries and territories, 1990–2017: A systematic analysis for the Global Burden of Disease Study 2017. *The Lancet (British edition)*, *392*(10159), 1789–1858. https://doi.org/10.1016/S0140-6736(18)32279-7

American Psychiatric Association. (2013). *Diagnostic and statistical manual of mental disorders* (5th ed.). Washington, DC: American Psychiatric Association. https://doi.org/10.1176/appi.books.9780890425596

American Psychological Association, Presidential Task Force on Evidence-Based Practice (2006). Evidence-based practice in psychology. *American Psychologist*, *61*(4), 271–285. https://doi.org/10.1037/0003-066X.61.4.271

Angus, L. (2012). Toward an integrative understanding of narrative and emotion processes in emotion-focused therapy of depression: Implications for theory, research and practice, *Psychotherapy Research*, *22*(4), 367–380. https://doi.org/10.1080/10503307.2012.683988

Angus, L., Goldman, R. N., & Mergenthaler, E. (2008). One case, multiple measures: An intensive case-analytic approach to understanding client change processes in evidence-based, emotion-focused therapy of depression. *Psychotherapy Research*, *18*(6), 629–633. https://doi.org/10.1080/10503300802430673

Baez, L. M., & Heller, A. S. (2020). Impact of age at onset on the phenomenology of depression in treatment-seeking adults in the STAR* D trial. *Journal of Affective Disorders*, *262*(1), 381–388. https://doi.org/10.1016/j.jad.2019.10.036

Birmaher, B., Brent, D., & AACAP Work Group on Quality Issues. (2007). Practice parameter for the assessment and treatment of children and adolescents with depressive disorders. *Journal of the American Academy of Child & Adolescent Psychiatry*, *46*(11), 1503–1526. https://doi.org/10.1097/chi.0b013e318145ae1c

Bodden, D. H. M., Stikkelbroek, Y., & Dirksen, C. D. (2018). Societal burden of adolescent depression, an overview and cost-of-illness study. *Journal of Affective Disorders*, *241*, 256–262. https://doi.org/10.1016/j.jad.2018.06.015

Chandra, A., & Minkovitz, C. S. (2006). Stigma starts early: Gender differences in teen willingness to use mental health services. *Journal of Adolescent Health*, *38*(6), 754-e1–754-e8. https://doi.org/10.1016/j.jadohealth.2005.08.011

Choi, B. H., Pos, A. E., & Magnusson, M. S. (2015). Emotional change process in resolving self-criticism during experiential treatment of depression. *Psychotherapy Research*, *26*(4), 484–499. https://doi.org/10.1080/10503307.2015.1041433

Dean, S., Britt, E., Bell, E., Stanley, J., & Collings, S. (2016). Motivational interviewing to enhance adolescent mental health treatment engagement: A randomized clinical trial. *Psychological Medicine*, *46*(9), 1961–1969. https://doi.org/10.1017/S0033291716000568

Elliott, R. (2012). Emotion-focused therapy. In P. Sanders (Ed.), *The tribes of the person-centred nation, 2nd edition: An introduction to the schools of therapy related to the person-centred approach* (pp. 103–120). PCCS Books.

Elliott, R., Watson, J. C., Goldman, R. N., & Greenberg, L. S. (2004). *Learning emotion focused therapy: The process-experiential approach to change*. American Psychological Association.

Foroughe, M., Ashley, A., Neela, I., Darking, S., & Bell, S. (2023). *Emotion focused therapy: A randomized case series of clinical outcomes* [Manuscript submitted for publication]. Department of Psychology, York University.

Gayes, L. A., & Steele, R. G. (2014). A meta-analysis of motivational interviewing interventions for pediatric health behavior change. *Journal of Consulting and Clinical Psychology*, *82*(3), 521–535. https://doi.org/10.1037/a0035917

Gendlin, E. T. (1996). *Focusing-oriented psychotherapy: A manual of the experiential method*. Guilford Press.

Goldman, R. N., Greenberg, L. S., & Angus, L. (2006). The effects of adding emotion-focused interventions to the client-centered relationship conditions in the treatment of depression. *Psychotherapy Research*, *16*(5), 536–546. https://doi.org/10.1080/10503300600589456

Goldman, R. N., Vaz, A., & Rousmaniere, T. (2021). *Deliberate practice in emotion-focused therapy*. American Psychological Association.

Greenberg, L. (2014). The therapeutic relationship in emotion-focused therapy. *Psychotherapy*, *51*(3), 350–357. https://doi.org/10.1037/a0037336

Greenberg, L. S. (2017). Emotion-focused therapy of depression. *Person-Centered & Experiential Psychotherapies*, *16*(2), 106–117. https://doi.org/10.1080/14779757.2017.1330702

Greenberg, L. S., Elliott, R., & Foerster, F. S. (1990). Experiential processes in the psychotherapeutic treatment of depression. In C. D. McCann & N. S. Endler (Eds.), *Depression: Developments in theory, research and practice* (pp. 157–185). Wall & Emerson.

Greenberg, L. S., Rice, L. N., & Elliott, R. (1993). *Facilitating emotional change: The moment-by-moment process*. Guilford Press.

Greenberg, L. Warwar, S. H., & Malcolm, W. M. (2008). Differential effects of emotion-focused therapy and psychoeducation in facilitating forgiveness and letting go of emotional injuries. *Journal of Counseling Psychology*, *55*(2), 185. https://doi.org/10.1037/0022-0167.55.2.185

Greenberg, L., & Watson, J. (1998). Experiential therapy of depression: Differential effects of client-centered relationship conditions and process experiential interventions. *Psychotherapy Research*, *8*(2), 210–224. https://doi.org/10.1080/10503309812331332317

Greenberg, L. S., & Watson, J. C. (2006). *Emotion-focused therapy for depression*. American Psychological Association.

Joormann, J., & Stanton, C. H. (2016). Examining emotion regulation in depression: A review and future directions. *Behaviour Research and Therapy*, *86*(1), 35–49. https://doi.org/10.1016/j.brat.2016.07.007

Korczak, D. J., & Goldstein, B. I. (2009). Childhood onset major depressive disorder: Course of illness and psychiatric comorbidity in a community sample. *The Journal of Pediatrics*, *155*(1), 118–123. https://doi.org/10.1016/j.jpeds.2009.01.061

Kramer, U., & Pascual-Leone, A. (2016). The role of maladaptive anger in self-criticism: A quasi-experimental study on emotional processes. *Counselling Psychology Quarterly*, *29*(3), 311–333. https://doi.org/10.1080/09515070.2015.1090395

Lafrance Robinson, A., McCague, E. A., & Whissell, C. (2014). "That chair work thing was great": A pilot study of group-based emotion-focused therapy for anxiety and depression. *Person-Centered & Experiential Psychotherapies*, *13*(4), 263–277. https://doi.org/10.1080/14779757.2014.910131

Lewinsohn, P. M., Petit, J. W., Joiner Jr., T. E., & Seeley, J. R. (2003). The symptomatic expression of major depressive disorder in adolescents and young adults. *Journal of Abnormal Psychology*, *112*(2), 244. https://doi.org/10.1037/0021-843X.112.2.244

Maalouf, F. T., Atwi, M., & Brent, D. A. (2011). Treatment-resistant depression in adolescents: Review and updates on clinical management. *Depression and Anxiety*, *28*(11), 946–954. https://doi.org/10.1002/da.20884

Maughan, B., Collishaw, S., & Stringaris, A. (2013). Depression in childhood and adolescence. *Journal of the Canadian Academy of Child and Adolescent Psychiatry*, *22*(1), 35–40.

Mental Health Commission of Canada. (2015). *Taking the next step forward building a responsive mental health and addictions system for emerging adults*. www.mentalhealthcommission.ca/sites/default/files/Taking%252520the%252520Next%252520Step%252520Forward_0.pdf

Miller, W. R., & Rollnick, S. (2013) *Motivational interviewing: Helping people to change* (3rd ed.). Guilford Press.

Paivio, S. C., & Greenberg, L. S. (1995). Resolving "unfinished business": Efficacy of experiential therapy using empty-chair dialogue. *Journal of Consulting and Clinical Psychology*, *63*(3), 419–425. https://doi.org/10.1037/0022-006X.63.3.419

Pos, A. E., & Greenberg, L. S. (2007). Emotion-focused therapy: The transforming power of affect. *Journal of Contemporary Psychotherapy*, *37*(1), 25–31. https://doi.org/10.1007/s10879-006-9031-z

Rogers, C. R. (1957). The necessary and sufficient conditions of therapeutic personality change. *Journal of Consulting Psychology*, *21*(2), 95–103. https://doi.org/10.1037/h0045357

Salgado, J., Cunha, C., Monteiro, M., Goldman, R., & Greenberg, L. S. (2019). Emotion focused-therapy for depression. In L. S. Greenberg & R. Goldman (Eds.), *Clinical handbook of emotion-focused therapy* (pp. 293–314). American Psychological Association.

Schäfer, J. Ö., Naumann, E., Holmes, E. A., Tuschen-Caffier, B., & Samson, A. C. (2017). Emotion regulation strategies in depressive and anxiety symptoms in youth: A meta-analytic review. *Journal of Youth and Adolescence*, *46*(2), 261–276. https://doi.org/10.1007/s10964-016-0585-0

Schore, A. N. (2003). *Affect dysregulation & disorders of the self.* Norton Professional Books.

Segrin, C. (2000). Social skills deficits associated with depression. *Clinical Psychology Review*, *20*(3), 379–403. https://doi.org/10.1016/S0272-7358(98)00104-4

Shahar, B., Carlin, E. R., Engle, D. E., Hegde, J., Szepsenwol, O., & Arkowitz, H. (2011). A pilot investigation of emotion-focused two-chair dialogue intervention for self-criticism. *Clinical Psychology & Psychotherapy*, *19*(6), 496–507. https://doi.org/10.1002/cpp.762

Sherry, S. B., Richards, J. E., Sherry, D. L., & Stewart, S. H. (2014). Self-critical perfectionism is a vulnerability factor for depression but not anxiety: A 12-month, 3-wave longitudinal study. *Journal of Research in Personality*, *52*, 1–5. https://doi.org/10.1016/j.jrp.2014.05.004

Singh, T., Pascual-Leone, A., Morrison, O. P., & Greenberg, L. (2021). Working with emotion predicts sudden gains during experiential therapy for depression. *Psychotherapy Research*, *31*(7). 895–908. https://doi.org/10.1080/10503307.2020.1866784

Solmi, M., Radua, J., Olivola, M., Croce, E., Soardo, L., Salazar de Pablo, G., Shin, J., Kirkbride, J. B., Jones, P., Kim, J. H., Kim, J. Y., Carvalho, A. F., Seeman, M. V., Correll, C. U., & Fusar-Poli, P. (2022). Age at onset of mental disorders worldwide: Large-scale meta-analysis of 192 epidemiological studies. *Molecular Psychiatry*, *27*(1), 281–295. https://doi.org/10.1038/s41380-021-01161-7

Spirito, A., Esposito-Smythers, C., Wolff, J., & Uhl, K. (2011). Cognitive-behavioral therapy for adolescent depression and suicidality. *Child and Adolescent Psychiatric Clinics*, 20(2), 191–204. https://doi.org/10.1016/j.chc.2011.01.012

Stern, D. N. (1985). *The interpersonal world of the infant: A view from psychoanalysis and developmental psychology*. Routledge.

Thapar, A., Collishaw, S., Pine, D. S., & Thapar, A. K. (2012). Depression in adolescence. *Lancet*, *379*(9820), 1056–1067. https://doi.org/10.1016/S0140-6736(11)60871-4

The Counselling Channel. (2016, July 25). *Emotional deepening process* [Video]. YouTube. https://youtu.be/kNRg2DFtgOw.

Weerasekera, P., Linder, B., Greenberg, L., & Watson, J. (2001). The working alliance in client-centered and process-experiential therapy of depression. *Psychotherapy Research*, *11*(2), 221–233. https://doi.org/10.1093/ptr/11.2.221

Whelton, W. J., & Greenberg, L. S. (2005). Emotion in self-criticism. *Personality and Individual Differences*, *38*(7), 1583–1595. https://doi.org/10.1016/j.paid.2004.09.024

Wickersham, A., Dickson, H., Jones, R., Pritchard, M., Stewart, R., Ford, T., & Downs, J. (2021). Educational attainment trajectories among children and adolescents with depression, and the role of sociodemographic characteristics: Longitudinal data-linkage study. *The British Journal of Psychiatry*, *218*(3), 151–157. https://doi.org/10.1192/bjp.2020.160

World Health Organization. (2013). *Global health estimates summary tables: YLDs by cause, age, and sex*. www.who.int/mental_health/evidence/atlas/mental_health_atlas_2014/en/

Zuroff, D. C., Igreja, I., & Mongrain, M. (1990). Dysfunctional attitudes, dependency, and self-criticism as predictors of depressive mood states: A 12-month longitudinal study. *Journal of Cognitive Therapy and Research*, *14*, 315–326. https://doi.org/10.1007/BF01183999

7

Emotion Focused Therapy for Youth with Borderline Personality Disorder

Mirisse Foroughe and George A. Langdon

> What's better after therapy? My child doesn't want to die every day! This therapy has literally saved her life and our family. Her daily mood has also improved and is more stable, she doesn't cry as often or scream and have meltdowns. More pleasant to be around. Same person—still huge social problems and now we know the reason but she is accepting herself and has hope that she can feel better and learn to be okay with living life. EFT has changed all of our lives. I want EFT for myself, my marriage, and our whole family.
>
> (Mother of 16-year-old girl with BPD)

Borderline Personality Disorder

Borderline personality disorder (BPD) presents as one of the most pervasive personality disorders today, accounting for up to 25% of inpatient psychiatric populations, making it the most common Axis II affective disorder seen in clinical settings (Hecht et al., 2014; Levy et al., 2018; Lieb et al., 2004; Smits

DOI: 10.4324/9781003218968-7

et al., 2017). Research has shown that 9–40% of returning inpatient utilizers of psychiatric services carry the diagnosis (Harned et al., 2006). Owing to the nature of BPD behaviours and symptoms, individuals diagnosed with the disorder are generally viewed as some of the most challenging clients for a clinician to treat (Harned et al., 2006). Linehan (1993a) outlines the diagnostic symptoms for BPD through the five most commonly seen areas of dysregulation within the clinical population. First, individuals with BPD often experience a chronic sense of emptiness and/or a consistently unstable sense of self (*dysregulation of the sense of self*). Second, individuals with BPD regularly exhibit highly reactive emotional responses, usually during brief but very intense periods of overwhelming affect (*emotion dysregulation*). Third, they tend to experience brief periods of uncontrollable dissociation in times of overwhelming stress (*cognitive dysregulation*). Fourth, individuals with BPD commonly present with an inability to control impulsive urges, engaging in behaviours that frequently include self-injury or suicidal behaviours, with the rate of self-injurious and suicidal behaviour estimated to range from 69% to 80% within the population (Harned et al., 2006), as well as various forms of indirect self-harming behaviours such as substance abuse, gambling, reckless driving, and spending sprees, to name a few (*behavioural dysregulation*). Finally, those with the diagnosis are often characterized by a pervasive pattern of unstable intrapersonal identity (*intrapersonal instability*) as well as interpersonal relating, including friendships, family ties, and romantic relationships (*interpersonal dysregulation*). Within the interpersonal realm is perhaps where considerable therapeutic challenges lie. And yet, it is in spite of copious interpersonal tension, extreme oscillations between idealization and devaluation, desperate efforts to avoid perceived abandonment, and the accompanying series of maladaptive behaviours that the therapeutic relationship must be built, maintained, and eventually—hopefully amicably—concluded.

Dialectical Behaviour Therapy and BPD

While no specific type of psychotherapy for the treatment of BPD is recommended by the American Psychiatric Association, a majority of the empirical research into treating the disorder has been focused on implementing Linehan's (1987) dialectical behaviour therapy (DBT) model (Oldham, 2006; Warwar et al., 2008). DBT is a cognitive-behavioural treatment for BPD that was developed based on the biosocial theory of the disorder's etiology (Harned et al., 2006). Linehan (1993a) used this theory to conceptualize the disorder as the result of the ongoing interactions between an individual with high emotional vulnerability and a consistently invalidating environment, be it subjectively perceived or objectively verifiable. DBT is organized in terms of two leading principles: a focus on problem-solving that is geared towards troubled behaviours and a strong emphasis on the dialectic reasoning behind interpersonal and intrapersonal cognition (i.e., the client's understanding of themself and their connection to others, their social motivations, and their perception of others' social motivations; Linehan, 1987). Perhaps the most critical dialectic within the treatment is that of acceptance and change: the patient must be accepted as they are, both by the therapist and by themself, while simultaneously seeking and working towards therapeutic growth (Linehan, 1987). They are doing their best *and* they need to do better; both realities are true at once.

DBT uses dialectics such as these to validate the client's understandings of their surrounding reality and the emotions they experience, as well as to help the client integrate them into the broader context of self-acceptance and personal growth (Harned et al., 2006). Much like traditional cognitive therapy, DBT is "directive and intervention-oriented" (Linehan, 1987, p. 272). The treatment typically involves teaching patients various skills to help them cope with and overcome struggles in problem areas that are most commonly associated with BPD. These skills include *mindfulness*, *distress tolerance*, *emotion regulation*, and *interpersonal effectiveness*. DBT places a lot of its focus on the intentional, systematic practice of thoughts and behaviours to help bring a person's attention to the current moment, their physical body, and a more balanced state of energetic, attentional, and emotion regulation. Therapeutic tasks include teaching the skills to help them cope with their presenting symptoms and difficult situations they may encounter in their day-to-day lives. Skills training emphasizes coping-based strategies such as putting one's face in cold water to reduce physical reactivity and, in turn, emotional reactivity; checking the facts around a situation to determine the appropriateness of one's emotional response; and using a prescribed sentence structure when making a request of another person (Linehan, 1993b).

Emotion Focused Therapy for BPD

If emotion dysregulation is conceived as a core deficit in BPD, effective processing of emotion can be a useful mechanism for psychotherapeutic change. Emotion processing is certainly a component of DBT and DBT-informed treatments for BPD; however, it is not a central focus in the way that skills training and dialectical reasoning are currently conducted (Warwar et al., 2008). Additionally, while targeting aspects of emotion regulation is a key element of DBT, the therapy's outcome goals largely target the mediation and reduction of parasuicidal and other dysfunctional behaviours (Linehan, 1993b). As such, the use of emotion as a mediator of change in DBT is most focused in its relation to the maladaptive behaviours that are being addressed (i.e., if an emotion is highlighted during therapy, it is usually to help identify the common maladaptive behaviour that accompanies it, and to figure out which DBT skill would be most appropriate to address the behaviour). Further, while DBT incorporates mindful practices through emotional awareness and acceptance, the emphasis on coping-based skills highlights the patient's vulnerabilities and the need for ongoing coping, in stark contrast to EFT's focus on transforming emotions. In other words, DBT emphasizes emotion regulation, not emotion transformation. DBT's efficacy in employing emotional awareness as a mediator of meaningful therapeutic change has yet to be demonstrated (Warwar et al., 2008). Given that DBT was filling the critical need for an intervention to support individuals with suicidal, self-injurious, and out-of-control behaviour, and that personality disorders have been widely thought to be persistent throughout a person's lifetime, it is understandable that DBT's focus on skills-based coping has become the standard treatment for BPD. Given the safety risks and need for immediate relief of distress in BPD clients, therapy should begin with establishing structure and stability.

In this chapter, we aim to combine the stabilizing impact of a coping-based intervention with the transformative potential of EFT, optimistically aiming for full recovery when working with youth (Baardstu et al., 2020; Pos & Greenberg, 2012; Zohar et al., 2019). Using the principles introduced by Greenberg, Pos, Warwar, and others, we outline the clinical application of a Phase 2 therapy for the treatment of BPD in youth aged 13–17. We offer process considerations for implementing EFT gradually, overlapping with a Phase 1 intervention such as DBT.

Before starting therapy with an adolescent, it is advisable to meet with their caregivers in order to obtain relevant background knowledge and strategize as to if, when, and how to involve caregivers in the treatment process. Many DBT programmes have a parent component, and we believe that engaging parents is both wise and compassionate—we can reduce treatment-interfering behaviours (TIBs) and provide much-needed support to parents. Without parent engagement, parent TIBs can inadvertently erode treatment gains and perpetuate symptoms—see Figure 7.1.

A Humanistic Stance

EFT therapists, like most therapists with a humanistic stance, tend not to focus on pathology and are less likely to diagnose their therapy clients with personality disorders. This reluctance to pathologize makes sense, given the humanistic emphasis on the health-seeking part of the client, and helps avoid the pitfalls of pathologizing, overidentifying with a disorder, as well as relationship power imbalances that have been associated with more traditional therapeutic models. It is easier to uphold humanistic relationship conditions when therapists do not assume the position of an all-knowing, healthy "expert" with the authority to label a client with a personality disorder. However, the reality of clients presenting with extreme instability in their relationships, their view of themselves, and their emotions and behaviour makes it necessary for EFT

Figure 7.1 The Voice Inside: You're Lazy.

practitioners to be able to support highly distressed clients in a systematic way. Pos and Paolone (2019) stress that the diagnosis of *personality disorder*, even if we don't believe this label is describing something "real" about the client, must still be considered within EFT practice because it (a) offers structure and a coherent framework, based on which the client and their family can better understand extreme symptoms; (b) underscores an appropriate sense of urgency and gravity regarding the potentially life-threatening and often developmentally disruptive impact of BPD symptoms; (c) presents a therapeutic challenge to the depathologizing and transdiagnostic approach of EFT therapists, and embracing this challenge can lead to growth in our therapeutic capacity; and (d) provides young patients with a coherent explanation for the intense suffering that they may be experiencing, which can be useful and highly validating in the first phase of therapy. Through this lens, we can regard it as humanistic to provide the structure, support, and relief that can come with a formal diagnosis of BPD, while adhering to the principle of supporting the health-seeking part of our client.

An Integrative Approach

Critchfield and Benjamin (2006) have summarized the American Psychological Association's (APA) Task Force review on the best practices for the psychosocial treatment of personality disorders (PDs) in stating that effective treatments must be *integrative* and include the following four leading principles: (1) providing clients with acceptance, empathy, and congruence through strong therapeutic alliances; (2) forming long-term, emotionally salient relationships; (3) offering therapeutic interventions that complement clients' functional impairment and readiness to change; and (4) establishing a treatment structure that is able to balance directiveness with acceptance within the therapeutic intervention. As a treatment modality, EFT embodies these principles with its in-depth focus on empathic responding, emotion process, primary relationships, and the therapeutic bond, as well as client–therapist agreement on the tasks and goals of therapy. EFT's concentration on process also allows for the integration of any supportive content from other interventions, programmes, or family-based support. Through the emphasis on emotion transformation, EFT can complement the excellent contribution that has been made by coping and acceptance-based approaches, such as DBT, CBT, mindfulness, acceptance and commitment therapy, and compassion-focused therapy, all of which have cognitive principles and processes at their core.

EFT's emphasis on supporting adult clients to access, identify, and transform their maladaptive emotion states (Greenberg, 2002) has proven effective in treating depression (Greenberg & Watson, 2006), emotional trauma (Greenberg et al., 2008; Paivio & Pascual-Leone, 2010), and couples' distress (Greenberg & Goldman, 2008; Johnson, 2004). In the past decade, EFT has been applied to the treatment of personality disorders, particularly BDP (Pos & Greenberg, 2012). Our work with youth has demonstrated that EFT processes can be successfully applied to youth with BPD, resulting in therapeutic progress in terms of emotion processing, improved relationships, and better behaviour.

EFT for Youth with BPD

Flexible Two-Phase Model for Youth

EFT-Y for BPD has two overarching phases: stabilization and transformation. The two phases encompass the three-phase trauma framework (Herman, 2001; Ford & Courtois, 2013), which has become the gold standard in therapeutic practice for complex trauma (e.g., Blue Knot, 2012). These two phases of EFT-Y for BPD occur in a staggered sequence, beginning with coping skill implementation and followed by the gradual integration of emotion focused therapy, allowing the therapist to push forward towards emotion transformation when possible but revert to restabilization when necessary. The flexible two-phase model acknowledges the non-linear nature of trauma treatment, which often moves "forward" towards therapeutic growth but with numerous setbacks along the way, often with a "two steps forward, one step back" pattern.

The tasks of **Phase 1** centre around **stabilization**, which borrows heavily from coping-based approaches such as trauma-focused CBT, DBT, and mindfulness, but can also include other interventions that may improve emotion regulation, including eye movement desensitization and redirection (EMDR) and clinical hypnotherapy. In Phase 2, tasks are centred around transformation, which follows EFT's six phases, covered in detail in Chapters 1 and 2.

Emotion Schemes

A core organizing concept within EFT is the **emotion scheme**. Pos and Greenberg (2012) conceptualize emotion schemes as "dynamic integrations of multiple levels of functioning (perception, sensation, cognition, affect, physiological changes) influenced over time by culture, learning and experience" (p. 85). The activation of emotion schemes during therapy sessions is an essential component of therapeutic change as it helps facilitate clients' experiencing, attending to, making meaning of, and, ultimately, transforming their emotion states (Pos, 2013). As EFT clinicians, we work differently with each of the four distinct categories of emotion, including primary adaptive, primary maladaptive, secondary, and instruction emotions.

Primary adaptive emotions represent generally healthy and immediate emotional responses to circumstances that assist the individual in organizing appropriate actions/reactions in order to tend to basic survival needs. Therapists typically work to help clients explore these emotions, helping to access accurate self-appraisals and adaptive needs.

Primary maladaptive emotions also represent immediate responses to surrounding circumstances; however, they usually stem from learned responses from previous, and most commonly traumatic, experiences. These emotions are most often explored in the historical context within which they were once adaptive, before the client is assisted in transforming them through accessing appraisals, needs, and new emotions that are adaptive within their present circumstances.

Secondary emotions are reactions that our clients have to the experience of their primary emotions (e.g., fear of shame, anger in regards to fear, and so on). We can recognize and explore secondary emotions with an aim of deepening

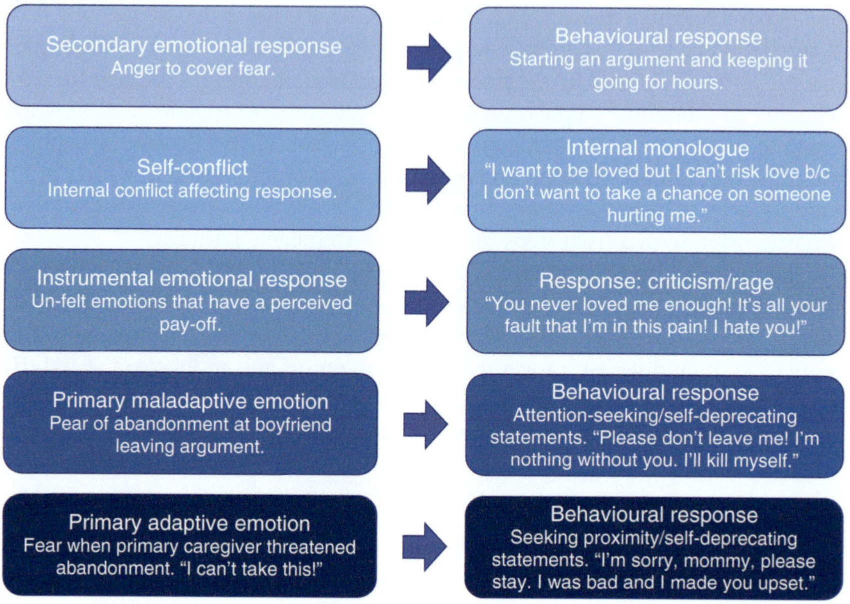

Figure 7.2 Example of Primary Maladaptive Emotions in BPD.

and following the client's emotional experience to reach the underlying primary emotion.

Instrumental emotions are used to obtain an outcome or manipulate the immediate environment (crying to avoid punishment or laughing in order to avoid feeling shame). Clients with BPD often find that their instrumental emotions are reinforced because they are effective at accomplishing a desired effect or avoiding an undesired consequence. Even if others react negatively to their instrumental emotions, any reaction is better than feeling alone or abandoned. We have to work hard to reinforce the expression of primary emotions in therapy, without judging our client for engaging in instrumental behaviour.

Emotion Assessment

What to Assess

When we conduct an emotion assessment for youth with BPD, we are asking ourselves to observe and attend to *what*, *how*, and *how much* they feel. This includes the basic emotions that they are presenting with as well as the emotion schemes that have developed over time as they tried to feel certain ways and not others. Initially, the work with youth with BPD involves approaching, allowing, and expressing feelings. Even these tasks can be highly threatening for youth in therapy with BPD, for whom anger can serve as a cover for more vulnerable emotions:

> I was furious coming into the first few sessions. I thought I would lose control, yell things I don't mean, and that it would be totally overwhelming, like I wouldn't be able to handle it and would hurt someone or myself or something and they'd just lock me away where I belong.
>
> (Thom, age 14)

Another part of the emotion assessment is *assessing the youth's current comfort level with emotion* so that we can provide appropriate support as we offer opportunities for them to notice their own emotional experiences. As our assessment progresses, we can differentiate between different categories of emotion (i.e., primary adaptive, primary maladaptive, secondary, and instrumental) as well as emotion schemes and how to interfere in these processes effectively.

How to Assess

From the first moments of the first session, the emotion assessment of the client begins. We follow what our clients says and does, what they pay attention to, the emotions they display behaviourally and how these fit or do not fit with what they acknowledge verbally. In our response to the client, we facilitate movement from an external to an internal focus, and from vague, global distress to specific, differentiated feelings. EFT process research has revealed that clients are eight times more likely to focus on emotion if our response ends with a similar focus (Greenberg, 2021). For example, if a youth says: "I was really scared when I didn't get a text back from my friend right away; I thought something horrible had happened to her or that she was angry with me for some reason," many therapists respond with a question about when they saw their friend last and what they did together, to which the youth often responds with more "content" or non-experiential information. With an EFT framework, if we respond to the same content with, "Wow, and they always reply right away so this is out of character for them? You mentioned that you were feeling really *scared*," they will be much more likely to follow our focus on their experiential, emotional process. What this tells us is that our responses are important, influential, and capable of drawing the youth's attention to their own internal processes. Most youth will begin by narrating an event or experience, focusing primarily on who was involved and what each person said or did. With targeted responses, we can help youth move to a deeper level of experience (see Table 7.1).

In our emotion assessment, we use all our empirical senses as well as our own gut reactions to notice and draw out the youth's emotional experience.

Table 7.1 Levels of Experience.

Level of Experience	*Client Statement*	*Therapist Response*
External Focus (Behaviour)	My mom keeps talking to me like I'm a child	What does that mean to you?
External Focus (Meaning)	She thinks I'm stupid or incompetent	Tell mom
Internal Focus (Meaning)	It's like you don't even know me or believe in me	Tell her how that makes you feel
Internal Focus (Primary Emotion)	Angry, hurt	I feel angry and I feel sad that you think I can't do anything right

While most therapists are accustomed to taking notes tracking the content of what the client is saying, it can be especially helpful to track the process of how a client with BPD is presenting and what you notice about them, and internally within yourself, as they talk. Videotaping sessions is invaluable for EFT training and practice, as so much of the nonverbal behaviour and live emotion process cannot be captured by even the most prolific note-taker. As well, it is very difficult to be fully present and in contact with our client when we are writing notes. As EFT depends on in-session processes, effective timing, and empathic attunement, it is optimal not to take notes throughout the experiential portion of a session. Therapists may wish to videotape sessions, then write a note from memory, followed by reviewing the session recording. If videotaping is not possible, another option would be audio recording sessions, so that the content, tone, cadence, and vocal changes can be tracked.

Transdiagnostic Approach: Core Empathic Responses

The underlying difficulty with appropriately regulating emotions is common to all psychiatric disorders and mental health difficulties. Whether our young client enters therapy with a pre-existing diagnosis or we are the first to communicate one to them, a core message within the EFT model is that we are not diagnosing them as a person, but diagnosing the state that they find themselves in. Viewing clients in this way, even when there is a diagnosis of BPD, allows them to believe that recovery is possible, and that productive emotion processing can help them get there. The first and most critical EFT intervention that we will employ with BPD clients is empathic responding. While a fulsome review of emphatic responding is provided in Chapter 2, there are valuable considerations to be made for youth with BPD.

Empathic Affirmation

Youth with BPD seek abundant empathic validation and reassurance. It is helpful for therapists to convey acceptance, understanding, and compassion in ways that are specific, humanizing, and honest. However, agreeing with everything a client says or providing overly positive praise does not fit within empathic affirmation and can backfire. Youth with BPD are astute observers of our nonverbal cues and may sometimes misinterpret these cues—for example, believing that we don't want to spend time with them if we look at the clock, feeling uncared for and disliked if they see us yawn or hear us sigh, and concluding that we are not really interested in them if we glance quickly at and superficially praise some artwork that they are sharing with us. In all of these situations, taking the time to genuinely listen to the youth's concerns and expressing affirmation of their experience with a high degree of attention to detail can make all the difference.

Validation

The practice of validation in therapy is a critical therapist skill, especially considering that youth with BPD report feeling invalidated much of the time, and even more so that chronic invalidation has been argued to be one of the core aspects of BPD etiology (Linehan, 1993a). Validation is the unconditional acceptance of feelings and is a crucial component of EFT's empathic affirmation process. Rebellion follows rejection (Ginott et al., 2009), and the acceptance that validation provides is the opposite of rejection, with the potential of encouraging cooperation from the youth. It involves letting the youth know that you understand where they are coming from, and that their emotions, thoughts, needs, and reactions make sense. It is the process of being non-judgemental and uttering phrases of acceptance. It is important to note that validation in EFT-Y is focused on the client's effort, values, and emotional experience—it does not necessarily involve agreement with the content of what they have shared. The therapist can work to validate the client's emotional experience itself, rather than the content surrounding it (e.g., if the client says, "Everyone hates me," the therapist obviously wouldn't say "Yes, everyone hates you" to validate, they would say "You've worked so hard to be loved and accepted and still don't experience the love that you want in your relationships"). The therapist thus reinforces that the youth is entitled to their emotional response and experience with a clear message that there is nothing wrong or deficient with emotional reactions, even if they are considered behaviourally undesirable—for example, "Yes, when you are this angry, of course you have a hard time calming yourself down, that is completely normal." Validation is particularly important at a time when the youth shares vulnerable feelings, such as newly expressed primary emotion. Using validation will allow youth to explore their emotional responses more willingly, as they will gradually feel less ashamed, less judged, and less compelled to justify their feelings (Greenberg, 2010). Ultimately, the main function of validation is to legitimize effort, values, and emotional experiences and support youth to continue to explore how they construct their experience and their interactions. Validation also builds alliance, as it allows the youth to see the therapist as a safe and understanding person (Greenberg, 2010).

Empathic Attunement

Empathic attunement is best described through metaphors such as taking a walk in the person's shoes or joining them on the same wavelength (Bohart & Greenberg, 1997). This refers to the process of emotional and kinaesthetic (using your body) responding to the youth's current experiences. Attunement refers to an accepting stance that tries to "lean into" the client's experience—in other words, what it must feel like to be the youth in that moment. The goal is to communicate, in every way possible, that you are clearly tracking and following the client's experience. To this end, close attention is paid to both the content of a youth's responses and the manner in which they are expressed—how are they feeling as they speak? What do their voice, breath, face, and body do as they share their experiences (Bohart et al., 1997)? As an EFT therapist, a primary goal is to actively immerse yourself in the client's world, using your verbal and nonverbal communication to convey understanding (Elliott et al., 2004). Attunement responses are often short utterances and body language that join with what the youth is experiencing in the moment. Your facial expressions, tone, and bodily sensations can match or mirror the intensity of the client's experience (Bohart et al., 1997). For instance, if a youth demonstrates a quicker rate of speech accompanied by a nervous look on their face when relating a distressing situation, you can approach, but not fully mirror, this intensity in your response by nodding quickly in agreement, opening your eyes wider, sitting up straight, and moving closer to them. Importantly, empathic attunement is the basis for all empathic responding (Elliott et al., 2004) because it requires us to feel what they feel, or at least imagine ourselves in their place.

Reflection

Empathic attunement also includes the process of reflection. Reflection, as described by Carl Rogers, gives the therapist the opportunity to repeat the youth's sentiments back to them, in a paraphrased or expanded version, while validating the experience and ensuring that they feel heard and understood (Elliott, 2012). As with the case for empathic attunement, the goal of reflection is to clearly convey to the youth that you are listening closely, both seeing and hearing them.

Evocative Responding

Exploratory questions are used to encourage self-exploration. This involves the therapist asking when, what, where, and how questions to bring up the youth's primary emotions and gain a deeper understanding of their experience (Elliott et al., 2004). Exploratory reflections include open-edge and growth-oriented responses, ending the therapist response with attention to the leading edge of the client's internal experience or to aspects of the client's experience that are focused on a desire for change or growth (Elliott et al., 2004). The therapist elicits and captures the implicit aspects of a youth's experience in a tentative, open-to-being-corrected manner. EFT-Y therapists often ask questions about the youth's present experience, including internal responses and reactions to in-session dynamics—for example, (a) "What's happening right now, as you say, 'I can't take this anymore?' What's that like for you?" (b) "Your face just seemed to change now; can you tell me what is happening for you?" The main functions of evocative responding are to increase awareness and expand elements of experience to help reorganize the experience, but also to access unclear or marginalized elements of experience and encourage exploration and engagement.

Evocative responding originates from the Latin word *evocare*, meaning "to call" (Lebow, 2012). Empathic evocation involves the therapist's use of dramatic and expressive language, often extrapolating from what the client has already shared and speaking in the client's voice (Elliott et al., 2004). The purpose of this technique is to assist the youth in accessing or deepening experiences, meanings, and emotions (Elliott et al., 2004). Using metaphors and vivid imagery is helpful and allows for the possibility of retrieving new information (Bohart & Greenberg, 1997). In an interaction with youth with BPD, we might use empathic evocation less often if youth are readily emotionally activated. Conversely, if youth tend to employ deactivating strategies, are dismissive of emotional pain, or have difficulty expressing vulnerability, empathic evocation can serve as a highly challenging but highly effective intervention.

Heightening

Heightening is the process of repeating the youth's sentiments or using imagery to make their experience more vivid (Elliott et al., 2004). The therapist highlights specific responses or interactions to intensify the youth's emotional experience—for example,

- "So, it feels like you're drowning … so when you think of your friends laughing at you and not caring about what you have to say, you feel like you're drowning in an ocean of pain and nobody sees, nobody seems to care."
- "It seems like this is incredibly difficult for you, like standing there and trying to speak to someone, anyone, just to know you're not alone, but no one can understand you. You feel so alone when this comes up, and it's

unbearable and makes you think that you don't want to be on this earth anymore."

- "So, when you're at this birthday party, you feel like you don't really belong there, you get thoughts like 'I'm so awkward. No one here even likes me. Everyone must think I'm such a loser.' This makes you feel worthless, unimportant, so you resort to drinking or hurting yourself, numbing yourself to make these thoughts stop."

When evocative empathy is used to heighten or deepen what the client has shared, it can enable the client to better engage with their inner experience, as it is made more evident.

Empathic Conjecture

Empathic conjectures are guesses or hypotheses made by the therapist regarding the youth's unexpressed thoughts and feelings (Elliott et al., 2004). The therapist can offer insight and share their perspective using a nonauthoritarian approach (Bohart & Greenberg, 1997). For instance:

> "Of course you panic and feel fear when you argue with your best friend. If this person abandons you, you might feel like you will be alone again, and like you might not even be worth being loved or cared for because you're 'overly dramatic,' or 'too needy,' or just simply not good enough."

Empathic conjectures are useful in guiding young clients to explore their experiences more thoroughly and to put these experiences into words (Elliott et al., 2004). In other words, the therapist works on the "leading edge" of a youth's experience to move them forward in their experience such that a new meaning can emerge. Often, these conjectures address the attachment fears related to self and others. The therapist should ask fit questions—meaning "does that fit?"—to determine the accuracy of their interpretations (Elliott et al., 2004): for example, (a) "You don't believe that you will ever gain control over your emotions, and they will continue to ruin your life and your relationships, is that right?" (b) "I am getting the idea that underneath your anger you may feel some fear. Am I getting that right, that really you are feeling fear and sadness, and you are acting angry because admitting that is too hard?" The main functions of this process are to promote a more intense awareness of emotional experience, meanings, or action tendencies.

Experiential Exercises: Emotional Preparation

Another evocative exercise that can be employed for youth with BPD is emotion focused chair work. Experiential exercises such as chair work can be intensely evoking and quite useful for this population because they do not require an adult-level grasp of intellectual concepts and bypass cognition to get to the heart of the matter. Before attempting any experiential exercises, therapists should ensure that safety and stability are reasonably strong in the therapeutic relationship. For clients with BPD, we recommend at least six therapy sessions with a focus on establishing a foundation of safety and stability, drawing in large part from the first stage of EFT for trauma (EFT-T), covered in detail in Chapter 8. Among the primary goals of these foundational sessions for youth with BPD are: (1) building an emerging alliance with the youth; (2) establishing agreement on therapeutic goals and associated tasks; (3) clear agreement on the treatment plan and a discussion of its anticipated length, course, common setbacks, and mechanisms for ongoing monitoring and evaluation of progress; (4) a plan for restabilizing and regulating if emotions feel out of control, and agreement to leave sufficient time in the session to support regulation and debriefing (at least 15 minutes) before ending the session. The therapist takes on primary responsibility for maintaining safety and stability, including ending chair work in time to allow for an appropriate debrief. While these practical aspects may seem like small details, they contribute substantially to an overall sense of stability, predictability, and security in the therapeutic process for youth with BPD. Whereas in other relationships, with peers or adults, youth with BPD can find themselves becoming highly emotionally dysregulated without the other person taking steps to recognize and respond to the signs of dysregulation, the EFT-Y therapist should provide an exceptionally safe and responsive environment, with firm and predictable boundaries that are maintained through the toughest emotional storms. Having a caring adult provide both emotional validation and predictable structure is an obvious yet critical part of the healing process.

Emotion Competence in BPD

Clients with BPD and personality disorders in general have been well known to struggle with emotional dysregulation (Linehan, 1993a), at least in part owing to the activation of early maladaptive attachment representations from primary caregivers (Crowell et al., 2009; Derbidge & Beauchaine, 2014; Fonagy et al., 2000, 2003; Hecht et al., 2014; Mosquera et al., 2014), coupled with struggles in areas of cognitive understanding of self and others, often referred to as a struggle with *mentalization* (Fonagy et al., 2011, 2018; Gergely et al., 2002).

An important aspect of treatment for clients with BPD is for them to become aware of and be able to express their primary emotions, and to differentiate between maladaptive and adaptive emotional responses (Warwar et al., 2008). As described by Pos (2013), adaptive primary emotions provide the client with important information and signal them to take action. For clients with BPD, primary maladaptive emotions can seem ubiquitous and are experienced quite intensely by the youth—and, in turn, by the therapist. Increasing awareness of these maladaptive primary emotions is the first step in transforming them into more integrated and adaptive emotion schemes (Warwar et al., 2008), but it can be the most challenging step for a client with BPD. Having over-responded to their own emotions and those of others around them for a significant amount of time in their young lives, youth can respond with extreme self-protective behaviours when challenged to simply acknowledge and allow these emotions instead of engaging in avoidant (dismissing, shutting down, running away, threatening, or engaging in self-harm) or defensive (blowing up, fighting, yelling, deflecting) behaviours. One of the central premises in EFT is that emotion sits at the centre of self-organization, and that salient changes in activated emotion schemes are the source of changing self-organization (Pos & Greenberg, 2012). In other words, when we can support youth to be in contact with their feelings, they can begin the emotion transformation process.

In general, and in BPD even more so, maladaptive emotions are experienced often throughout the day and can occur and reoccur without change. These can be core feelings of sadness, worthlessness or inadequacy, abandonment, and often explosive anger. They often do not alter or evolve in response to changing circumstance, nor do they provide the client with BPD with any adaptive solutions to problems; they often lead to repetitive cycles of maladaptive interpersonal interactions that both create and reinforce the client's sense of being victimized and trapped by their close personal relationships (Warwar et al., 2008). For this reason, the effective use of the therapeutic relationship in EFT cannot be over-emphasized in the treatment of BPD. The EFT therapist must offer an empathically attuned and genuine relationship while attending to the core difficulties of emotional processing in order to effectively engage clients in interventions designed to address these struggles (Pos & Greenberg, 2012). As such, the therapist is viewed as an emotion coach, working to actively collaborate with the client throughout the process (Greenberg & Warwar, 2006). However, it must be noted that, owing to their particular types of self-organization and emotional volatility, clients with BPD will typically not engage in interventions in expected ways (Pos & Greenberg, 2012). At times, clients with BPD will react to common emotional prompts in paradoxical ways—such as exploding in anger when the therapist empathizes with their sadness. The EFT therapist, then, must be *perceptive* and *adaptive* in the ways in which they use and alter EFT-TAU (treatment as usual), to offer clients with BPD the opportunity to regulate, structure, and mentalize their experiences based on their specific emotional states and inner conflicts, without fear of losing the therapeutic relationship (Pos & Paolone, 2019).

EFT Chair Work and BPD

Clients with BPD will often suffer from chronic states of self-conflict or dialectical processing difficulties, as they split and oscillate between rigidly defined and opposing self-states (Linehan, 1993a). In EFT, a self-split conflict marker typically calls for a two-chair task, which can help integrate, for example, a dominant and hostile relationship between two opposing self-organizations into a relationship of mutual acceptance. As Pos and Greenberg (2012) outline, during a two-chair intervention, emotion schemes that belong to two discrete self-organizations are brought into an interpersonal dialogue, with each self's needs being expressed from within each chair.

EFT therapists employ several approaches to help clients activate and integrate their self-organizations (Pos & Greenberg, 2012). The activation of the more dominant self-organization typically involves: (1) over-emphasizing the presumed superiority of the Self Critic through amplified expression (e.g., "You did a terrible job at school today!"); (2) focusing a critical aspect of the client's emotional scheme into a core criticism (i.e., "You're completely worthless!"); and (3) articulating the nonverbal or attitudinal position of the Critic (e.g., acting out the stern, disapproving look or putting it into words, including its tone, attitude, and posture) to enliven its expression (Pos & Greenberg, 2012). To deepen the experience in the "experiencing chair," the therapist may: (1) neutralize the Experiencer's efforts to diffuse the Critic Self's attack, instead guiding the client to allow, accept, and contactfully feel the impact of the attack; (2) help facilitate and maintain the client's feeling of interpersonal safety, to allow the client to direct their full attention towards their internal experience, instead of monitoring their interpersonal space and surroundings; (3) use an empathic response to reflect understanding and acceptance of the client's experience, guiding their attention inwards again; (4) help the client in the construction of emotional meaning by describing and capturing experiences in words; and (5) assist the client in regulating difficult emotions through empathic validation and understanding, as well as helping to provide social and emotional feedback (Elliott et al., 2004; Pos & Greenberg, 2012).

Resolution occurs if a new adaptive relationship respecting the emotional needs of both sides emerges. This type of resolution is coherent with the dialectical principal in DBT, within which self-conflict is overcome and transformed so that the client can both accept the current state of being and strive for growth (Linehan, 1993a). Through the resolution of opposing self-organizations, EFT chair work has the potential to provide clients with a sense of emotional structure and adaptive functioning, mitigate emotional polarization and overactivation, as well as providing a stronger sense of self-coherence (Pos & Greenberg, 2012). Youth with BPD often struggle in all these domains, typically being wary and mistrustful of their emotions and often experiencing discomfort or even panic in the face of emotional experience (Crowell et al., 2009; Linehan, 1933a; McMain et al., 2008). For this reason, Pos and Greenberg (2012) argue that clients with BPD are "both in great need of and potentially likely to gain substantially from two-chair work" (p. 87) and have found that, if the structure and groundwork are adequately prepared, this intervention is able to provide the client with BPD an opportunity to experience, express, and reflect on their emotions in safe and empathic surroundings. As we have emphasized, the therapist must establish and maintain a close working alliance with the client with BPD, as clients will more willingly and effectively face and accept overstimulating emotions in the context of a stable and consistent therapeutic alliance (Warwar et al., 2008; Pos & Paolone, 2019). By providing unconditional positive regard, safe contact, and transparent willingness to help, the therapist can work to meet previously unmet needs for acceptance and support and help regulate core maladaptive feelings such as fear, shame, and helplessness for the BPD client. These experiences of safety and support in the face of challenging emotional experiences have the potential to transform the client's core maladaptive interpersonal emotion schemes, which often withhold youth with BPD from engaging meaningfully in therapy.

How Can Chair Work Be Different for This Population and What to Do about It

A common problem for EFT chair work when working with clients with BPD and PDs in general is that they are often most vulnerable to emotional overarousal within interpersonal contexts, which obviously include the therapist–client relationship (Pos & Paolone, 2019). However, while overarousal can be an obstacle for the client effectively engaging in chair work, an *optimal* level of arousal contributes to the client's ability to experience their emotions in greater depth (Greenberg et al., 2007), identify important needs, and engage in the meaning-making that can transform the youth's entrenched narrative. Pos and Paolone (2019) note that optimal emotion arousal can be achieved by effectively scaffolding the client's capacity to engage in the task at hand (chair work). They echo Wood et al. (1976) in stating that, when scaffolding is done correctly, it (1) helps maintain the client's engagement in the chair work, (2) helps to simplify the chair task in order to match the client's current level of emotional functioning, (3) emphasizes important aspects for success in the chair task, (4) assists in creating an environment in which the client's overarousal is appropriately regulated, and (5) works to demonstrate components necessary to resolve the chair task through modelling. Some notable scaffolding strategies for chair work with emotionally dysregulated clients such as ones with BPD can include (a) using a relational or systemic model of resolution when engaging in chair work, as opposed to a an individual one; (b) using various regulating-emotion-with-emotion techniques (Pos & Greenberg, 2012), such as sharing the client's emotional atmosphere, using humour, and expressing your own positive feelings towards the client; and (c) using the therapeutic relationship to assist the client in regulating their affect (Pos & Paolone, 2019).

Case Example: Scaffolding

The following dialogue is from Session 6 with 16-year-old Anisha, using just the first prompt from EFT's **current interpersonal conflict** chair exercise, which asks the client to imagine the person with whom they are experiencing conflict.

Therapist: Imagine the "mean girl" from your class in the chair. What do you see?
Anisha: What do I see? I see her staring at me, her eyes are glaring all over me and finding every flaw and she's smirking, holding back her snotty laughter, looking down on me, disgusted at how totally gross and pathetic I am.
Therapist: What happens in your body when you see her do that?
Anisha: I want to die. I want to kill her and then I want to die.
Therapist: It's like anger on fire, or …
Anisha: Yeah, like a 10-alarm fire. Nothing makes me more angry than this. Her face.
Therapist: Where do you feel it right now? What do you sense in your body and face?
Anisha: My face is so hot, so hot right now. My jaw is clenching, my firsts are clenching, my shoulders are tight, my chest is full of … like a tidal wave. And my heart is racing. My legs want to run and I want to punch her.
Therapist: What is this feeling? Speak from the heat in your face.
Anisha: It's … I'm so angry, this is crazy! She's not even here, she's lucky she's not because I would seriously punch her right now, like I don't even care.
Therapist: Yeah, the anger is so overwhelming, 10-alarm fire … and your face, the heat, you said before that you want to die …
Anisha: For a split second and then I want to kill her.
Therapist: Speak from the heat in your face, Anisha. What is it telling you?
Anisha: [Tearful] It's total annihilation. I feel ashamed of myself, ashamed of how I look, ashamed of who I am, what I wear, why I even exist. Like I'm nothing.

Gaining practice with modulating sensory experiences in this way, with the support of the therapist in the therapeutic space, allows youth to come into contact with slightly more tolerable versions of the same sensations that often overcome them in moments of distress: to feel what it's like when a peer is staring at them, to experience the feelings in session but to have awareness that they are having an experience right now and have their therapist's support as they go through it. As youth with BPD often have intensely heightened emotional memory, with vivid colours and fulsome affect reactions as if the event being imagined is happening again, right in that moment, they may need minimal evocative prompting to contact emotion. Access to emotion comes quickly and powerfully. What requires the therapist's focused attention in this segment is ensuring that the client gains access to their primary emotion; the therapist repeatedly asks about physical or sensory experiences and facilitates the connect between these sensations and the client's emotions. Although anger was the secondary maladaptive emotion dominating the dialogue, repeated prompts to pay attention to the client's sensation of heat in her face helped to access underlying shame. From this point, with a primary maladaptive emotion identified, there are several possible pathways, based on the client's tolerance: (1) move to expressing the shame directly to the imagined Other in the empty chair; (2) switch to an Open for Business empty-chair dialogue with a primary caregiver or supportive other in the empty chair; (3) practise a coping-based strategy in the moment (e.g., using a down-regulating strategy such as smelling their favourite soothing scent) in preparation for using the same strategy outside session.

What If the Client "Agrees" with the "Other" Chair?

There are a few problematic assumptions EFT therapists often make when attempting to work with BPD clients through experiential interventions (Pos & Greenberg, 2012). The first assumption is that the opposing self-organization is the "bad" or "culprit" side of the client that engages in maladaptive processes such as self-interruption or self-criticism. In fact, we cannot judge either side as being good or bad, and it is the lack of integration or synthesis between the parts of the Self that serves to maintain the youth's maladaptive functioning. Their behaviour is often a result of the interaction between both sides of the split, with one side claiming that "nobody cares about you" and the other side experiencing intense shame and anger, lashing out at others and leaving the youth isolated and more likely to feel uncared for. Second, EFT therapists often assume that provocations from the Self Critic will eventually result in the setting of internal boundaries by the Experiencing Self (i.e., as the therapist attempts to focus the Experiencing Self towards deeper feelings and needs, they believe the client will access their primary assertiveness and bring about internal resilience in forms of limit-setting or demands for the coercive self). However, clients with BPD often do not spontaneously display internal resilience during chair work, even after continuous and considerable emotional support from the therapist in an effort to engage in them in building adaptive resilience (Pos &

Paolone, 2019). The more typical response is that the client will agree with the Self Critic and engage in self-attack (Pos & Greenberg, 2012).

What to Do?

When a client with BPD engages in intense self-attack while in session (e.g., harsh self-judgement), Pos and Greenberg have noted four likely responses from the Experiencing Self. The client either: (1) agrees with the self-judger wholeheartedly (i.e., splits and polarizes in the self-judgemental state); (2) becomes hostile towards the self-judger (i.e., views them as all-black); (3) freezes in the face of the process and becomes demoralized and hopeless (i.e., a more shameful and fragile self becomes activated); or (4) becomes confused and disorganized. In this case, and in EFT with BPD clients in general, the therapist can refrain from identifying a bad or good self and work to relate to both self-organizations as equally important parts of the self in conflict, continuously directing each chair towards the client's primary needs while also maintaining an effective interpersonal dialogue (Pos & Greenberg, 2012). The therapist must accept the client's knowledge and expertise on themselves as their own. Pos and Greenberg (2012) further claim that, in agreement with Gergely et al. (2002), the stronger the client's sense of their own subjectivity is, the easier it will be for them to experience the salience and validity of their own emotional experience. Clients with BPD have been known to either unconditionally accept or reject the therapist's perspective, and the EFT therapist must not attempt to act as an expert in interpreting the client's needs but encourage the client to pave their own emotional path, exemplifying the emotionally validating environment that clients with BPD feel they have lacked (Pos & Greenberg, 2012).

Clinical Application

Client details: Felicia, age 16
Diagnosis: Borderline personality disorder
Identifying the marker: In the first few minutes of the session, Felicia was asked to share a brief update about the week that had just passed, knowing that we would be transitioning to experiential exercises based on what seemed most salient for her today. She was quick to share that she felt better this past week, and there had been more stability than in previous weeks. However, she had noticed that she has not been covering up her feelings as she usually does, and this felt "nice for me but unpleasant for other people." She reflected that the empathy she has received, particularly in the form of validation and empathic conjecture, has helped her realize that "it takes a lot of effort to be

on the same social plane as other people," and that, when she doesn't put in active effort to be socially pleasant, she feels less pressure and a sense of relief. Finally, when asked if she would be willing to explore memories from younger years when she felt she had to pretend to be happy and show a "pleasant" self to others, Felicia agreed that she would be willing to go back to these memories and "see what's there."

Therapist: Picture your mom in the empty chair. What happens for you when you see her?

Felicia: I feel sad [Felicia was visibly tearful].

Therapist: There's sadness when you picture Mom … do you have a sense of where this sadness is in your body?

Felicia: I feel so bad for Mom, she works so hard, and this is what she gets.

Therapist: There's feeling bad for Mom and … any other feeling you notice right now?

Felicia: Empathy for Mom … frustration? Can't find a word for the other feeling …

Therapist: Okay, it's something like frustration or …

Felicia: Yeah, not sure.

Therapist: Let's try something if you can. Picture Dad in the chair instead. What happens for you when you see him?

Felicia: Wow, it's like he's unapproachable, untouchable … there's fondness, don't want to hurt him. He's a sensitive dude. We are allies.

Therapist: Okay, and how do you feel inside yourself?

Felicia: Just understanding him. Empathy again.

Therapist: Okay, let's try Mom again. See Mom and this time tell her how things have been for you. Let her know the pain that you've been in just trying to feel pleasant.

Felicia: I can't do that.

Therapist: What happens when you try? What's the "can't" part right now?

Felicia: I just don't want to go down that road.

Therapist: Right, okay—you don't want to go down that road … because if you do go, what might happen?

Felicia: I don't think I want to tell Mom anything like that.

Therapist: Okay, it's understandable. Maybe part of you wants to protect Mom right now or maybe it's really hard to tell her. Let's try putting Mom in a soundproof booth and she's content, doesn't see what you are feeling. Come over here [therapist motions to empty chair] and be the part of you that stops you from expressing yourself to Mom.

Felicia: Don't let somebody into your brain space.

Therapist: Right, scare her some more. What's the worst that can happen?

Felicia: [Interrupted by coach critic] You should be able to do this. Why can't you find the words? This is embarrassing. Just do it.

Therapist: Just allow the coach voice but go back to being the part that makes her feel she can't do it in the first place. She's not allowed to upset anyone.

Felicia: It's precarious. You have to protect yourself.

Therapist: Tell her some more. Really scare her.

Felicia: Protect yourself.

Therapist: Right, because if you don't … tell her what will happen if she doesn't protect.

Felicia: If you share, it will feel gutted—gut a fish, open it up, it's all there.

Therapist: Yes, you will feel gutted. You'll be exposed and gutted … and what will happen next? What will that mean for her?

Felicia: It's a lot to have to cover back up in order to function.

Therapist: Right, but what will it feel like for her? What would happen to her when she's gutted?

Felicia: The discomfort would be intolerable, there would be nowhere to go.

Therapist: She'll have nowhere to go … like she will be lost? Alone? Stuck, or?

Felicia: Status quo [Felicia drew a big breath]: this is so frustrating. It's the whole part that tells me not to do this, not to even allow myself to do this here and now. I hate her.

Therapist: It's understandable, she wants to protect you from feeling overwhelmed or gutted right now, even as we speak. I know part of you gets frustrated with this all, and we accept that part, but let's keep going with this process.

Felicia: Okay, I just want to say that I don't like being unable to do something.

Therapist: Right, of course, okay … you don't like that this is so hard do to, and that you stop yourself, so there's this criticism of that whole process … but can you come back to scaring yourself just for right now? Or is the interruption getting in the way?

Felicia: No, I can do it. Okay. So, it's like, don't open up because it's going to take so much to put yourself back together. You're going to feel headless, takes so much time to find every shrapnel. You'll feel invalidated, not listened to, abandoned, hated, loathed. Don't show your pain because you'll never get help with it. You'll feel embarrassed, trapped, there's a lot of scrutiny.

Therapist: Switch chairs. In this chair, having heard the part that warns you not to show pain, what happens for you? Tell her how it feels to hear that?

Felicia: Nothing happens. Well, I agree with her. She is keeping me from making a fool of myself.

Therapist: Okay, exactly—can you thank her? Let her know how it feels to agree with her.

Felicia: Thanks but no thanks too. When you do this to me, I feel inhuman, numb.

Therapist: Inhuman … it's hurtful—so it's partly like, "No thanks, I don't want this"?

Felicia: No, it's not a bad feeling, I'm not bothered by it.

Therapist: What do you feel most in your body right now?

Felicia: Feel mostly grateful.

Therapist: Okay, so you feel partly grateful and thankful to the self-interruption part … and what else do you feel. What is the "no thanks" part?

Felicia: I feel a little sad in a pity way. Like the emotion areas are inaccessible. It's hard to talk about real things. Hard to really feel. [Tearful, voice cracking] … I think I accepted that this was a useful way to function in the world [crying] … I'm not satisfied with living this way anymore.

Therapist: Okay, that makes sense—it makes sense to have accepted this way of functioning out of necessity. But now there's part of you that has had enough of living this way … it's like "I'm tired of not being able to feel what I really feel" or something like that?

Felicia: Yes, exactly—I'm tired, and sad, and terrified about how it will feel to actually be connected to myself again. But I want that and I'm ready for it no matter how hard it might be. I can't just be an automaton anymore.

Clinical Observations

Clinical progress is always relative to where a client started. Supporting youth with BPD is no exception to this principle, and the pathway of "progress" is often winding, bumpy, and foggy. However, small successes can lead to a stronger bond, a greater willingness on the part of youth to make changes, and bigger breakthroughs. In the interaction above, Felicia was much more open to emotional processing after the self-interruption chair work than she had ever been in any therapy session. Still, she was several steps away from fully expressing her core maladaptive emotions because, as soon as we approached them, she pulled back and began to identify with the self-interrupter again, denying her feelings. From the therapist's clinical observation notes, there was markedly less interpersonal tension in the therapist–client relationship in this session than in previous ones. The therapist noted feeling more like they were working together on Felicia's true path, even though it was slow, cumbersome, and painful. Building upon this initial journey, the challenge of facing difficult emotions can be attempted, reattempted again and again, and overcome.

Conclusion

EFT interventions, including attuned empathic responses and evocative tasks, can support youth with BPD to integrate their conflict self-organizations, assisting in the exploration processing of emotion through genuine, robust, and playful therapist responses. Youth with BPD are often outwardly angry but experience internal chaos, and they are not often skilled at knowing what they need to do about their predicament. The end goal of therapy is for a youth to identify and differentiate their core feelings and channel them in a more productive manner, in the service of their own emotional, social, and behavioural functioning. If and when youth can handle whatever emotion or situation or thought comes their way, without shutting down, over-responding, or acting out, they begin to experience success in daily life. Through an "upward spiral" of trust, structure, and socio-emotional competence, their predicament is largely resolved. For youth with BPD, working directly with emotions should be seen as a critical element of, if not the primary strategy in, the psychotherapeutic treatment of BPD, after necessary safety and stability have been established. Just as they have been for adults with BPD (Warwar et al., 2008), emotion focused approaches can be integrated into traditional therapies for BPD to move beyond mere coping with suffering. With our young clients, more than any other population, the possibility for meaningful change is often within reach.

Practical Tips for Working with Clients with BPD

1. Always treat your client with BPD as if they are the expert on themselves, because they are. You are there to support them in learning new ways of relating to themselves and others, but you are also there to learn.
2. Be mindful of over-validation. Most clients with BPD have grown up with considerable amounts of emotional invalidation, and, while it is important to validate their emotions, blanket validation of every emotion can feel disingenuous and appear like invalidation all over again. Be careful and specific and focus on the part of their experience with which you can genuinely empathize.
3. Meet your clients where they are, not where you would like them to be. If they say their world is ending (which they often might say), don't try to convince them that things will be fine; help them prepare how they will manage their emotions even if the worst-case scenario happens. EFT-Y is an intervention that can build tremendous emotional tolerance, competence, and capacity.
4. Be mindful of your tone. For example, when a client with BPD is presenting with anger, a calming tone will not necessarily have a calming effect; it might even feel invalidating. Again, meet your client where they are at, get angry along them, just one notch less, and then lead them back down a few notches.
5. Regulation, flexibility, and tolerance can be "taught" through your relationship and your empathic responding. As a Phase 2 therapy, EFT-Y

can teach through the relationship versus the explicit strategies taught in coping-based therapies.

6. Use the acronym EVE (effort, values, and emotional experience) to remember to validate the client's feelings more specifically and deeply. Validate effort: "You've been working so hard to make friends"; validate values: "Of course you were devastated—you care a lot about your close relationships"; validate emotion experience: "When you stood there on your own and everyone else at the party was in a group, it obviously felt so alone and embarrassing!"
7. Be mindful of all kinds of extreme emotions, not just negative ones. While clients with BPD can feel very high levels of sadness, anger, shame, and fear, they can also feel high levels of joy, inspiration, love, and confidence that may not be healthy or balanced.
8. Don't be afraid of using humour! Laughing about difficult things normalizes them and can help create a sense of safety and connection. It can also diffuse anger and speak the unspoken tension in a given moment.
9. If you are in Phase 1 of therapy, stay the course. Youth with BPD may offend you, be offended by you, fire you, rehire you, break down or shut down in your office, storm out or refuse to leave. Expect the extremes and work towards a more stable "middle ground," so that you can build a foundation of stability on which you can attempt transformation.
10. Sometimes, no matter what you do, clients with BPD will terminate therapy unilaterally. Express respect for their decision and emphasize your open-door policy, if and when they want to return—more often than not, they will return if they feel safe to do so.

References

Baardstu, S., Coplan, R. J., Karevold, E. B., Laceulle, O. M., & von Soest, T. (2020). Longitudinal pathways from shyness in early childhood to personality in adolescence: Do peers matter? *Journal of Research on Adolescence*, *30*, 362–379. https://doi.org/10.1111/jora.12482

Blue Knot. (2013). *Understanding trauma fact sheets*. Blue Knot. https://professionals.blueknot.org.au/resources/key-concepts-for-working-with-a-trauma-lens/understanding-trauma/

Bohart, A. C., & Greenberg, L. S. (Eds.). (1997). *Empathy reconsidered: New directions in psychotherapy*. American Psychological Association. https://doi.org/10.1037/10226-000

Critchfield, K. L., & Benjamin, L. S. (2006). Principles for psychosocial treatment of personality disorder: Summary of the APA Division 12 Task Force/NASPR review. *Journal of Clinical Psychology*, *62*(6), 661–674. https://doi.org/10.1002/jclp.20255

Crowell, S. E., Beauchaine, T. P., & Linehan, M. M. (2009). A biosocial developmental model of borderline personality: Elaborating and extending Linehan's theory. *Psychological Bulletin*, *135*(3), 495. https://doi.org/10.1037/a0015616

Derbidge, C. M., & Beauchaine, T. P. (2014). A developmental model of self-inflicted injury, borderline personality, and suicide risk. In *Handbook of developmental psychopathology* (pp. 521–542). Boston, MA: Springer.
Elliott, R. (2012). Emotion-focused therapy. In P. Sanders (Ed.), *The tribes of the person-centred nation* (pp. 103–130). Ross-on-Wye.
Elliott, R., Watson, J. C., Goldman, R. N., & Greenberg, L. S. (2004). *Learning emotion-focused therapy: The process-experiential approach to change*. American Psychological Association.
Fonagy, P., Gergely, G., Jurist, E. L., & Target, M. (2018). *Affect regulation, mentalization, and the development of the self*. Routledge.
Fonagy, P., Luyten, P., & Strathearn, L. (2011). Borderline personality disorder, mentalization, and the neurobiology of attachment. *Infant Mental Health Journal*, *32*(1), 47–69. https://doi.org/10.1002/imhj.20283
Fonagy, P., Target, M., & Gergely, G. (2000). Attachment and borderline personality disorder: A theory and some evidence. *Psychiatric Clinics*, *23*(1), 103–122. https://doi.org/10.1016/S0193-953X(05)70146-5
Fonagy, P., Target, M., Gergely, G., Allen, J. G., & Bateman, A. W. (2003). The developmental roots of borderline personality disorder in early attachment relationships: A theory and some evidence. *Psychoanalytic Inquiry*, *23*(3), 412–459. https://doi.org/10.1080/07351692309349042
Ford, J. D., & Courtois, C. A. (2013). *Treating complex traumatic stress disorders in children and adolescents*. Guilford Press.
Gergely, G., Fonagy, P., Jurist, E., & Target, M. (2002). Affect regulation, mentalization, and the development of the self. *International Journal of Psychoanalysis*, 77, 217–234.
Ginott, H. G., Ginott, A., & Goddard, H. W. (2009). *Between parent and child: The best-selling classic that revolutionized parent–child communication*. Harmony.
Greenberg, L. S. (2002). Integrating an emotion-focused approach to treatment into psychotherapy integration. *Journal of Psychotherapy integration*, *12*(2), 154. https://doi.org/10.1037/1053-0479.12.2.154
Greenberg, L. S. (2010). Emotion-focused therapy: A clinical synthesis. *FOCUS*, *8*(1), 32–42. https://doi.org/10.1176/foc.8.1.foc32
Greenberg, L. S. (2021). *Emotion Focused Therapy Level 3 Institute* [PowerPoint Slides]. York University, Toronto, Ontario.
Greenberg, L. S., Auszra, L., & Herrmann, I. R. (2007). The relationship among emotional productivity, emotional arousal and outcome in experiential therapy of depression. *Psychotherapy Research*, *17*(4), 482–493. https://doi.org/10.1080/10503300600977800
Greenberg, L. S., & Goldman, R. N. (2008). *Emotion-focused couples therapy: The dynamics of emotion, love, and power*. American Psychological Association.
Greenberg, L. S., & Warwar, S. H. (2006). Homework in an emotion-focused approach to experiential therapy. *Journal of Psychotherapy Integration*, *16*(2), 178. https://doi.org/10.1037/1053-0479.16.2.178
Greenberg, L. J., Warwar, S. H., & Malcolm, W. M. (2008). Differential effects of emotion-focused therapy and psychoeducation in facilitating forgiveness and letting go of emotional injuries. *Journal of Counseling Psychology*, *55*(2), 185. https://doi.org/10.1037/0022-0167.55.2.185
Greenberg, L. S., & Watson, J. C. (2006). *Emotion-focused therapy for depression*. American Psychological Association.
Harned, M. S., Banawan, S. F., & Lynch, T. R. (2006). Dialectical behavior therapy: An emotion-focused treatment for borderline personality disorder.

Journal of Contemporary Psychotherapy, *36*(2), 67–75. https://doi.org/10.1007/s10879-006-9009-x

Hecht, K. F., Cicchetti, D., Rogosch, F. A., & Crick, N. R. (2014). Borderline personality features in childhood: The role of subtype, developmental timing, and chronicity of child maltreatment. *Development and Psychopathology*, *26*(3), 805–815. https://doi.org/10.1017/S0954579414000406

Herman, J. (2001). *Trauma and recovery: From domestic abuse to political terror*. Basic Books.

Johnson, S. (2004). *The practice of emotionally focused marital therapy: Creating connection*. New York: Bruner.

Lebow, J. L. (2012 [2005]). *Handbook of clinical family therapy*. John Wiley.

Levy, K. N., McMain, S., Bateman, A., & Clouthier, T. (2018). Treatment of borderline personality disorder. *Psychiatric Clinics*, *41*(4), 711–728. https://doi.org/10.1016/j.psc.2018.07.011

Lieb, K., Zanarini, M. C., Schmahl, C., Linehan, M. M., & Bohus, M. (2004). Borderline personality disorder. *The Lancet*, *364*(9432), 453–461. https://doi.org/10.1016/S0140-6736(04)16770-6

Linehan, M. M. (1987). Dialectical behavior therapy for borderline personality disorder: Theory and method. *Bulletin of the Menninger Clinic*, *51*(3), 261.

Linehan, M. M. (1993a). *Cognitive-behavioral treatment of borderline personality disorder*. New York: Guilford Press.

Linehan, M. (1993b). *Skills training manual for treating borderline personality disorder* (Vol. 29). New York: Guilford Press.

McMain, S., Wnuk, S., & Pos, A. (2008). Enhancing emotion regulation: An implicit common factor among psychotherapies for borderline personality disorder. *Psychotherapy Bulletin*, *43*, 29–35.

Mosquera, D., Gonzalez, A., & Leeds, A. M. (2014). Early experience, structural dissociation, and emotional dysregulation in borderline personality disorder: The role of insecure and disorganized attachment. *Borderline Personality Disorder and Emotion Dysregulation*, *1*(1), 1–8. https://doi.org/10.1186/2051-6673-1-15

Oldham, J. M. (2006). Borderline personality disorder and suicidality. *American Journal of Psychiatry*, *163*(1), 20–26. https://doi.org/10.1176/appi.ajp.163.1.20

Paivio, S. C., & Pascual-Leone, A. (2010). Emotion-focused therapy for trauma treatment model. In S. C. Paivio & A. Pascual-Leone, *Emotion-focused therapy for complex trauma: An integrative approach* (pp. 33–54). American Psychological Association. https://doi.org/10.1037/12077-002

Pos, A. E. (2013). Emotion focused therapy for avoidant personality disorder: Pragmatic considerations for working with experientially avoidant clients. *Journal of Contemporary Psychotherapy*, *44*(2), 127–139. https://doi.org/10.1007/s10879-013-9256-6

Pos, A. E., & Greenberg, L. S. (2007). Emotion-focused therapy. The transforming power of affect. *Journal of Contemporary Psychotherapy: On the Cutting Edge of Modern Developments in Psychotherapy*, *37*(1), 25–31. https://doi.org/10.1007/s10879-006-9031-z

Pos, A. E., & Greenberg, L. S. (2012). Organizing awareness and increasing emotion regulation: Revising chair work in emotion-focused therapy for borderline personality disorder. *Journal of Personality Disorders*, *26*(1), 84 107. https://doi.org/10.1521/pedi.2012.26.1.84

Pos, A. E., & Paolone, D. A. (2019). Emotion-focused therapy for personality disorders. In L. S. Greenberg & R. N. Goldman (Eds.), Clinical handbook of emotion-focused therapy (pp. 381–402). *American Psychological Association*. https://doi.org/10.1037/0000112-017

Smits, M. L., Feenstra, D. J., Bales, D. L., Vos, J., Lucas, Z., Verheul, R., & Luyten, P. (2017). Subtypes of borderline personality disorder patients: a cluster-analytic approach. *Borderline Personality Disorder and Emotion Dysregulation*, *4*(1), 16. https://doi.org/10.1186/s40479-017-0066-4

Warwar, S. H., Links, P. S., Greenberg, L., & Bergmans, Y. (2008). Emotion-focused principles for working with borderline personality disorder. *Journal of Psychiatric Practice*, *14*(2), 94–104. https://doi.org/10.1097/01.pra.0000314316.02416.3e

Wood, D., Bruner, J. S., & Ross, G. (1976). The role of tutoring in problem solving. *Child Psychology & Psychiatry & Allied Disciplines*, *17*, 89–100.

Zohar, A. H., Zwir, I., Wang, J., Cloninger, C. R., & Anokhin, A. P. (2019). The development of temperament and character during adolescence: The processes and phases of change. *Development and Psychopathology*, *31*(2), 601–617. https://doi.org/10.1017/S0954579418000159

8
EFT-Y for Parent and Youth Trauma

Mirisse Foroughe, Robert T. Muller, and Lucas Liu

When working with trauma in a youth or their caregiver, there are important steps to help reach the point where productive therapy can begin. In community or outpatient mental health settings, there can be many obstacles in the way, both practical and emotional. Practical challenges include reaching clients to schedule appointments, having clients arrive to session—on time—building trust, setting goals, and having enough stability in the client's life to make space for effective therapy. Emotionally, there may be understandable fear and concern about engaging in a process that can intensely expose vulnerabilities. In addition to the therapeutic bond, emotion focused therapy (EFT) requires agreement on goals and tasks, including tasks that may evoke strong emotions and memories. Before therapy can begin, a trauma-informed approach to identifying and addressing obstacles to the work can be helpful for the client's sense of safety and for the clinical process. The more knowledge we have about what these obstacles will look and feel like, the more we can prepare ourselves and our clients for the bumpy road ahead.

 DOI: 10.4324/9781003218968-8

Obstacles to Trauma Therapy for Youth

One of the first obstacles to trauma therapy for youth is identifying trauma. Many youth seeking treatment for anxiety, depression, behavioural problems, or social difficulties also have histories of intrafamilial or interpersonal trauma that are not necessarily identified within the list of presenting concerns. Once underlying trauma is identified, acquiring the youth's consent to work on this aspect of their experience can be a formidable challenge. Often, youth have great difficulty engaging in treatment modalities targeting trauma symptoms (Pettit et al., 2020; Fiorini et al., 2022). They may find the treatment process to be emotionally overwhelming, painful, or shaming, and they may disengage to varying degrees to avoid the discomfort associated with recalling painful or overwhelming experiences. In these cases, it can be difficult for emotion focused therapy to progress, as clients work hard to protect themselves from what they expect will be an intolerable experience. Therapists, in response to a client's avoidance, may seek to protect their client from discomfort and may understandably question whether EFT can be attempted. While behavioural modalities can provide much needed coping skills for clients avoiding emotional distress, successful treatment of behavioural symptoms can leave youth without relief from the underlying emotional experiences that led to symptoms in the first place. It may only be a matter of time before they exhibit new symptoms as they adopt alternative maladaptive ways of coping with their emotional pain.

Tania was a 12-year-old girl when she presented for treatment for anxiety and panic after several years of intrafamilial trauma. For the next three years, from age 12 through 15, Tania received 41 sessions of CBT for anxiety, a full year of DBT skills training and individual therapy for teens, and a series of medications to address daily anxiety, weekly panic attacks at home, and difficulty falling asleep. Treatment was weekly and intensive and involved a multidisciplinary care team including psychology, psychiatry, and pediatrics. While some symptoms would abate at some points, by age 15 Tania met criteria for clinical depression, suicidality and self-harm, as well as generalized anxiety disorder (GAD). Her parents opted to try EFT-Y because it was different from any other therapy that she had tried and, in their estimation, "nothing so far had worked." After engaging in her first eight-week EFT process, Tania reported that she "learned more about myself in these eight sessions than in the past three years." She painted a portrait of an empty chair that was used in some of our experiential exercises, including split chair and empty-chair work. She entitled her painting "The Dreaded Chair" and suggested that we, as therapists in the EFT-Y programme, could show it to other youth feeling unsure about trying chair work.

Figure 8.1 The Dreaded Chair, by Tania, 15.

Another youth, Julia, age 14, provided a comment that she wanted to share with other young people considering or starting EFT:

> I'll tell you straight, it's not going to feel good, but you'll be able to feel what's really there, which is honest and true for you. You're not going to want to do it because it's really awkward and you might be scared that you won't survive facing how you really feel. But after you do the chairs thing, it's not as scary or awful as you thought. The best part is, you won't be living in fear of your own feelings anymore. So next time you do the chairs, you might still feel awkward but you will be less afraid of it. You will survive, and you will feel your feelings and then they go through your body and you'll feel a huge relief because this storm that you thought was going to kill you actually passes and you'll survive, and you'll feel stronger and more clear and so much lighter.

To effectively support youth with the emotional memories that they experience as traumatic, we can go beyond behavioural treatment targets to the lived experience within, allowing for deeper processing of emotion and reducing the need for maladaptive symptoms. While their first experiences with EFT will likely feel awkward, embarrassing, and intensely emotionally evocative, youth can benefit from moving through these intense feelings with your support, your attuned presence with them, and your confidence that they can face their core emotions and survive.

Working with Emotion in Trauma Therapy for Youth

As we consider the application of the EFT process to youth struggling with trauma, the extensive literature on **emotion focused therapy for trauma**

(EFTT) serves as our foundation. EFTT is an adaptation of EFT for clients with histories of complex, relational trauma (Paivio & Pascual-Leone, 2010). For youth, EFTT can serve as an alternative to existing trauma therapies such as cognitive-behavioural therapy (CBT) and exposure therapy. The ways in which emotion focused therapy departs from cognitive and behavioural therapies can be particularly useful for youth struggling with trauma. Specifically, EFTT emphasizes experiential processing, employs a semi-structured interview approach, progresses through phases based on the client's emotional processing, and moves beyond any judgements about the logic or reasonableness of the youth's thoughts. The semi-structured nature of EFTT allows for therapists to adjust the pacing based on the client's presentation, prioritizing the cultivation of safety and strengthening of the therapeutic relationship before progressing into later phases of the therapy (Paivio & Pascual-Leone, 2010).

Once the therapeutic relationship and goals of therapy have been established, we gently begin the journey to clarify the tasks that will support emotion transformation for this particular youth. Each individual client's emotional landscape will be unique and will require a personalized road map. Although this need for personalized process-oriented therapy can be a challenge for therapists accustomed to the uniform structure of therapies such as CBT, there are helpful EFT structures to guide our work with youth experiencing trauma: (1) a **phase-based approach**, (2) **empathic responding**, (3) **attuning to nonverbal communication**, (4) **emotion focused case formulation**, and (5) **evocative interventions**.

In their recalling of traumatic events, we can look for what is salient by watching their nonverbal communication as they remember and retell and by asking about the most painful parts of the experience for them. By evoking the memory and orienting the client to their internal experience, we can track the experience along with them. **Experiential re-enactments** can help evoke secondary and primary maladaptive emotions and support youth to move through the sequential emotion transformation phases using trauma retelling, chair work, imaginal confrontation, as well as empathic exploration (Greenberg & Pascual-Leone, 2006). We follow the four basic phases of EFTT (Paivio & Pascual-Leone, 2010), which take place over 8–16 weekly, individual one-hour sessions for youth. In our experience, some clients with trauma experience reduced emotional and behavioural symptoms with one 8-week course of therapy. However, other youth require a slower progression through the phases of therapy and an additional 8-session course of therapy.

Phases of Therapy: What to Do and When to Do It

- **Phase 1:** *Establish a secure therapeutic relationship* with safety, compassion, and empathic responding. Collaborate with the youth on the goals of therapy and develop your case formulation. This typically takes up the first three sessions.

- **Phase 2:** *Reduce fear and shame* by engaging in imaginal confrontations, which can include two-chair dialogues and empathic exploration.
- **Phase 3:** *Resolve trauma and attachment injury* by accessing anger and sadness in imaginal confrontations.
- **Phase 4:** *Termination.* Wrap up therapy with final imaginal confrontations and discussing the youth's experience of therapy. During the final imaginal confrontation, prompt the youth to contrast it with earlier experiences during therapy.

Intervention Strategies: How to Do It

In working with youth trauma, as we begin to focus attention on the youth's core wound or maladaptive emotion, we take on a partially directive role by asking the youth to recall the events that they experienced as traumatic. The purpose of this recall is to access the encoded memories, which also contain the trauma-related emotions that will lead to the emergence of the core maladaptive emotion. We do not know precisely what this emotion will be, although we can make guesses and hold our story of the client tentatively, as we continue to learn more about their internal process. As EFT requires us to empathically respond to the emotions that we are "seeing" rather than just the verbal content that we are hearing, attunement to nonverbal behaviour can be particularly helpful.

Empathic Responding

In the Rogerian tradition, empathy has been defined as imaginative entry into the world of the other person (Dymond, 1949). Empathic responding is the primary intervention used throughout all phases of EFTT and is particularly applicable for helping youth with histories of complex trauma to regulate their emotions, as affect dysregulation is common among these clients (Paivio & Laurent, 2001; Paivio & Pascual-Leone, 2010). Empathic responses can be used to both magnify and reduce the strength of emotions, which can be used to help the youth regulate when highly distressed, as well as to access underlying feelings of hurt and anger (Paivio & Laurent, 2001) that can lead to adaptive emotion transformation. For example, evoking anger may increase the youth's assertiveness or help them to feel more entitled to be treated well by others. While empathic responding is presented in detail in Chapter 3, in this chapter we apply key aspects of the intervention to practise with youth and caregivers experiencing trauma.[1]

Empathic Affirmation

Empathic affirmation is central throughout work with youth and caregivers with a history of trauma as they often struggle with shame, worthlessness, and vulnerability (Paivio & Pascual-Leone, 2010). It is also helpful as a way of allowing clients to express the more negative or "unspeakable" aspects of their traumatic experiences. A client may share a deeply painful memory for the first time, allowing the therapist an opportunity to respond with empathic affirmation of the experience as well as the associated emotions, which may seem to be confusing and even contradictory. A survivor of sexual abuse may feel angry at their abuser and ashamed at themselves at the same time. Given how vulnerable our clients can be in the initial phase of therapy, the therapist should focus on establishing a secure, empathically responsive relationship before engaging in deeper exploration (Khayyat-Abuaita & Paivio, 2019). Empathic affirmations can help us foster a sense of togetherness so that our client feels that we are on their side. For example, after listening to the client share a traumatic intrafamilial memory from their childhood, the therapist can say: "You went through so much at such a young age." Of course, some youth will dismiss affirming comments by employing deactivating strategies, such as a positive wrap-up (e.g., "It's all good though!" or "What doesn't kill you makes you stronger!"). In these moments, we can follow the client's emotion pathway again and affirm the new feeling that is being alluded to. For example, we can affirm how difficult it may be to even talk about these feelings, concede the complexity of how they might be feeling (i.e., feeling sad in regard to painful childhood memories but appreciative of how their caregiver prepared them for hardships in life), or wonder if there is some guilt or dishonour when they acknowledge the caregiver's past behaviour in session right now.

Validation

An often-discussed form of affirmation is validation: the practice of unconditionally accepting feelings. Put another way, we don't argue with feelings; feelings are always valid (Ginott, 1965). Validation entails communicating to the client that you recognize their perspective, and that their feelings, needs, and responses are justified. Having received validating responses, the client will be more likely to explore their emotional reactions without feeling judged or embarrassed. Validation is easiest to do with "because" statements:

> "It makes sense that you feel worried because you haven't talked about this for years, and because you want to be strong for your family, and because maybe you're concerned that the feeling will be overwhelming, and you'll lose control or get stuck in it."

Empathic Attunement

Empathic attunement can be understood as putting oneself in another person's position, both emotionally and physically (Bohart & Greenberg, 1997). It means responding with the feelings and actions that match our client's internal experiences. The therapist uses all forms of communication to attune to the client, watching closely, listening carefully, and paying attention to how a client is expressing themselves in addition to what they are expressing (Bohart & Greenberg, 1997). Using verbal and nonverbal behaviour, the therapist can create a sense of shared experience and connectedness (Elliott et al., 2004). This can be accomplished by closely reflecting body language, tone, posture, and the intensity of the client's expressions (Bohart & Greenberg, 1997). For example, when a client is sharing a painful experience, the therapist can track the story with curious facial expressions and match the pace of the story in their verbal responses (Bohart & Greenberg, 1997). Empathic attunement is the foundation of all empathic responding (Elliott et al., 2004), because we need to see, hear, feel, and know our client if we are going to be able to join and empathize with them.

Reflection

Reflection conveys empathy. A key element of Carl Rogers's client-centred therapy, reflection allows the therapist the chance to reiterate the client's thoughts in a paraphrased and enlarged form, confirming the experience and making sure they feel heard.

Reflecting Underlying Emotions

Reflecting underlying emotions involves recognizing emerging emotions and integrating them into the cycle that the client and therapist have identified and clarified together (Pos & Greenberg, 2007). The fundamental benefit of reflecting emotions is that it reveals emotional reactions behind interactional situations and concentrates the therapeutic process. For example, "When you and Dad argue and you tense up, it's like there's this fear there for you … am I getting that right?"

Empathic Conjecture

Empathic conjectures are the therapist's speculations about the client's unshared feelings (Elliott et al., 2004). They allow us to imagine how the client is feeling, wonder about their experience, or suggest a perspective (Bohart & Greenberg, 1997). We offer conjectures tentatively, with openness to the client accepting the suggestion or not. By "trying on" our conjecture, the client engages deeply with their own experience; if the suggestion does not "fit," this is also a useful insight for the client as they try and put their new understanding into their own words (Elliott et al., 2004). To ensure that the client feels safe and welcome to determine if our suggestion is relevant for them, we can offer conjecture together with tentativeness or a question ("It's like there is a loneliness or something like that behind your frustration. Does that fit?"). For clients with a history of trauma, as therapists we may feel reluctant to risk conjecture and opt to stay within the relatively "safer" empathic responses, such as validation. However, empathic conjecture can provide clients with permission to speak the unspeakable and the confidence that we will be able to support them through even the most difficult-to-approach experiences, memories, and feelings. We can embark on empathic conjecture with the utmost sensitivity and care, but it is often useful to take the risk nonetheless. Given how difficult it can be for our clients to speak about traumatic events, attuning to their nonverbal communication is of critical importance.

Attending to Nonverbal Communication

As therapists, we often train extensively for listening to our clients and recording what they say to us—their **"told" experience**. In order to appreciate their **lived experience**, which refers to their internal, sometimes untold reality, we can also pay attention to what clients show us through their nonverbal behaviour (Goldstein, 2019). In general, we know that up to 65% of communication takes place on a nonverbal level—this includes tone of voice, timing, and emphasis in speech as well as what the client's face and body are doing and not doing (Burgoon, 1994; Burgoon et al., 2021). In clinical populations and for clients with a history of trauma, the relative importance of nonverbal communication can be much greater than in the general population. For example, behaviour that indicates self-soothing (e.g., wrapping their arms around themselves, stroking their scalp, rubbing their hand) can indicate that a client is feeling sad, lonely, or otherwise distressed. Dismissive or distancing behaviour (e.g., rolling their eyes, changing the subject, placing objects between themselves and the therapist) can indicate that a particularly threatening topic has been raised. Given that traumatic memories are often coded nonverbally (e.g., a visual image of an angry parent's face), and that many attachment-related experiences occur before a child's language is fully developed, attending to nonverbal behaviour can be highly relevant for working with trauma.

Before making any inferences based on a client's nonverbal communication, we must establish a nonverbal baseline for their behaviour so that we can recognize departures from that baseline (Foley & Gentile, 2010). This can be done by paying attention to our client's behaviour when they are talking about neutral topics—often before the session begins—for example, "How was the drive here?" or even the cliché, "How's the weather outside today?" Baseline behaviour varies greatly from person to person. For example, you may have a client who constantly taps their foot when they are bored. For another client, foot-tapping may only happen when a distressing topic is brought up, such as discussion of early childhood experiences. It is important to be conservative and use caution when interpreting nonverbal behaviour. It is well accepted in the field of nonverbal communication that we cannot make a meaningful interpretation based on a single behaviour (e.g., foot tapping when a difficult topic is raised); we can be much more confident when two or more nonverbal cues cluster together (e.g., uncharacteristic foot tapping and throat clearing and changing the subject away from the topic; DePaulo et al., 2003; Navarro & Karlins, 2008). There are several categories of nonverbal behaviours that we can become familiar with, so that it's easier to notice and track them during our clinical sessions.

Affect Display

Affect display includes macro and micro expressions. Macro expressions are prolonged facial expressions. Micro expressions are very brief and often signify an emotion that the person wants to mask or neutralize to appear more socially appropriate (Ekman & Friesen, 1969). Commonly, micro expressions display the seven universal emotions: joy, anger, sadness, fear, surprise, disgust, and contempt (Ekman, 1971). It can be tricky to spot these, because they happen quite quickly. While some therapists are naturally able to notice micro expressions, it is also possible to train this ability through practice. As well, videotaping sessions can be extremely valuable so that we can watch certain moments of the video at slow speed or still frames, especially in places where we recall feeling a sense of incongruence between what the person was saying and how we felt hearing it. For example, when asked about their childhood, a parent makes a brief expression of fear but go on to state that their experiences were "just fine."

Gestures

Gestures are physical movements which involve using the body or limbs—for example, pointing, waving, and beckoning. Gestures can be used with communicative intent, acting as a signal which conveys a specific message. It is helpful to notice if gestures do or don't "fit" with what is said—is the gesture congruent with the client's verbal communication or the story they are relating? An example of incongruence is a client saying, "I don't blame her for what she's done," while pointing at their child in an agitated manner. Some gesture types include:

- **Emblems:** Emblems are gestures with a direct verbal translation (Hans & Hans, 2015). These include nodding, shaking your head, shrugging, giving a thumbs up, a peace sign, and so on. It is notable when a client who typically responds verbally suddenly shifts to using emblems, such as nodding "yes" or "no" or shrugging their shoulders. This may be a sign that they are feeling too emotionally activated to respond verbally or that they may be in contact with an emotional memory that is taking up some of their focus and cognitive processing bandwidth.

Table 8.1 Types of Gestures.

	Emblems	*Illustrations*	*Manipulators*
Have a precise meaning	✓	✗	✗
Meaning is known to a specific group	✓	✗	✗
Individual differences of meaning	✗	✓	✓
Conveys specific meaning without words	✓	✗	✗
Usually performed deliberately	✓	✗	✗
Difficult to inhibit	✗	✗	✓

Adapted from www.paulekman.com/nonverbal-communication/types-of-gestures/

- **Illustrators:** Illustrators are actions that we use to add emphasis to what we are communicating—for example, using our body to emphasize specific words or phrases (e.g., pointing, slamming a hand down, waving our hand dismissively). Using these actions can add a great deal of nonverbal context to verbal communication. Compared with emblems and gestures, illustrators occur more automatically, and people often don't realize that they have used an illustrator unless it is brought to their attention.
- **Manipulators:** In the context of therapy, manipulators occur when clients engage in an action involving a body part to self-soothe, fidgeting, rocking their leg, or rubbing their hands. They are "manipulating" a part of their body, and this may indicate some degree of nervousness or distress.

Adaptors

Adaptors refer to gestures that are used to release nervous energy (e.g., swinging leg, scratching face, tapping, rubbing arms, leaning in or away, biting lips, clicking pen; Hans & Hans, 2015). Adaptors are often used to self-soothe as a response to feelings of anxiety or unease. When clients demonstrate adaptors in session, it is a possible indication that a sensitive topic has been broached.

Barriers

Barriers are when a client places an item between you and them; this may indicate distancing behaviour—for example, if they grab an object and hold it in their lap or zip up their jacket. This can be done as a protective gesture, to "shield" themselves from others when they are feeling vulnerable or fearful.

Paralinguistics

Speech also includes some nonverbal aspects that we can pay attention to as therapists. Paralinguistics is the analysis of vocal signals beyond the meaning or verbal content (Foley & Gentile, 2010). This includes the volume, pitch, and tone of our client's speech, as well as pauses, latency in responding, the use of speech fillers (e.g., "um" or "you know"), laughing, interrupting, or scoffing. A client's lack of memory of an event is also a paralinguistic marker that may mean something clinically. Moreover, not responding to a question or attempting to distract from the topic with humour or sarcasm can indicate possible self-protection and represent distancing behaviour. Another common distancing marker is insistence on a lack of memory and the insignificance of the past: "I don't recall anything about my childhood. It was just normal."

Proxemics

Proxemics, which refers to the physical space between the client and therapist (Foley & Gentile, 2010), can be used to observe attachment-seeking versus distancing manoeuvres of the client. Does the client sit near you and lean in towards you, or do they sit as far away as possible and have objects in between the two of you, such as a bag, jacket, or bottle? If distancing and protective objects are noticed when vulnerable topics are brought up, they can be recorded as part of our overall understanding of the client's emotional experience in the session.

Kinesics

Kinesics, which includes micro expressions and other movements of the body, can also be monitored to assess when a client's emotions may be activated. For example, brief micro expressions of dread or anger can indicate that a sensitive topic is being touched on. A parent who crosses their arms during a retelling of a past memory may be engaging in a self-protective movement to physically block themselves from the therapist (Goldstein, 2019).

Building our knowledge and practice with nonverbal behaviour generally, and nonverbal indicators of emotion activation specifically, can go a long way when working with youth and caregivers experiencing the effects of trauma. We can learn to notice, attend to, track, record, and respond to the nonverbal information that clients are sharing with us, informing everything from our empathic response in the moment to the overall purpose and pace of treatment. At first, trying to take note of what the client is showing us nonverbally may seem overwhelming, on top of attending to their verbal content. In the practice of EFT, we will gain greater capacity in this area and more efficiency in recognizing the valuable information that is often right in front of us.

Evocative Interventions

Activating and Challenging

Working with trauma necessarily includes working with avoidance. Given how painful emotional, physical, and sexual trauma can be for the individual, it makes sense that many clients try and avoid the pain however they can. At the same time, it is only *if* they can feel their pain while in session with us that we then have access to work with and facilitate emotion transformation. In this process, as EFT-Y therapists working with youth and caregivers, we engage in a contemporaneous process of activating the client's attachment system and challenging their defensive avoidance. Pacing is especially important in this work, and the best pace is a gradual one of **activating and challenging**, within the client's tolerance (Muller, 2010). Before activating and challenging clients (both youth and parents alike), we must, of course, ensure the **therapeutic relationship** is safe enough to discuss their painful memories. The client needs to have confidence in our ability to provide the **psychological containment** they need, so that they can take the risk of opening up about their trauma (Muller, 2018).

The risk of **over-challenging** an avoidant client is that the process might evoke emotions that are too intense, leading the client to feel out of control, potentially pulling themselves back from the therapy and refusing to engage deeply in future sessions, or leading them to over-disclose, feel scared and/or ashamed, and possibly terminate therapy early. If there is an intense outpouring of emotions or of "rushing into" the therapeutic work, it is the therapist's responsibility to slow down the client, provide structure, and pause some topics for the time being (Muller, 2018). It is then crucial that we do revisit the story or topic again soon, perhaps in a partial and measured way, as it reassures the client that you can handle their story, thus providing containment. Revisiting the painful topic shows the client that you both value the emotionally taxing story that they shared and that their disclosure was important. As discussed earlier in the chapter, and as is common in trauma therapy, therapists can offer further structure for working with difficult topics, speaking openly with clients regarding how, when, and how much they can expect to work on these topics. In addition, our EFT lens encourages attunement with nonverbal cues of emotion activation, which are particularly helpful when working with clients for whom communicating assertive boundaries may be difficult. We can attune to the client's capacity and tolerance for activation, moment by moment, leading to more timely and effective interventions.

On the other hand, **under-challenging** our client can enable avoidance and result in ongoing discussions of "safer" and less emotionally activating topics (Muller, 2018). Sessions in which clients are under-challenged tend to be dull and cyclical. The message that clients may receive in these situations is that their emotions are truly too much to handle, even for their therapist. When deactivation and defensive strategies are unaddressed, the client will not have enough meaningful contact with their emotions to make change possible. Reinforcing EFT theory, psychotherapy research has shown that treatment outcome is better when there is greater expressed affect than defence in a session (McCullough, 2001; Taurke et al., 1990).

Evocative Responding

There are several functions of evocative responding: (1) to retrieve new information; (2) to increase the client's awareness of their own emotions; (3) to facilitate contact with emotional experience; and (4) to access meanings and emotional schemes (Elliott et al., 2004). As therapists, we can evoke by enquiring about the client's current emotional state or felt sense, including through the use of dramatic and expressive language that amplifies the client's feelings. For example, in response to a perceived shift in the client's emotional state as they talk about a memory of arguing with a parent, we can ask: "What is happening right now as you talk about the fight you had with your mother?" or "What do you notice in your body right now?" or "What happened just now as your shoulders tensed up?"

Heightening

Heightening refers to intensifying a client's experience by restating the situation in a vivified way ("You had enough, you were done"; Elliott et al., 2004), highlighting specific parts ("When your dad calls you a brat, maybe it's like a slap in the face or a betrayal of the trust you have"), or using imagery to make their emotions more concrete ("This memory is frightening ... it's like being on the edge of a cliff or ..."). Heightening an experience helps a client more clearly confront it. It amplifies and calls attention to critical emotions and provides the client with new ways of understanding an important experience.

Clinical Considerations for EFTT with Youth

As with any cycle, breaking the intergenerational cycle of trauma and relational insecurity can be facilitated by targeting one of many specific components within the cycle (see Figure 8.2). EFT can intervene through the treatment with youth directly, through parent therapy, or through a parent–child dyad seen separately or in joint sessions. In addition to the intervention strategies outlined thus far in this chapter, EFT-Y chair work tasks, including two-chair and empty-chair, can be employed (see Chapter 2). One such task is the Open for Business chair sequence.

Intervention Strategies in Practice: Open for Business

Catherine began her journey in therapy at the age of nine. Her mother brought her to the first session, reporting that Catherine was very sensitive and had self-regulation difficulties. In the first few years of therapy, Catherine was very difficult to engage in conversation—she responded best to unstructured play and resisted attempts at anything goal-oriented, didactic, or solution-focused. When she did converse, she often talked about how much she disliked her older brother and how annoying he

Table 8.2 Summary of Therapeutic Tasks.

Technique	*When to Use*	*How to Use*	*Example*
Empathic responding	In all phases of EFTT Reduce feelings of extreme distress in youth Invoke emotions in youth Help youth recognize their emotions	Understand and accept with non-judgemental stance Normalize and validate what they went through During middle phase of therapy, if the youth is catastrophizing or avoiding, the therapist can exaggerate the youth's internal messaging (e.g., "Don't let your feelings show—push them down" or "It would kill you to remember that pain") to invoke a reaction from the part of the client which does not catastrophize or avoid (Paivio & Laurent, 2001)	Phrases such as "Of course" or "No wonder that …" or "It makes sense that …" (Paivio & Laurent, 2001)
Imaginal confrontation	Introduce in Phase 2 of EFTT after establishing secure therapeutic relationship. This is typically the fourth session Utilize throughout remainder of therapy ~5 sessions on average are imaginal confrontation (IC) (Khayyat-Abuaita & Paivio, 2019)	Using an empty chair, the youth is instructed to imagine someone involved in past negative experiences of trauma. The youth talks to the empty chair about their feelings and thoughts, which the therapist prompts them to stay attentive to Imaginal confrontation can be done without a chair by imagining the process in their head	The youth tells the empty chair, imagining the perpetrator there, how it felt to have been the subject of their abuse This evokes difficult emotions for the youth, which the therapist helps clarify and express The youth is supported in speaking their unmet needs (e.g., "I deserved to be protected and cherished") and alternative ways of seeing themselves and the perpetrator in that moment (e.g., "I was just a child")

(*continued*)

Table 8.2 Cont.

Technique	*When to Use*	*How to Use*	*Example*
Empathic exploration of trauma material	Introduce in Phase 2 of EFTT, which typically begins at Session Four Utilize throughout remainder of therapy	Utilize empathic responding when exploring memories of trauma Trauma is explored by the youth sharing their thoughts and feelings related to the experience	The youth describes thoughts and feelings related to the shame they experienced when they were not able to protect a loved one from a traumatic event The therapist uses empathic responding to identify the emotion they were feeling and what made them feel that way
Experiential focusing or two-chair enactments	Use in Phases 2 and 3 of EFTT	Two-chair enactments can allow the youth and therapist to evoke emotions related to intra- and interpersonal conflicts Use two chairs to create an empty chair enactment, or one in which the therapist sits in the other chair	The youth sits in one chair and describes their maladaptive, critical thoughts involving memories of trauma Sitting in the other chair, the youth can articulate their authentic feelings and what they need from their critical self The youth imagines their perpetrator in the other chair and engages in an experiential confrontation

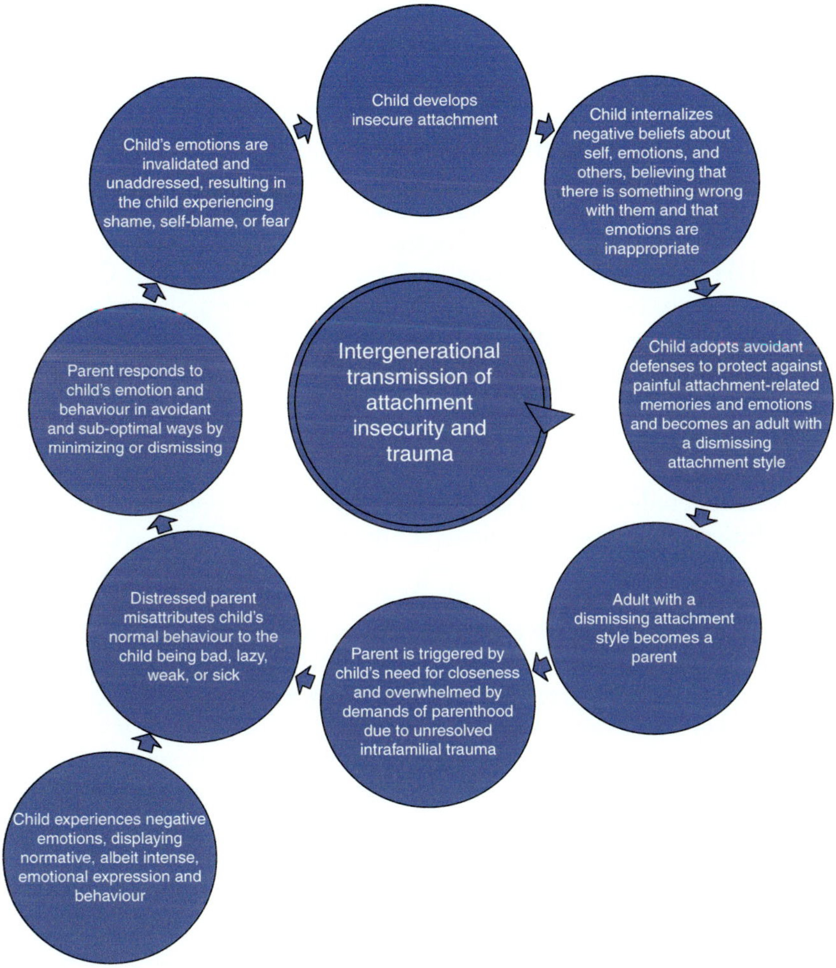

Figure 8.2 The Intergenerational Cycle of Attachment Insecurity and Trauma.

was. By age 12, Catherine was presenting with signs of depression and struggling socially at school. She was friendly with people but often felt slighted in social situations, did not feel comfortable talking or working in groups, and did not have any close friendships forming. On the recommendation of her therapist, Catherine was assessed for autism. Although her parents were sceptical, Catherine was ultimately diagnosed with autism spectrum disorder (ASD) and embraced this new understanding of herself. However, soon after the relief of finally receiving a diagnosis that explained so much about her and what she had experienced throughout her life, Catherine's depression worsened. She began to share more about her relationship with her brother: how he berated her regarding her physical appearance and weight, had bullied her for years without adult intervention, and how she felt trapped and helpless at home with him each day while their parents worked late into the evening. When her parents were advised that Catherine was feeling so negative about experiences with her brother, they withdrew her from therapy for two years. At age 15, after medications and ADHD coaching were tried and did not provide relief, Catherine's parents brought her back to therapy with a new diagnosis: complex trauma. Although she was hesitant, Catherine agreed to try an emotion focused approach to therapy.

Session Excerpt

Client details at time of OFB intervention: Catherine, age 15
Clinical diagnoses: Childhood depression, ADHD, ASD, complex trauma
Identifying the marker: Catherine started the session talking about school that day, which was her typical start to sessions. A few minutes into session, Catherine didn't want to talk about school anymore. She appeared frustrated and sad and, when asked, said she was working very hard to hold her feelings inside. She shared that she was thinking about her childhood experiences and couldn't remember "if it really happened." She experienced an intrusive voice that she identified as her mother's, saying that she was being too sensitive.

Therapist: Come over here and be the part of Mom that made you upset. Be Mom and give yourself the message she gave you … like "Don't be so sensitive," or …

Catherine: [Mom's voice] You're being selfish, you were too sensitive, it wasn't so bad, it was the way you took it.

Therapist: [Mom's voice] You're selfish and too sensitive and you interpreted things incorrectly—so it was your fault. Is that what Mom's message was?

Catherine: Yes. She doesn't want to destroy the extended family's impression of James.

Therapist: Okay, so she protects your brother, James—what about you? What was the message you received?

Catherine: Well, first of all, did it really happen? What did it constitute? Can you convince me that any of it actually happened?

Therapist: What do you remember happening?

Catherine: I remember James calling me fat, storming into my room uninvited ... I remember dissociating.

Therapist: It was very painful ... you can doubt the details of what happened, but you remember the impact, how it made you feel. What hurt the most?

Catherine: Feeling that I was the problem. That's still what hurts the most.

Therapist: Right ... so Mom's message was "You're the problem, not James"?

Catherine: Always.

Therapist: Tell Mom. Picture her again in the empty chair. Tell her what you remember.

Catherine: [Looking at empty chair, tears flow] I remember you left me alone with him for hours every day. I never had any safety from him. And when I told you what he was doing, you shut me down every time. You made me feel like a crazy person.

Therapist: I felt like I was crazy ... tell her what that was like for you.

Catherine: I felt trapped. Nobody limited his power at all.

Therapist: Trapped and shut down ... that's what hurt the most? Can you feel it now, what that was like?

Catherine: ... No, I can't [5 second pause], I can remember but I can't feel it now.

Therapist: Switch and be your mom in those moments—how did she shut you down?

Catherine: [Mom's voice] Don't be ridiculous. You're being so sensitive. It's not so bad and all siblings fight.

Therapist: And what's the underlying message about you? Your feelings aren't real or this is your fault?

Catherine: Yes, both.

Therapist: Be Mom and say it the way she did—maybe not those words but how did she convey this to you? What was the look on her face?

Catherine: [Mimics dismissive/condescending face and posture] Oh, please Catherine! Your little feelings are ridiculous. What you feel is not real.

Therapist: Say that again, in Mom's voice.

Catherine: [Mimics dismissive/condescending face and posture] What you feel is not real!

Therapist: Switch [motions to self chair]. How does it feel now, as you hear that?

Catherine: [Tearful] Sad and very lonely.

Therapist: Tell Mom [motions to empty chair].

Before attempting the Level 3 OFB task, described above in the session with Catherine, it is important to try Levels 1 and then 2, as they can be adequately evocative for some clients. As well, debriefing at the end of a youth's session can be incredibly helpful, preparing them for the potential for experiencing a higher degree of emotion in the days that follow as well as discussing the pros and cons of sharing insights from their therapy sessions directly with family members. In these debriefing conversations, it may become apparent that the youth is planning to tell their parents what they "realized" in therapy that day. Other youth may not have any plans but may find themselves in an interaction that triggers something they experienced in the session, which can lead to an unexpected outburst. The risk in both of these situations is that the youth may not receive the kind of response that they are hoping for from their family member, and this may lead to disappointment and even emotional harm. Before the client leaves the session, it is wise to discuss what the pros and cons of sharing session experiences might be, and what response they wish versus are likely to receive from family members. Engaging parents in the therapy process can also go a long way to prevent misattunement and prepare parents for the EFT process in general. Sometimes, such as when there have been traumatic experiences in their parent's own history, we may determine that directly supporting the parent can support the overall process for the youth, as well as their clinical outcomes. Whether we offer occasional parent communication, direct parent therapy, or something in between, our efforts can reduce the likelihood of the family's unintentional **treatment interfering behaviours** (TIBS; Foroughe et al., 2018; Strahan et al., 2017), which, as already discussed, may impact the therapy process and outcome and even counteract the positive changes that therapy provides. This is especially the case when youth and caregivers are being impacted by a cycle of intergenerational trauma.

Why Consider Working with Caregiver Trauma?

Caregiver Need

The intergenerational transmission of attachment insecurity and trauma is a well-researched phenomenon (Crawford & Benoit, 2009; Isobel et al., 2019); youth presenting with complex, interfamilial trauma often have at least one parent or caregiver with a history of complex trauma as well. While, in many cases, it is possible successfully to use EFT-Y with youth on their own, in other cases it may be clinically advantageous—even necessary—to engage one or both parents in the treatment process (see Chapters 4 and 5 for a detailed overview). Parents and other caregivers can struggle to provide validation and support for youth in therapy. Difficult emotions may arise such as feelings of helplessness, fear of failure, and overwhelm, as caregivers attempt to regulate their own emotions (Foroughe & Muller, 2012, 2014; Foroughe et al., 2018). When a caregiver's default is to disengage and use avoidance and distancing behaviours to steer clear of painful emotions and attachment memories (albeit for self-protection), this may point to a **dismissing-avoidant attachment style** (Muller, 2010; Slade, 2004).

Even if we suggest it, parents with a dismissing-avoidant attachment style, developed to protect them from painful attachment-based memories, may be reluctant to seek individual therapy on their own (Dozier, 1990; Vogel & Wei, 2005). Often, having a child in therapy is a parent's first exposure to any form of counselling or therapy—in many cases, it will be their only such exposure. As a result, it can be a key opportunity to engage the parent in a therapeutic process.

Therapy-Induced Relational Strain

To the extent that therapy opens up difficult feelings, bringing painful or overwhelming memories closer to the surface, it can be highly threatening and activating for individuals with a history of trauma and can place strain on their close relationships. Children and teens with experiences of complex trauma are often highly dysregulated and reactive and can suffer from feelings of invalidation. As therapists, we are understandably supportive of their perspective and validate and affirm their feelings. We are trained to tune into the transference experiences of both our clients and ourselves, so as to effectively contain difficult feelings and respond empathically, even when our clients may be reacting negatively towards us. However, when youth are engaged in treatment and accessing emotions that are related to their family dynamics, other family members may react less than enthusiastically to the youth's new insights and behaviours. These reactions from family members, in combination with the youth's emotional vulnerability, create a perfect storm for post-therapy blow-ups with caregivers.

Imagine a teen has learned through therapy to take more responsibility for their behaviour and walk away from arguments, taking a few minutes to practise coping strategies instead of reacting impulsively. When this teen storms off mid-conversation to go suddenly to their room, parents or other family members can interpret this behaviour as disrespectful and unintentionally interfere with the youth's new health-seeking behaviour. In several other chapters throughout this manual, we have referred to this type of parent response as a TIB—a treatment interfering behaviour that a parent can unintentionally engage in (Foroughe et al., 2018; Strahan et al., 2017). Once viewed through this lens, it becomes clearer that negative reactions to the youth's health-seeking behaviour are much more likely to occur when parents and families do not know what changes to expect from the youth in therapy, are not sure how to support the youth or manage their own emotional reactions, and continue to respond in the same way as they had in the past.

TIBs as a Function of Intergenerational Trauma

The presence of TIBs is a sign that something is interfering with the parent's internal desire to support their child. EFT posits that the only thing that can change an emotion is another emotion. In this case, the only thing that can

Figure 8.3 It Happened at Dinner.

change a caregiver's desire to support their child is a **caregiving interfering emotion** (CIE). Every TIB has a CIE underlying it. CIEs may be a result of a parent's own emotional history or simply be due to an "emotional mismatch" between the parent responses and the child's needs. Parent–child emotional mismatches on their own are not uncommon, but they may be a cause for concern if there is difficulty overcoming this mismatch and tuning into what is needed for the youth struggling with their mental health. While problematic parental responses can be very frustrating for therapists, they indicate that a parent is struggling with a CIE, and that there is an opportunity to provide parents with support to identify and transform their own emotional reactions. For parents with a history of trauma, fear is a common CIE. If a parent has endured events that were immediately terrifying and in which they were overpowered and unable to protect themselves, a fear-based response would have been adaptive at the time. However, if that person is now a parent of a teen with an explosive temper and needing clear boundaries, fear can be an obstacle to an adaptive response—see Figure 8.4.

At some point in a caregiver's past, their avoidant behaviours may have served an adaptive purpose. Freezing up helped them avoid further bullying and injury; dissociating helped them survive abuse; being the clown helped lift the family's mood; acting out helped keep harmful people away; and so on. However, for caregivers supporting a child through mental health struggles, under-responding through avoidant or distancing behaviour is usually unhelpful (Muller, 2009), as is over-responding with anger, criticism, and defensiveness. When a parent needs to protect themselves from acknowledging or addressing their child's emotions or needs, this can create the conditions that unfortunately perpetuate the intergenerational cycle (Muller, 2018). As well, caregivers who are not engaged in some way in their child's therapy may

Figure 8.4 Toughen Up.

express a negative attitude towards therapy, refute the therapist's perspective, mistrust the process, and even pull their child out from therapy prematurely (discussed in more detail in Chapter 4). As a therapist, understanding how to manage caregiver emotions and provide targeted support can be crucial to working with parents and youth. This doesn't mean you have to become the therapist for every parent or caregiver; there are many possible options that can be helpful.[2] It doesn't even have to be you (the youth's therapist) that provides parent EFT. The critical part is just that the parent receives support from someone with whom you can communicate and collaborate (with consent from the parent and child), creating the best conditions for the parent–child relationship, caregiver well-being, and the youth's therapeutic outcomes.

Whether through greater emotional awareness, accessing the type of emotional state that will be most adaptive in meeting a child's need, or processing the impact that their own traumatic memories are having on their current parenting, EFT for parents can provide relief, confidence, and a renewed sense of energy to face the difficulties that lie ahead. This process can intervene in the cycle of intergenerational transmission of emotion avoidance (Dias & Ressler, 2014; Schickedanz et al., 2018).

Emotion Focused Intervention Strategies with Caregivers

Preparing Caregivers

By engaging the parent to anticipate and manage painful memories that arise at home when dealing with their child's difficult emotions and behaviour, we can provide a secure environment to acknowledge and process the painful experiences that parents themselves have experienced that may be interfering with new caregiver responses. Likely, these painful experiences were pushed down for good reason. Often, parents tell us that they were doing just fine until becoming a parent or until their child presented with challenges that they had never expected. They may even acknowledge that their child reminds them of one of their own parents, a sibling, or themselves as a child. For instance, when a child comes to their father for support when they feel scared, the father may be reminded of his own memories of being ignored as a child when he expressed strong negative emotions. As an individual with a dismissing-avoidant attachment style, he may claim that his parent's distancing behaviour "made him stronger" and may ignore his own child's cries for support: see Figure 8.6.

By allowing parents an opportunity to address the emotional memories that are driving their current under- or over-response, EFT for parents can disrupt the intergenerational transmission of attachment insecurity and trauma. The mechanism of action is emotion transformation, which is the core change process within EFT. If we accept that the parent's emotions (particularly CIEs)

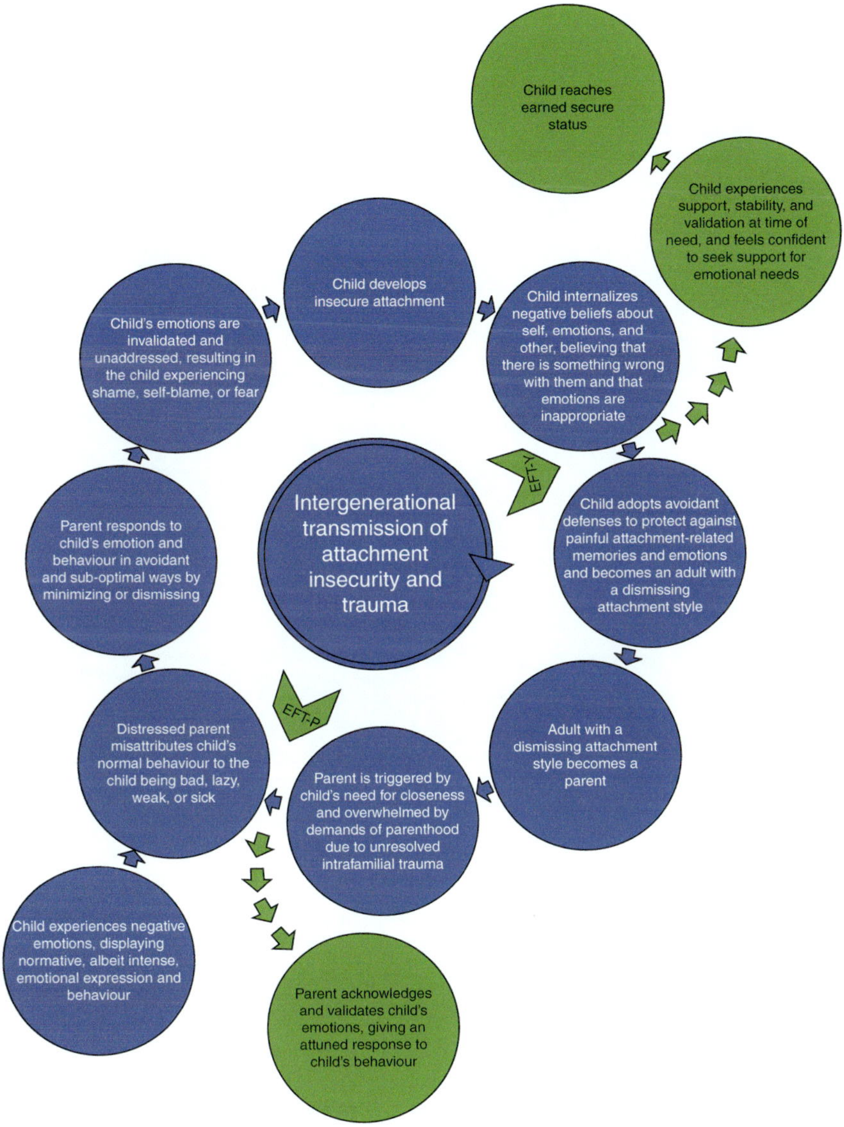

Figure 8.5 The Impact of EFT-Y Interventions on the Intergenerational Cycle of Attachment Insecurity and Trauma.

Figure 8.6 | Turned Out Okay TIB.

are relevant to their child's therapy, take a non-judgemental stance towards parents, and demonstrate compassion and transparency in our communication with parents, we can turn parents into allies. At the very least, we can help reduce TIBs. In the best-case scenario, parents become more present and emotionally engaged with their child and partner with us in the therapeutic process.

Caregiver Deactivating Strategies

Deactivating behaviour refers to anything that can reduce or avoid emotional activation and contact with painful or overwhelming emotions. When engaging parents with a history of trauma, the therapist can look for avoidant behaviour, both verbal and nonverbal, by paying close attention to the parent's communication during initial consultations, interviews, as well as brief encounters. When talking about their own emotional history or childhood, or when talking about their own child's feelings and needs, parents can verbally minimize any painful experiences by speaking of these topics in a light and dismissing manner: "I turned out okay," "Nobody has a perfect childhood," "She's a tough cookie, she'll be fine," "Anyway, it doesn't matter all that much." Parents can also talk of what is an objectively negative experience and yet paint it as a positive experience, such as describing physical abuse from their parent as a "learning experience" and stating that it was actually good for them to have endured it, because it made them more resilient or self-disciplined: "What doesn't kill you makes your stronger" or "Getting the belt made you learn right from wrong and kids these days don't learn that." Sometimes, pronoun shifts from "I/me" to "you/we" or "they/kids/people" can signify distancing behaviour: "You do your best with what you've got" or "That's ancient history." At other times, overly stereotyped and impersonal statements are common as a defensive response: "Life is tough," "You get what you get, and you don't get upset," or "It is what it is."

Parents struggling to keep painful memories at bay may also change the topic to avoid discussing troubling topics that are uncomfortable for them to discuss. Other avoidant parents may report lapses in memory of their childhood or state that their childhood memories are unimportant for discussion (Alexander et al., 1998; Kohn et al., 2012; Slade, 1999). Further, to maintain a positive view of their parents, avoidant parents can idealize their view of their own parents—for example, by describing them as wonderful and inspiring, despite contradictory evidence that they were abusive. Overall narrative inconsistencies can emerge when avoidant parents discuss their experiences of trauma or are asked to recall specific examples from memory. The adult attachment interview (AAI) can be a very useful clinical tool to access attachment history and observe deactivating strategies. In addition to improving long-term outcomes for caregivers with a history of trauma (Cordeiro et al., 2022), the AAI is a long-standing research tool and has recently been utilized in studies of defensive nonverbal behaviour in parents and caregivers (Goldstein, 2019). Table 8.3 provides a summary of common defensive strategies that parents can use to deactivate and avoid negative emotions arising from attachment-related memories.

Conclusion

EFTT provides a framework for us to explore experiences of trauma with a phase-based, semi-structured approach. A secure therapeutic relationship, in which there is safety and psychological containment, must be established before exploring trauma material. With parents, we can also provide a safe and secure environment where they feel valued as a caregiver and work on attuning to their child's emotional needs, which may sometimes require exploring their own emotional history. As therapists, we can note when a painful or overwhelming emotional memory may have been brought up by recognizing our client's deactivating strategies and distancing behaviour. We work to simultaneously activate emotion and challenge blocks, remaining aware of the risks of over- or under-challenging clients. This must be done

Table 8.3 Common Defensive Strategies.

Defence	*The Client in Therapy*
Defensive exclusion of painful memories	• Difficulty recalling certain memories from childhood • Description of relationships with attachment figures are vague Example: "I don't really remember anything from my childhood. It was pretty good overall"
Minimization	• Portrays trauma and attachment experiences as less impactful or emotionally significant • Describes experience as "normal" Example: "She didn't really need to go to the hospital. Honestly, it's normal for kids her age to seek attention. She's fine now," a father says, despite multiple hospitalizations for his child's suicide attempts
Positive ending	• Explaining that a negative story had a positive influence on their life • A form of minimization Example: wrapping up a story of abuse or neglect with a positive life lesson: "Being left alone all the time taught me to be independent and take care of myself. Kids these days are too coddled"
Idealization	• Describes one or both parents in extremely positive terms that are not consistent with the specific events or memories described • It's not uncommon for the abusive or emotionally absent parent to be idealized Example: a mom who, just moments earlier, was described as violent and depressed, later in the AAI is, out of nowhere, described in this way: "Yeah, mom was a pretty impressive lady … You know … Putting up with the crap he threw her way"
Intellectualization and talking around feelings	• Diverts attention from emotions by focusing instead on cognitive aspects of experiences, non-attachment related themes, or activities Example: may focus on or altogether change the topic to non-threatening issues, such as financial or legal difficulties
Self-perception as self-reliant, independent, strong, and normal	• Help-rejecting and defensive • Struggles to acknowledge the need for help, or may seek help for symptoms (e.g., difficulties sleeping or concentrating at work) Example: the parent may distance or isolate themselves rather than seek support when dealing with stressful situations

Table 8.3 Cont.

Defence	*The Client in Therapy*
Distancing language	• Uses words or general phrases to distance themselves from attachment-related content Example: a client, describing her reaction to her father's violent outbursts, suddenly distances herself by switching to the pronoun "you": "You just knew not to get in his way"
Activity-centered pursuits	• Engaging in work or chore-related activities to avoid painful emotional experiences related to attachment Example: in response to a child's request for attention, the caregiver may instead choose to engage in a task as it is less emotionally taxing
Distancing behaviour	• Placement of objects between themselves and the therapist • Micro expressions of dread or sadness • Nonverbal behaviours which occur after attachment is discussed, which are different from their nonverbal baseline • Lateness, scheduling difficulties, cancelled appointments, leaving early, refusing to be present during child's sessions Example: once the therapist brings up experiences of childhood, the caregiver begins to fidget. There is a lack of eye contact as caregiver engages in self-soothing behaviour

Adapted, with permission, from Cordeiro et al. (2018), pp. 106–107.

at a pace that is tolerable for the client, and the therapist must be sensitive to the risk of either over- or under-challenging during trauma therapy. While working with clients experiencing trauma can be challenging for us as therapists, emotion transformation can intervene in the intergenerational cycle of attachment insecurity and trauma, allowing our clients to live fuller lives with less suffering.

Practical Tips

Do:

- Pay attention to nonverbal communication even more than you usually do: trauma is often stored in the body, and it can be hard to access language to express such intense memories and experiences
- Cultivate safety in the therapeutic relationship before activating painful memories.

- If a trauma is mentioned early in therapy, honour the telling and return to the topic later once safety is established.
- Consider if, when, to what extent, and how to involve caregivers in youth therapy.
- Recognize habitual deactivating (avoidance) strategies that youth or caregivers may use to manage painful emotions or memories; gradually reduce or replace with deliberate deactivating strategies (relaxation, validation, etc.).
- If a client demonstrates distress in session, slow down therapy, use deliberate deactivating strategies, and focus on strengthening the therapeutic relationship.
- Provide consistency and stability: schedule sessions at the same time each week, keep the space and contents consistent, begin on time, and provide notice if you anticipate any changes.
- Check in with clients regarding their comfort in the space where sessions are held—offer options if available; ask about any privacy concerns if they are joining you virtually.

Don't:

- Attempt to rush the client into talking about painful experiences before establishing adequate trust, safety, and psychological containment.
- Focus only on the youth in their therapy without considering TIBS and potential parent communication, support, or involvement.
- Attribute parents' avoidant defensive strategies to malicious or intentional motives.
- Be complicit with avoidant defensive strategies that youth or caregivers present.
- Proceed to later phases of trauma therapy when a client is still showing intense distress.
- Dive into emotion transformation before working to relax their nervous system first.
- Forget to be aware of your own nonverbal communication, emotion blocks, and potential trauma history that may impact your experience of working with a particular client.

Notes

1 The use of present tense "experiencing trauma" here is intentional and acknowledges the reality of ongoing impact, continuing after an event occurred and impacting our client in the present.

2 See Chapter 5 for a detailed overview of involving caregivers in parent–child therapy.

References

Alexander, P. C., Anderson, C. L., Brand, B., Schaeffer, C. M., Grelling, B. Z., & Kretz, L. (1998). Adult attachment and long-term effects in survivors of incest. *Child Abuse & Neglect*, *22*(1), 45–61. https://doi.org/10.1016/S0145-2134(97)00120-8

Bohart, A. C., & Greenberg, L. S. (Eds.). (1997). *Empathy reconsidered: New directions in psychotherapy*. American Psychological Association. https://doi.org/10.1037/10226-000

Burgoon, J. K. (1994). Nonverbal signals. In M. L. Knapp & G. R. Miller (Eds.), *Handbook of interpersonal communication* (2nd ed., pp. 229–285). Sage.

Burgoon, J. K., Guerrero, L. K., & Floyd, K. *Nonverbal communication* (2nd ed.). Routledge. https://doi.org/10.4324/9781003095552

Cordeiro, K., Rependa, S. L., Muller, R. T., & Foroughe, M. (Ed.). (2018). EFFT and trauma: Engaging the parent with a dismissing attachment style. In *Emotion Focused Family Therapy with Children and Caregivers: A Trauma-Informed Approach* (pp. 106–107). Routledge.

Cordeiro, K., Wyers, C., Oliver, M., Foroughe, M., & Muller, R. T. (2022). Caregiver maltreatment history and treatment response following an intensive emotion focused family therapy workshop. *Clinical Psychology & Psychotherapy*, *29*(5), 1728–1741. https://doi.org/10.1002/cpp.2739

Crawford, A., & Benoit, D. (2009). Caregivers' disrupted representations of the unborn child predict later infant–caregiver disorganized attachment and disrupted interactions. *Infant Mental Health Journal*, *30*(2), 124–144. https://doi.org/10.1002/imhj.20207

DePaulo, B. M., Lindsay, J. J., Malone, B. E., Muhlenbruck, L., Charlton, K., & Cooper, H. (2003). Cues to deception. *Psychological Bulletin*, *129*(1), 74–118. https://doi.org/10.1037/0033-2909.129.1.74

Dias, B., & Ressler, K. (2014). Parental olfactory experience influences behavior and neural structure in subsequent generations. *Nature Neuroscience*, *17*, 89–96. https://doi.org/10.1038/nn.3594

Dozier, M. (1990). Attachment organization and treatment use for adults with serious psychopathological disorders. *Development and Psychopathology*, *2*(1), 47–60. https://doi.org/10.1017/S0954579400000584

Dymond, R. F. (1949). A scale for the measurement of empathic ability. *Journal of Consulting Psychology*, *13*(2), 127–133. https://doi.org/10.1037/h0061728

Ekman, P. (1971). Universal and cultural differences in facial expressions of emotion. In J. K. Cole (Ed.), *Nebraska Symposium on Motivation* (pp. 207–283). Lincoln: University of Nebraska Press.

Ekman, P., & Friesen, W. V. (1969). Nonverbal leakage and clues to deception. *Psychiatry*, *32*(1), 88–106.

Elliott, R., Watson, J. C., Goldman, R. N., & Greenberg, L. S. (2004). *Learning emotion-focused therapy: The process-experiential approach to change*. American Psychological Association. https://doi.org/10.1037/10725-000

Fiorini, G., Saunders, R., Fonagy, P., Impact Consortium, & Midgley, N. (2022). Trajectories of change in general psychopathology levels among depressed adolescents in short-term psychotherapies. *Psychotherapy Research: Journal of the Society for Psychotherapy Research*, 1–12. Advance online publication. https://doi.org/10.1080/10503307.2022.2040751

Foley, G. N., & Gentile, J. P. (2010). Nonverbal communication in psychotherapy. *Psychiatry*, 7(6), 38–44.

Foroughe, M., Dolhanty, J., Mithal, P., & Lafrance, A. (2018). Development and core components of EFFT. In M. Foroughe (Ed.), *EFFT with Children and Caregivers: A Trauma-Informed Approach* (pp. 45–62). Routledge.

Foroughe, M., & Muller, R. T. (2012). Dismissing (avoidant) attachment and trauma in dyadic parent–child psychotherapy. *Psychological Trauma: Theory, Research, Practice, and Policy*, *4*(2), 229–236. https://doi.org/10.1037/a0023061

Foroughe, M. F., & Muller, R. T. (2014). Attachment-based intervention strategies in family therapy with survivors of intra-familial trauma: A case study. *Journal of Family Violence*, *29*(5), 539–548. https://doi.org/10.1007/s10896-014-9607-4

Ginott, H. G. (1965). *Between parent and child: New solutions to old problems.* New York: Macmillan.

Goldstein, L. (2019). *Nonverbal and paralinguistic behaviours during the adult attachment interview: The construction of a novel coding system* [Master's thesis, York University]. https://hdl.handle.net/10315/36729

Greenberg, L. S., & Pascual-Leone, A. (2006). Emotion in psychotherapy: A practice-friendly research review. *Journal of Clinical Psychology*, *62*(5), 611–630. https://doi.org/10.1002/jclp.20252

Hans, A., & Hans, E. (2015). Kinesics, haptics and proxemics: Aspects of non-verbal communication. *IOSR Journal of Humanities and Social Science*, *20*(2), 47–52.

Isobel, S., Goodyear, M., Furness, T., & Foster, K. (2019). Preventing intergenerational trauma transmission: A critical interpretive synthesis. *Journal of Clinical Nursing*, *28*(7–8), 1100–1113. https://doi.org/10.1111/jocn.14735

Khayyat-Abuaita, U., & Paivio, S. (2019). Emotion-focused therapy for complex interpersonal trauma. In L. S. Greenberg & R. N. Goldman (Eds.), *Clinical handbook of emotion-focused therapy* (pp. 361–380). Washington, DC: American Psychological Association. http://dx.doi.org/10.1037/0000112-016

Kohn, J. L., Rholes, W. S., & Schmeichel, B. J. (2012). Self-regulatory depletion and attachment avoidance: Increasing the accessibility of negative attachment-related memories. *Journal of Experimental Social Psychology*, *48*(1), 375–378. https://doi.org/10.1016/j.jesp.2011.06.020

McCullough, L. (2001). Desensitization of affect phobias in short-term dynamic psychotherapy. In M. F. Solomon, R. J. Neborsky, L. McCullogh, M. Alpert, F. Shapiro, & D. Malan (Eds.), *Short-term therapy for long-term change* (pp. 54–82). W. W. Norton.

Muller, R. T. (2009). Trauma and dismissing (avoidant) attachment: Intervention strategies in individual psychotherapy. *Psychotherapy: Theory, Research, Practice, Training*, *46*(1), 68–81. https://doi.org/10.1037/a0015135

Muller, R. T. (2010). *Trauma and the avoidant client.* W. W. Norton.

Muller, R. T. (2018). *Trauma and the struggle to open up.* W. W. Norton.

Navarro, J., & Karlins, M. (2008). *What every body is saying* (Vol. 27, p. 90). Harper Collins.

Paivio, S. C., & Laurent, C. (2001). Empathy and emotion regulation: Reprocessing memories of childhood abuse. *Journal of Clinical Psychology*, *57*(2), 213–226. https://doi.org/10.1002/1097-4679(200102)57:2<213::aid-jclp7>3.0.co;2-b

Paivio, S. C., & Pascual-Leone, A. (2010). *Emotion-focused therapy for complex trauma: An integrative approach.* American Psychological Association. https://doi.org/10.1037/12077-000

Pettit, J. W., Bechor, M., Rey, Y., Vasey, M. W., Abend, R., Pine, D. S., Bar-Haim, Y., Jaccard, J., & Silverman, W. K. (2020). A randomized controlled trial of attention bias modification treatment in youth with treatment-resistant anxiety disorders.

Journal of the American Academy of Child and Adolescent Psychiatry, *59*(1), 157–165. https://doi.org/10.1016/j.jaac.2019.02.018

Schickedanz, A., Halfon, N., Sastry, N., & Chung, J. P. (2018). Parents' adverse childhood experiences and their children's behavioral health problems. *American Academy of Pediatrics*, *142*(2): e20180023. https://doi.org/10.1542/peds.2018-0023

Slade, A. (1999). Attachment theory and research: Implications for the theory and practice of individual psychotherapy with adults. In J. Cassidy & P. R. Shaver (Eds.), *Handbook of attachment: Theory, research, and clinical applications* (pp. 575–594). Guilford Press.

Slade, A. (2004). Two therapies: Attachment organization and the clinical process. In L. Atkinson & S. Goldberg (Eds.), *Attachment issues in psychopathology and intervention* (pp. 181–206). Erlbaum.

Strahan, E. J., Stillar, A., Files, N., Nash, P., Scarborough, J., Connors, L., Gusella, J., Henderson, K., Mayman, S., Marchand, P., Orr, E. S., Dolhanty, J., & Lafrance, A. (2017). Increasing parental self-efficacy with emotion-focused family therapy for eating disorders: A process model. *Person-Centered & Experiential Psychotherapies*, *16*(3), 256–269. https://doi.org/10.1080/14779757.2017.1330703

Taurke, E. A., Flegenheimer, W., McCullouoh, L., Winston, A., Pollack, J., & Trujillo, M. (1990). Change in patient affect/defense ratio from early to late sessions in brief psychotherapy. *Journal of Clinical Psychology*, *46*(5), 657–668. https://doi.org/10.1002/1097-4679(199009)46:5%3C657::AID-JCLP2270460519%3E3.0.CO;2-G

Vogel, D. L., & Wei, M. (2005). Adult attachment and help-seeking intent: The mediating roles of psychological distress and perceived social support. *Journal of Counseling Psychology*, *52*(3), 347–357. https://doi.org/10.1037/0022-0167.52.3.347

GLOSSARY

Activating and challenging: the process of activating a client's attachment system and challenging their defensive avoidance.

Affect reconsolidation: a process in which a memory itself is altered in the process each time something is remembered.

Anxiety split: also known as the two-chair worry dialogue, this chair work can be used as a first pass to assist a youth in understanding where their worries and anxiety stem from. The worry can be viewed as the self's attempt to protect against experiences that would remind them of underlying, painful emotions they are trying to avoid.

Attachment rupture narrative: how the client sees the breakage in attachment security between themselves and their caregiver. This can include the client's perspective of how factors such as neglect or trauma have contributed to damaging their relationship with the caregiver.

Attuning to nonverbal communication: being aware of one's facial expressions, tone of voice, and body language.

Body sculpting: practising empathy and validation by listening to a client attentively, responding in an attuned manner, tolerating negative emotions, and conveying nonverbal messages.

Coach critic: the voice in a client's head that fears the emotions that the client is experiencing and attempts to have the client avoid them at all costs. This is one side of the self-criticism split.

Collaborative case formulation: an approach to developing an understanding and narrative as to why a client is in therapy and what their presenting concerns are. In this approach, the therapist works with the client to develop a shared understanding of their unique situation.

Conflict split: an umbrella term that describes a conflict between two parts of the self (e.g., the harsh critic and the coach critic).

Current interpersonal conflict: conflict that occurs between two or more individuals who work together in groups or teams.

Dismissing-avoidant attachment style: an attachment style which parents use to protect themselves from painful attachment-based memories. Individuals with this attachment style are not likely to seek individual therapy on their own.

Emotion: a complex state that results in physical and psychological change, influences an individual's thoughts and behaviours, and alerts them to threats and to actions that will help them survive.

Emotion marker: client behaviours that indicate the emotional state of the client and provide a guide for which particular technique would be appropriate for the therapist to use.

Emotion schemes: a whole experience of a certain emotion state and what is then activated in one's body and mind.

Emotion transformation: one of the main goals of EFT is to transform maladaptive emotions to learn how to access the adaptive ones.

Emotional blocks: when the emotions of the caregiver interfere with caregiving efforts.

Empathic affirmation: a task used for youth who are struggling with self-related emotional pain such as shame, worthlessness, and vulnerability. It takes priority over any other task within the EFT therapeutic process.

Empathic attunement: the process of emotional and kinaesthetic responding to the youth's current experiences that uses an accepting stance in which the therapist tries to "lean into" their experience; the basis for all empathic responding.

Empathic support: a term that encompasses empathic affirmation and empathic attunement. It begins in the very first moments of contact with a client, as it supports the forming of a therapeutic bond and opens the door to further exploration of the youth's feelings as treatment progresses.

Emotion-focused therapy for trauma (EFTT): an evidence-based, short-term treatment for childhood abuse and neglect that posits the therapeutic relationship and emotional processing of trauma material as key mechanisms of change .

Emotion focused case formulation: aids therapists to both conceptualize core emotion schemes and follow markers across therapy that signify tasks aimed at emotional transformation.

Empathic responding: magnifies or reduces client emotions by conveying that you understand the client's experience and that they are valid.

Empty-chair work: a technique used to help clients fully express, and resolve suppressed, primary negative feelings towards others and explore the implicit meaning of past events with them.

Evocative interventions: provides the social context for growth and change; it is a combination of selected activities, which are catalysts to communication, and a particular approach to the process and content of the group.

Experiential focusing: a technique used when a client has an unclear or absent felt sense. This is used when the therapist would like to deepen a youth's level of experiencing by going below the surface emotions.

Experiential re-enactments: a number of exercises used to evoke secondary and primary maladaptive emotions and support youth to move through the sequential emotion transformation phases. This includes trauma retelling, split chair work, empty-chair work, imaginal confrontation, and empathic exploration.

Experiencing Self: the side of the self that is experiencing the emotions in the present moment.

Family systems perspective: this perspective takes on the view that an individual's functioning is not determined solely by intrapsychic factors but, rather, is reciprocally impacted by the relationships they hold with those around them, especially their family.

Felt sense: a deep understanding of what's going on in the body through the process of awareness.

Guiding attention: present-centred awareness exercises that help people focus attention on their current body sensations and feelings. Such awareness practices, which link sensory awareness and thinking, highlight the constructive nature of experience.

Harsh critic: the voice in a client's head that is cruel and aims to put down the client. This is one side of the self-criticism split.

Instrumental emotion: an emotion that is expressed purposefully to influence others and does not match what one is actually experiencing. For example, one may express sadness to manipulate someone or express anger to keep someone at bay.

Kinesics: used as tools to assess when the parent's attachment style is activated. These include micro expressions and bodily gestures.

Lived experience: what the client is actually feeling as opposed to what they're just saying about their experience.

Marker: identification of clients' statements.

Memory reconsolidation: how memories are changed.

Motivation: a made-up construct that describes the net effect of the conflict between two or more underlying emotions.

Neuroplasticity: when neurons that fire together, wire together.

Over-challenging: encouraging a client to open up about trauma before safety is established, leading to a sudden outpouring of intense, hard-to-control emotions. For avoidant clients, over-challenging can lead to early termination.

Parentectomy: a negative therapeutic approach that attempts to remove a parent from the therapeutic process under the assumption that the therapist is the expert who can take better care of the child without parental interference.

Phase-based approach: a recommended treatment option for individuals with complex trauma histories. It involves two stages of treatment, with one focusing on safety and stabilization and the second on trauma memory processing.

Primary emotion: the first feeling or reaction being felt in response to a change in an environment; can be considered either adaptive or maladaptive.

Primary adaptive emotion: an emotion that is biologically adaptive and gives immediately useful information, alerting one to details in the environment that require the most attention; for example, one may feel fear of an oncoming car or feel sadness about a loss.

Primary maladaptive emotion: an emotion that functions as a result of memory or trauma. It is concerned with what happened in the past ("then and there") as opposed to what is happening in the present ("here and now").

Problematic reaction point: a state in which the client is confused about why they felt a particular way in a situation.

Proxemics: the distance between the parent and therapist; can be used to observe distancing manoeuvres from the parent.

Psychological containment: the ability to hold difficult emotions brought up within therapy without becoming overwhelmed.

Reflection: a technique that therapists use to validate their client and show them that they're listening; involves the therapist paraphrasing what the client said with an emphasis on feeling.

Relational markers: used in relational thinking to explicitly convey the connections between idea components. They function as cohesive devices in discourse that guide participants to search for underlying connections between ideas.

Secondary emotion: an emotion that masks the primary emotion; a reaction to one's own reaction. For example, someone may feel ashamed of their own sadness or scared of their own anger.

Self-critic split: this two-chair work can be used to address an individual's harsh inner voice which criticizes their underlying thoughts and emotions.

Self-interruption: a state in which the client is avoiding or becoming emotionally distant during their therapy session.

Stabilization: defined as including resource interventions, grounding techniques, comprehensive history taking, trauma preparation, trauma mapping, trauma case conceptualization, and psychoeducation.

Sudden gains: rapid improvements in symptoms that occur within or between sessions.

Systematic evocative unfolding: a therapeutic task whereby the therapist encourages the client to explore and describe their personal narratives when they reach a problematic reaction point.

Transformative self-soothing: involves ways of being with the self to moderate and transform core pain. It is rooted in a client's ability—based on inner resources, probably derived from the internalization of compassion received from others—to soothe their own core painful, primary maladaptive emotions.

Therapeutic relationship: the relationship between therapist and client; can also be referred to as the therapeutic alliance.

Told experience: how the client describes their experience rather than the feeling they had during it.

Treatment interfering behaviours (TIBs): these consist of caregivers' behaviours that can interfere with, and are counterproductive to, treatment progress. Usually, these behaviours stem from caregivers' own histories of attachment insecurity and trauma with their parents.

Two-chair dialogue: a technique that involves having the client move back and forth between two chairs, each representing a conflict within the self. The client is asked to take on the role that is represented by the chair they are seated in.

Two-chair enactment: a therapeutic task whereby the therapist has the client act out their self-interruptions. This technique addresses self-interruptions.

Unfinished business: unmet needs within the client that haven't been fully processed and often contribute to their present concerns.

Under-challenging: allowing the client's avoidant defensive responses to go unchallenged in therapy can result in therapy that appears to go in circles, with the client making little progress.

Universal emotions: emotions which are observed cross-culturally and are useful for interpreting a client's affect display in therapy. They are joy, anger, sadness, fear, surprise, disgust, and contempt.

Validation: a process that involves being non-judgemental and uttering phrases of acceptance and is often accompanied by nonverbal behaviour; a crucial component of EFT and part of the empathic affirmation process, in which the therapist reinforces that both the parent and the child are entitled to their emotional responses and experiences.

Witness Your Parent: a task in which the client enacts the negative aspects of their caregivers when the client is having difficulty accessing and experiencing their negative feelings towards them.

INDEX

Note: Entries in **bold** refer to tables; entries in *italics* refer to figures.

For Product Safety Concerns and Information please contact our
EU representative GPSR@taylorandfrancis.com Taylor & Francis
Verlag GmbH, Kaufingerstraße 24, 80331 München, Germany